Great Escapes of the First World War

Great Escapes of the First World War

WITH AN INTRODUCTION BY J. R. ACKERLEY

Edited by

Rachel Bilton

Pen & Sword
MILITARY

AN IMPRINT OF PEN & SWORD BOOKS LTD.
YORKSHIRE – PHILADELPHIA

First published in Great Britain in 2018 by
PEN & SWORD MILITARY
an imprint of
Pen & Sword Books Ltd
Yorkshire – Philadelphia

ISBN 978 1 47388 7 732

Printed and bound in England by TJ International Ltd, Padstow, Cornwall

Pen & Sword Books Limited incorporates the imprints of Atlas, Archaeology, Aviation, Discovery, Family History, Fiction, History, Maritime, Military, Military Classics, Politics, Select, Transport, True Crime, Air World, Frontline Publishing, Leo Cooper, Remember When, Seaforth Publishing, The Praetorian Press, Wharncliffe Local History, Wharncliffe Transport, Wharncliffe True Crime and White Owl.

For a complete list of Pen & Sword titles please contact

PEN & SWORD BOOKS LIMITED
47 Church Street, Barnsley, South Yorkshire, S70 2AS, England
E-mail: enquiries@pen-and-sword.co.uk
Website: www.pen-and-sword.co.uk

Or
PEN AND SWORD BOOKS
1950 Lawrence Rd, Havertown, PA 19083, USA
E-mail: Uspen-and-sword@casematepublishers.com
Website: www.penandswordbooks.com

CONTENTS

List of Illustrations vii

Maps and Plans ix

Publishers' Note xi

The Authors xiii

Introduction   The Grim Game of Escape xvii

  1. Trapped in Belgium 1

  2. Beginners 13

  3. Tunnelling to Freedom 37

  4. Exploits of the Escaping Club 47

  5. Inveterate Escapers 59

  6. A Winter's Tale 71

  7. Fugitives in Germany 79

  8. What a Skeleton Key Will Do 89

  9. Through the Bathroom Floor 103

10. A Game of Bluff 115

11. An Unconducted Tour of England 129

12. Outwitting the Turk 143

13. Hide-and-Seek in Eastern Seas 155

14.   Through the Camp Sewer 167

15.   Escaping from England.. 175

16.   Rendezvous With a Submarine................................ 191

17.   Hazards of Escape... 199

LIST OF ILLUSTRATIONS

J. R. Ackerley

Harry Beaumont

H. A. Cartwright

Hugh Durnford

A. J. Evans

D. Grinnell-Milne

J. L. Hardy

M. C. C. Harrison

E. H. Jones

Heinz H. E. Justus

E. H. Keeling

Ernest Pearce

Gunther Plüschow

Hermann Tholens

Lawrence A. Wingfield

MAPS AND PLANS

Map of the Internment Camp At Burg Bei Magdeburg   15

Magdeburg Prison – 'Kriegsgarnisonarrestanstalt'   91

Sketch-Map Illustrating E. H. Keeling's Escape From Turkey   145

PUBLISHERS' NOTE

In the summer of last year the British Broadcasting Corporation organised a series of sixteen talks by men who escaped from Prison camps in the Great War, in which they described their escaping adventures. Of these sixteen talks, thirteen were given by Englishmen who escaped in Germany and Turkey, two by Germans who escaped in England, and one by a German who escaped from a British island in the Indian Ocean. So great was the interest aroused by these talks that it was decided to edit and publish them in volume form as a permanent record of escaping during the War, and to add to them two other exciting stories of war-time escape. The original sixteen stories, including the introduction by J. R. Ackerley, are published by arrangement with the British Broadcasting Corporation, to whom the publishers' thanks are due for their helpful co-operation. The two additional stories are "Beginners" by Captain H. A. Cartwright, which is reprinted from Major M. C. C. Harrison's and Captain H. A. Cartwright's book "Within Four Walls" by kind permission of the authors and the publishers Messrs. Edward Arnold and Company, and "Escaping from England" by Gunther Plüschow, which is reprinted from Gunther Plüschow's book "My Escape from Donington Hall" (The Bodley Head).

THE AUTHORS

Ackerley, J. R. Captain 8th East Surrey Regiment. Joined up in October 1914 at the age of 17. Wounded on the Somme 1 July 1916. Again wounded and taken prisoner in May 1917. Spent eight months in Germany first in hospital at Hanover, then at prison-camps of Karlsruhe, Heidelberg and Augustabad. Invalided to Switzerland, where he was interned for the rest of the war. Author of "Hindoo Holiday" (Chatto and Windus) and "The Prisoners of War", a play (Chatto and Windus).

Beaumont, Harry. Enlisted in the (Queen's Own) Royal West Kent Regiment, February 1904, and served with the 2nd Battalion November 1904 to November 1912 in China, Singapore and India. Transferred to Army Reserve December 1912. Rejoined as a private on outbreak of war in 1914 and went to France with 1st Battalion, which was part of original British Expeditionary Force. Transferred to R.F.C. in 1917.

Cartwright, H. A. Joined Middlesex Regiment 1906, Captain 1914, retired 1922. Legion d'Honneur 1918, M.C. 1918, Croix de Guerre Czechoslovaque, 1919. Joint author of "Within Four Walls" (Arnold), from which the following story is an extract.

Durnford, Hugh. Lieutenant R.F.A. 112th Brigade, 25th Division. Joined R.F.A. from India, 1915. With 112th Brigade in action on the Somme 7 July to 3 December 1916, commanding a battery for some of the period. In action at Ploogsteert 1916-17, Messines 1917 and Ypres 1917. Taken prisoner

5 August 1917 while endeavouring as F.O.O. for Brigade to establish touch with infantry front-line headquarters. Awarded M.C. for successful escape from Stralsund Camp in October 1918. Author of "The Tunnellers of Holzminden" (Cambridge University Press).

Evans, A. J. Joined Inns of Court O.T.C. 5 August 1914. Transferred to Intelligence Corps, crossed to France August 1914 as Temporary 2nd Lieutenant and took part in the Retreat. Joined Flying Corps in February 1915, observer in No. 3 Squadron till September 1915; awarded M.C. for continuing to observe while attacked by German aeroplane at Loos. Pilot in No. 3 Squadron in spring 1916, taken prisoner on 16 July 1916, after forced landing behind German lines. Escaped from Clausthal camp, recaptured on Dutch frontier. Escaped successfully into Switzerland after eighteen nights' walking. In command of No. 142 Squadron in Palestine in February 1918. Captured by Turks, and returned to Egypt at the Armistice. Awarded bar to M.C. for numerous attempts to escape. Author of "The Escaping Club" (The Bodley Head).

Grinnell-Milne, Duncan. Commissioned in Special Reserve Infantry 1914, seconded R.F.C. July 1915. Served as pilot with 16 Squadron in France until captured on 1 December 1915. Escaped from Germany April 1918. Served with 56 Squadron in France, commanding Squadron at Armistice and after. Awarded M.C., D.F.C. and bar. After the war served in Egypt, Palestine, Syria, Sudan and later in Experimental Section at Farnborough. Later Assistant Air Attaché, British Embassy, Paris. Retired from R.A.F. December 1925. Author of "An Escaper's Log" and "Fortune of War" (The Bodley Head), and of several other books.

Hardy, J. L. Left Sandhurst end of 1913 and joined Connaught Rangers. Went to France August, 1914. Taken prisoner end of August 1914. Escaped from Germany March 1918. Returned to France April 1918. Slightly wounded August 1918, badly wounded October 1918, with loss of leg. D.S.O., M.C. and bar. Author of "I Escape!" (The Bodley Head).

Harrison, M. C. C. Entered Army 2nd Royal Irish Regiment, 1906; Lieutenant 1908 Captain and adjutant 1914; Bt. Major 1919; Major 1923. Served in Expeditionary Force, severely wounded and prisoner in October 1914. After five attempts to escape from Germany, succeeded in September 1917 and rejoined his old Battalion in France in December. Acting Major and Second in Command February 1918. Temp. Lt.-Colonel March 1918. Wounded twice, mentioned in despatches three times, Brevet of Italian Silver Medal for Military Valour, D.S.O., M.C. and bar. Transferred to command 5th Bn. Royal Irish Regiment, Army of Rhine 1919. Instructor Sandhurst 1920-24. Transferred Royal Tank Corps 1923. Joint author of "Within Four Walls" (Arnold).

Jones, E. H. Enlisted as gunner in Volunteer Artillery Battery (Rangoon Contingent), June 1915. Served in Mesopotamia from June 1915 to April 1916. Promoted Corporal July 1915, Lieutenant I.A.R.O. September 1915. Taken prisoner on surrender of Kut, 29 April 1916. Got moved from Yozgad with C. W. Hill by feigning insanity 1918. Sent as insane to Constantinople and certified by Turkish officials for exchange. Promoted Captain I.A.R.O., 1919. Author of "The Road to En-Dor" (The Bodley Head).

Justus, Heinz H. E. Oberleutnant A.D. Joined the German Army as Fahnenjunker (Ensign) in the 15th Hussars, 4 August 1914. Sent to Western Front October 1914, then after few weeks to the Russian Front. Transferred 1915 to Hanoverian Fusiliers (No. 73 Regiment). Fought on the Somme, Vimy Ridge and in Flanders 1915-1917. Taken prisoner at Langemark by Irish Guards, 31 July 1917. In various English prison-camps 1917-18. Made several attempts to escape from England, for which he was three times court-martialled and spent Christmas 1918 in Chelmsford Prison. Sent back to Germany July 1919.

Keeling, E. H. Served in India, Mesopotamia (twice wounded, mentioned in despatches, M.C.), Russia, Black Sea, Syria, Anatolia, Armenia and Kurdistan. Taken prisoner by the Turks on the fall of Kut. Retired with rank of Lieut.-Colonel. Author of "Adventures in Turkey and Russia".

von Mücke, Hellmut. Served in the First World War as the Executive Officer and First Lieutenant of the German Light Cruiser SMS *Emden* of the Kaiserliche Marine (the Imperial German Navy). He successfully led a fifty-man party on a ten month long escape across the ocean on a stolen schooner. Mücke received the Iron Cross first class and also published two books about his escape during the war: *The Emden* and *The Ayesha*.

Pearce, Ernest. Enlisted on 23 February 1915, at age of 15 in 14th Yorks and Lancs. Regiment. Saw active service at the age of 17 in the 2/7th Sherwood Foresters. Taken prisoner 21 March 1918. Received M.M. for escaping from Germany.

Plüschow, Gunther. First Naval Flying Officer at Kiao-Chow, China, on outbreak of war. Escaped in his aeroplane from Kiao-Chow during the siege, November 1914, and travelled by steamer to San Francisco under assumed name. Sailed from New York on Italian steamer January 1915. Identified and taken prisoner by English authorities at Gibraltar, brought to England and interned in Donington Hall Camp, February 1915. Escaped 4 July 1915, to London, and managed to board a Dutch steamer at Tilbury by night. Reached Germany through Holland July 13th, 1915. Awarded Iron Cross 1st Class by the Kaiser for his successful escape from England. Author of "My Escape from Donington Hall" (The Bodley Head), from which the following story is an extract.

Tholens, Hermann, Korvettenkapitan, A.D. Entered German Navy 1900. Second in command of HMS "Mainz," 1914. Captured by English 28 August 1914, about 100 miles west of Heligoland after fight against four cruisers and thirty destroyers led by HMS "Arethusa," in which his ship was torpedoed and he himself was picked up after swimming for an hour. Taken to military hospital, Chatham, transferred to Dyffryn Aled, near Denbigh, N. Wales. Escaped and was recaptured and sent to Chelmsford Prison for three months. Sent to Switzerland, September 1917, interned there till May 1918.

Wingfield, Lawrence, A. joined R.F.C. September 1915, No. 12 Squadron, at St. Omer, January 1916, taken prisoner 1 July 1916, shot down whilst on bombing raid over enemy territory. M.C., D.F.C.

THE GRIM GAME OF ESCAPE

By J. R. Ackerley

Although I was a prisoner of war in Germany I never attempted to escape – in fact, as far as I can recall those times, which now seem so remote and unreal, I never even thought of doing so. Perhaps the fact that I was taken rather late in the War – in the middle of 1917 – had something to do with that, for by that time I may well have been too stunned and frightened to do anything more than "stay put". However, the reason does not matter, and there is worse to come, for not only did I not try to escape myself, but I do not remember that anyone else tried to escape from any of the three camps in which I found myself. Perhaps these two facts are to some extent related, for the Germans tried to segregate the "bad boys" – persistent escapers and such – into special camps where a stricter discipline and closer supervision were kept, and where the atmosphere of unrest they generated would not affect "good boys" – like myself.

So I am afraid that your disappointment in me as introducer of this volume of adventures will now be complete – and I share your disappointment with you, for I have lately been reading a great many books about escapes and meeting their authors, and I never had any idea that such exciting events were taking place in other camps, not only in Germany, but in England too, and all over the world. Indeed, they may actually have been afoot in my own camps, under my very nose, for all I know, for escapers seem to have learnt from sad experience that they must keep their plots darkly secret, not only on account of spies, who were sometimes put to mingle with them, but because their fellow-prisoners themselves couldn't be trusted not to gossip and let the cat out of the bag. This book is a collection of the stories of some of these escapades told by the escapers themselves, as far as they are able to compress the history of their exploits into the space allotted to them; for many of them attempted to escape a great many times before they actually succeeded in getting away, and months and months were often spent in elaborate preparation. There are a variety of stories – the stories of our own people who escaped from Germany and from Turkey, and the other side is here too, for German escapers in this country are also represented in this book.

Generally speaking, there seem to have been three separate problems connected with escaping – breaking camp, reaching the frontier and crossing the frontier, and the comparative difficulties attaching to these three problems varied with period, camp and country. Chance, of course, always played a pretty large part in each of them, but in the last two it sometimes took almost complete charge.

To break out of most of the camps in Turkey, for example, was not the most serious problem of the three. The real questions there, in the heart of Asia, were how to cross several hundred miles of waterless desert and mountainous, robber-infested country, and perhaps worse still, what on earth to do when one reached the Black Sea, or Marmora, or the Mediterranean, or whatever shore one was making for. Both these problems were very chancy indeed. One had to leave a lot – far too much – on the knees of the Gods, as Mr. E. H. Keeling will tell you. The difficulties and hardships were, in fact, so dark and incalculable that a number of prisoners in Turkey devised other methods of escape which involved securing the unconscious assistance of their captors themselves.

That is the story of Mr. E. H. Jones, of "The Road to Endor" fame, and he describes how he hoodwinked the Turks into setting him free. In these islands, too, there was one of those exceptional and daunting difficulties – the coast. Up to that point the escaper could foresee, calculate; the difficulties were, in fact, much the same as those confronting our own men in Germany; but then, at the coast, little more than chance remained. That is why so few of the prisoners we took managed to escape completely; it was due to our "splendid isolation," as one of them told me. He – Oberleutnant Heinz Justus – describes here his many attempts to solve this difficult question. But in Germany, and of course in other inland countries too, the three problems were, so to speak, more fairly set; although, as I have said, there was an element of chance in all of them, in none did it play so disproportionate and discouraging a part as in Turkey and England. The actual camp-breaking was undoubtedly, I think, the main problem in Germany, though the subsequent difficulties mustn't be under-estimated. They were very ticklish indeed, and required a very high degree of caution, patience and endurance; in fact, I believe that as many, if not more, attempts to escape were scotched outside the German camps as inside them. The distances to the frontiers varied, of course; but, long or short, the time the journeys took was greatly prolonged, since the escapers could only march by night and in a roundabout way across country, avoiding roads and villages. During the day-time – sixteen or seventeen hours – they had to lie up in hiding, in whatever cover came to hand before dawn broke. That may not sound much, but it was, I can well believe, the worst part of the whole journey. Try it, and see how long you can stick it, lying close in one place, and then imagine the effect on men who were hunted and hungry, and whose nerves were already ragged with anxiety and impatience. At this rate it sometimes took them as long as three or four weeks to reach the frontier, and they lived all this time on whatever condensed foods they could carry, eked out with raw vegetables from the fields. They got lost, hungry and tired; they were exposed to all weathers, and they became so dirty and unshaven that a single glimpse of them must inevitably have aroused suspicion and betrayed them. It was, in fact, a very nerve-racking journey, and the frontier problem, if they got that far, was even more ticklish, for how does one find a frontier in total darkness, in the country, with a compass and small-scale map? How does one find it, that's to say, especially when one is already fagged out and impatient, without blundering into the arms of one of the numerous, invisible sentries – who may be a yard or a mile away – or without attracting their attention by some small noise – the snapping of a twig? How the devil was one to know, as one crawled along, on hands and knees, in and out of ditches, whether one had reached and crossed it or not – for there was often nothing, deep in the country, to mark the boundary at all, except this close but invisible ring of sentries? Indeed, it sometimes happened that escapers did crawl across into safety without knowing it, and then, owing to some twist in the line, crawled back into Germany and captivity again.

So these two problems were by no means negligible; they required the greatest care and patience; but they did not require, I think, the *ingenuity* needed for breaking out of camp, and the escapers from Germany in this volume, since they have not a great deal of space at their disposal, will concentrate mainly upon that. That was the real nut; that was where the fun came in, and I think you will be amused and surprised at the skill with which they tackled it.

They burrowed under the defences of the camps like moles; they swooped over them like bats; they swam the moats in broad daylight under the noses of the sentries with their faces painted white and green to resemble water-lilies; they – but I must leave it to them to tell their own stories. But was there any expedient they did not think of? Any impudent trick they did not play – in all the countries concerned? No Rallies or Arséne Lupin can lay claim to anything like the resource, the ingenuity, the inexhaustible invention shown by these prison-breakers in their stories.

And not merely that. Consider too the patience and determination required. For these were seldom *reckless* acts, suddenly undertaken on the spur of the moment. They were usually most carefully planned, and months and months of thought and work went to their preparation. The smallest detail of disguise or equipment was painstakingly considered; the remotest adverse contingency prepared against as far as possible. And all the time they were being watched.

Imagine yourselves in these circumstances digging a hundred foot tunnel with a table-spoon, for instance, or cutting through an iron window-bar with a saw made out of a broken razor-blade, for it must be remembered, too, that they started their careers as prison-breakers with nothing, and the collecting together of tools and an escaping kit alone was a long and complicated business. Artful code messages were sent home in letters asking for such things as maps and compasses, which were smuggled back in the food parcels. Needless to say the contents of these parcels were most carefully examined before the prisoners were allowed to have them – tins of food were opened and emptied, and things prodable were prodded with skewers. But much of the contraband got through to them nevertheless. What couldn't be procured in this and other ways they had to make for themselves – more than that, they had to make the very tools with which they made them. And all out of nothing, out of odds and ends.

And that is what comes out most in these stories: patience and determination. For schemes which had taken months of hard work to prepare often failed at the last moment. The conspirators were suddenly ordered to another camp, or the tunnel fell in in its last few yards, or the plot was discovered, or the escapers, having achieved the first part of their plan and broken out of the camp, were retaken before they crossed the frontier. But no sooner had one of these schemes failed and the punishment for it been served, than another scheme was at once set afoot. They enjoyed it; undoubtedly they enjoyed it. It kept them going, and apart from the serious object of it all, they extracted from it a great deal of fun. The game – it was very like one of those board games we used to play as boys – the game was tireless. The camp was the board. Picture it. It varied in detail from place to place, but the general plan was always much the same. Here is a description of one prison camp, chosen at random.

"It was bounded all round by a fence of solid boarding, about eight feet high, with six strands of overhung barbed wire on top. Outside this was a twenty-strand barbed wire fence about ten feet high – in all about thirty-one miles of wire were used for a perimeter of six hundred yards. There was one sentry or more at every angle outside, and sentries inside at every point where buildings stood close to the board fence. There were big arc lights dotted about all over the inside and small electric lamps at about twenty yard intervals along the board fence..."

That is the kind of thing. Another camp might be an old fortress surrounded by a moat to add to the difficulties; but the general scheme of defence was much the same.

And inside, in blocks of buildings or huts, were the prisoners, men of all nationalities, intent on getting out. How did they do it? Sometimes, particularly in some of those special camps in which most of the persistent escapers were segregated, the problem that confronted them as they prowled round the defences – simulating innocent perambulation, but in reality keenly investigating for weak spots – the problem seemed insoluble. So many various attempts had already been made, even here, that the captors seemed wise to every possible move and had taken counter precautions. Extra sentries and arc lamps had been placed; Alsatian police dogs added; surprise searches were constantly made; extra roll-calls at particularly inconvenient times instituted. The situation seemed hopeless. Was there any move left? There was. It seems there always was. How was it done? The escapers themselves will tell you.

A good many of the books which have been published in all countries about escaping, especially those published during or soon after the war, are coloured with the animosities and prejudices of that time, and I believe that a number of their authors could now wish this otherwise.

This book, however, will not concern itself with the treatment of prisoners of war or the conditions in which they lived, excepting in so far as these are a relevant background to their adventures of escape. Prisoners of war were treated the same in every country that took part in the war, and when they received – as they occasionally did receive in all countries – real kindness and consideration, then we may be surprised and grateful that such good qualities managed to survive the poison and the pettiness of those times. That is the most that can be said. For war is not intended to bring out the best and kindest in men; the emotions it deliberately calls forth and fosters – hatred, fear, greed, revenge – are not pretty emotions and do not beget pretty manners. But in any case such matters are irrelevant to this book, for it was never from hardship or injustice, where they existed, that these men were escaping – though such conditions may sometimes have supplied a purely artificial stimulus.

Captain J. L. Hardy has an illuminating passage in his book, "I Escape!" He was one of the most persistent and daring escapers of them all – in fact he was known to the Germans as "that maniac Hardy"; and after one of his many attempts he was sent to a camp in Augustabad in the North of Germany. This is what he says about it: –

"I felt my captivity very much more at Augustabad than in any place where I have since been. The camp was a hotel which had been converted, and the food though not too plentiful, was good, while the staff were polite and our rooms clean and comfortable. I was only in the camp for ten days, but was perfectly miserable during the whole of that time, and I do not think I was hypersensitive in that it seemed to me abominable that I should be leading a life of comfort at such a time. It was never again my lot to find myself in a good camp, and of that I am glad..."

So you see that the urge to escape sprang from something much deeper than physical conditions; it sprang from a very deep human instinct indeed – the need for self-expression; and that is why these stories must appeal to all of us, for they touch a universal note which inspires our own actions, not only in war but in peace. Prisoners of war were on the shelf, and they felt it all the time. They were unimportant, they were unused, and especially to educated men that is a very dreadful thing indeed. It was not just being separated from countries, families, friends; it was not just being out of the war; it went deeper than that; it was a thwarting of the free and natural growth of individual life, and it has permanently stunted many a once eager and ambitious spirit.

This book, however, will not concern itself with that either – that gloomy general background of monotonous waiting and wasting – but one ought to remember it all the same so that these stories may not be taken as typical of the lives of prisoners of war. They are not by any means typical; they are very rare, for the vast majority of prisoners, I think, tried to find other means of escape – tried, that is to say, to preserve the balance and fitness of their minds in other ways: in writing, or reading, or friendships, or learning languages, or by taking up the various other pursuits and sports that their circumstances offered.

Although these stories spring, unfortunately, from the war and have that for their background, they are nevertheless side-issues – the tales of men who were "out of" the war – and I think they can and should be kept separate. For they have all the fascination, the glamour of the good adventure story. They are not concerned with the destruction of life and property; their direct object, as I have said, was the attainment of personal freedom, and that is a very inspiring and romantic thing. And another characteristic which, I think, distinguishes them from other war stories, is that in the risks these escapers ran there was usually that element – the sporting chance. They did, of course, run risks. The sentries might shoot; or the plan to escape may already have been discovered and an armed guard waiting in ambush; or one might be killed in the scuffle and excitement of recapture; or one might die of exposure or at the hands of brigands in the mountains and deserts of Turkey. There was certainly risk – and a number of fatalities did, in fact, occur, and a few attempted escapes ended in death.

But if I may say so without seeming to minimize the courage and achievements of these adventurers it was, so to speak, a fair and measureable risk, and the fear in their minds was not *primarily* a fear of death, but a fear of recapture. The danger, in fact, was not an indefinable, ubiquitous, helpless danger, such as that run, for instance, by a wiring party in No-man's land or raiders upon enemy trenches. Death would not drop from out of the skies or mine the ground under their feet. It was, comparatively speaking, locatable, accountable, and therefore a danger against which they could, to some extent, pit their wits. And that is the point: the success or failure of their efforts all through did largely depend upon their own skill and abilities; they could and did use their wits; they had usually what is called a sporting chance. But modern war itself can hardly be said to be liberal with its sporting chances; and the soldier in his trench or the sailor on his ship may be as clever as paint, but how far will that help him against gas and mines and long range guns?

The flying corps perhaps tasted something of this feeling of adventure of which I am speaking, when the stunts on which they were engaged were not too perilous. For they too, in their own specialised war of single combats, must have experienced this sense of personal endeavour and personal achievement, of self reliance and of the sporting chance. And that no doubt is why a better relationship existed between enemy air forces than among other arms. They were not required to live like rats in the ground, and did not therefore think of each other such. On the contrary there seems to have been a curious chivalry among them. They were dealing, between themselves, with individuals whose personal abilities and courage they were able to recognise and acknowledge, and the result was, as Captain Wingfield makes clear, that when they took their air-antagonists prisoner they generally showed them an almost ceremonial respect and courtesy, practically unknown among the other arms of the war.

Well, read these adventure tales. Perhaps they are the last war-escape stories that will ever be told, for it may not be fanciful to suppose that if ever there is another great war there will be no more prisoners – except in so far as nations can be imprisoned within the boundaries of their lands and dart about from end to end in their efforts to escape the poisons that fall from the sky.

CHAPTER ONE

TRAPPED IN BELGIUM

By Harry Beaumont

The hospital authorities gave me the job of nursing one the British officers. He was totally paralysed, and the Belgians could do very little for him. I nursed him until he died about three weeks later.

Doing this kind of work made me helpful to the Belgians and they used to give me the tip whenever the German officer came visiting. He always commenced at the officers' building, and by the time he arrived at our end, my bed was rolled up stowed away in the storeroom and I was well hidden in the scrap iron yard.

I went on dodging this fellow up to about the second or third week in October; then, one day, he checked the roll and suddenly discovered there was one man in that hospital that he had never seen. He was in a terrible rage and ordered Belgians to search the colliery and produce me. They knew, of course, where to find me, and I was taken before him. He glared at me, and in very good English said, "Why have you been absent from this hospital every time I've visited it?" I made the first excuse that came into my head: "I didn't know you were coming. I'm fond of fresh air and spend most of my time in the grounds." He said: "Fresh air! Fresh air! You'll get all the fresh air you want very soon! I shall send you to Stettin-on-Oder!" I said: "Thank you," and returned to my ward with something to think about.

I made up my mind there and then that I was not going to Stettin, but I had not the slightest idea what to do about it. Next day the answer came without my seeking. Lance-Corporal Arthur Heath, of my regiment – who was one of the patients – had got very friendly with a Belgian and his wife by the name of Neusy, who used to visit the hospital. Heath took me into his confidence. He told me that if he could get to the Neusys' house they were going to look after him, and get him out of the country when he was well enough.

He was shot through the thigh, and could not walk. Someone therefore would have to carry him from the hospital to the Neusys' house, and I was the man he chose to do the job. I said I would do it, but would the Neusys look after me too. Heath said he did not know, but thought it would be all right. We then started getting ready. Heath practised walking up and down the ward with a couple of sticks, and I looked round for a civilian suit.

Our ward was opposite the gas retorts and the stoker used to come in about 8 o'clock every night, change into overalls, and hang his suit up near the door. He worked until about 3 o'clock in the morning, and would then fall asleep until it was time to go home; so that suit was mine for the taking. On 26 October we were suddenly ordered to be in readiness to proceed to Germany at 10 o'clock on the following day, so there was now no time to be lost and we fixed 4 o'clock in the morning as the time for our escape. We arranged that as I was to do all the hard work, I should go to bed and Heath would keep awake and rouse me about ten minutes to four.

One of the patients in the hospital was a Prussian and this Prussian was in our ward. He was badly wounded, and seldom went to sleep, and I was very much afraid that he would see us going and give the alarm. But a funny thing happened. That night he beckoned me to his bedside to help him turn over, which I had often done before. As soon as I had made him comfortable, to my surprise he gripped me by the hand and placed his finger on his lips. This was his way of telling me that he knew what was going on and would keep silent. It was decent of him; we were just brothers in distress.

At ten minutes to four I was roused by Heath, who quietly left the ward on his crutches. I saw him clear and then went to the stokehold and bagged the stoker's suit. I emptied everything out of the pockets and tied them up in a bundle in the old chap's red handkerchief and left it on the hook beside him. I did not want to rob him of more than I could help. He was still dreaming about the end of the War when I crept away.

I joined Heath at the gate. He had discarded his crutches for his sticks, which had been put there for him overnight. The Neusys' house was about four miles away, and we had a rough sketch of the road to it on a sheet of ordinary notepaper. I carried Heath on my back; but it was no fun for him either as he was in great pain. At every turn of the road we struck a match and consulted our map. I well remember those matches; they were the old-fashioned twinklers of the "wait a minute" kind. After two hours, we reached our destination, which was the second house with iron railings in the Rue Calvary in the village of Petite Wasmes. We hadn't been able to warn the Neusys that we were coming and we found the outer gate was locked. So I scaled the wall and threw some gravel at the bedroom window. After two or three throws Neusy put out his head, and in a few moments we were inside.

Emil Neusy was a heavily built man with a fresh complexion and a jolly disposition. His wife Marie was a slim little woman with the heart of a lion. They seemed pleased to have us, and soon made us comfortable; but the difficulty was conversation. They knew no English, and we knew no French, so we had to talk to one another with our hands, which was a very slow job. However, we were not allowed to rest for long. At about 9 o'clock a Belgian from the hospital arrived in a very excited state, and the Neusys at once hid us behind some thick curtains. They then invited him into the room, and after a long and apparently heated conversation, he left the house again. Neusy went out soon after and came back with a cab and took Heath away. I followed almost immediately, led by Neusy's son, a boy of thirteen, who took me to some woods and told me to stay there until he came back for me. After dark that night I was collected and taken to a café on the outskirts of the wood, where I found Heath, who had also spent the day in the woods.

We spent several days together in the woods, returning to the café at night for food and shelter. Heath still suffered great pain from his wound and found it very difficult to move about. By this time German patrols and the Belgian police had got tired of searching the district for us, so we moved by easy stages to the village of Paturage, where we were put up for a time by a Madame Godart, a friend of the Neusys. We returned to the Neusys' house at the end of November.

By this time the food shortage was acute. Everyone was rationed, except us of course – but we had many friends by now and never went short.

We were already beginning to pick up a certain amount of French, which eased our position considerably, and Heath had been attended by a doctor and his wound was now on the mend.

One day Neusy showed me a British rifle and several rounds of ammunition which he had souvenired from the battlefields. I did not think it was a wise souvenir and said so, and advised him to get rid of it. I told him that if the house was searched it would be his death warrant and possibly that of others as well, and although he would not take this seriously at first I never let the subject drop until the rifle was eventually cemented into the wall under the window-sill of the front bedroom. The room was then repapered to remove any traces of tampering with the walls.

Just before Christmas 1914 the Germans began to realise that there were a good many British soldiers being hidden by the Belgians in occupied territory, so they issued a warning through the Local Authorities that any British soldier who gave himself up before a certain date would be treated as a prisoner of war; but that if he failed to surrender and was caught he would be shot as a spy whether in uniform or not. It also warned the inhabitants that the penalty for harbouring the enemy was death. I never saw this order, but it was discussed by the Neusys, and they decided to take the risk. So we sat tight.

About the middle of February, 1915, Marie received a visit from the mayor of the district. He said that it had come to his knowledge that two English soldiers were hiding in her house, and that as he was responsible for his district being clear they must go. He said he did not care where they went so long as they left the district. The same night I left for Paturage to live with Madame Godart again. Heath preferred to stay where he was.

A fortnight later a neighbour of the Neusys came round to me there and between fits of weeping told me that the Germans had taken Heath. This was very bad news, and as soon as it got dark that night I moved to a place called La Bouverie, about five miles distant, to the house of Madam Godart's mother. This old lady was eighty years of age. At dawn the next morning there was a terrific banging at the front door. I naturally thought the Germans had come for me, and was half-way out the window when I heard the voices of Heath and Emil Neusy.

Heath had not been caught after all, and this is what had happened at the Neusys' house. At 9 o'clock the previous morning, two German detectives had entered by the back gate. They had given the correct secret signal, which was the opening of the gate three times, which automatically gave three peals on the bell in the kitchen. They had then walked straight into the house, covered Marie Neusy with an automatic and said: "You've got English in your house." Marie had denied this at once, although Heath was in bed in the room above. However, the detectives had wasted no time in argument; one remained with Marie and the other started searching the house. Luckily for Heath he began from the cellar. Heath had heard their conversation and knew he was in a hole. He had no time to put on his clothes, so in only his shirt and socks he climbed out of the landing window and dropped on to the roof of the scullery, which jutted out from the kitchen. Unfortunately the slates of the roof gave way with a fearful crash and Heath nearly came through into the scullery. The German in the kitchen at once rushed to the back door. So did Marie. She got there first, turned the key in the lock and put her back to the door. There was a brief struggle and then the German pushed her aside and opened the door. Unfortunately – or fortunately – this was the moment chosen by Heath to jump off the roof. He jumped on top of the detective and they fell to the ground. Heath was up first and raced down the garden, zig-zagging from side to side, his shirt flapping in the wind. The German who was still on the ground, fired four shots at him, but never got a hit. Heath jumped a low wall into the neighbour's garden, at the top of which was another wall – a high one with glass on top. He leapt at this, but missed his hold.

By this time the German was after him and had reached the bottom of Neusy's garden, only a few feet away. He covered Heath with his automatic and said: "Hands up." Heath took no notice. He decided not to be an Englishman at any price. The German gave the order again, this time in French and up went Heath's hands.

Meanwhile the German inside the house had reached the landing window and saw what was happening outside. He at once started to shout orders to the one in the garden, who turned round to reply. This gave Heath another chance. He made one more leap at the wall, gained a hold, and was over the top. The

German in the garden turned round just in time to see his last leg disappearing. He had one more shot but was far too late.

Heath had then done a record sprint across a ploughed field, down a lane, and through a forge, until he came to a cottage. The back door stood invitingly open, so in he went and locked the door behind him. The good lady of the house came down from upstairs and had a bit of a shock to find a stranger with no trousers on seated in her kitchen. However, he explained his position, and she soon fixed him up with one of her husband's suits. Heath had left the house at dark and gone to Madame Godart's, where he found Neusy. They had remained there until next morning, when they came to me.

Marie Neusy was arrested and taken to Mons, where she was committed for trial. The Germans ripped her house to pieces and took away several hundred francs. They didn't, however, find that rifle, and for all I know it's there still. They left word with the maid that if Emil Neusy came to Mons for his money he could have it. He went next day and they arrested him too.

After a few days at La Bouverie, we returned to Madame Godart, where we anxiously awaited the result of the trial. Marie smuggled a letter to us from her prison, concealed in a piece of bread, in which she said we were not to worry about her, for what she had done was for her country and not for us. These were brave words from a woman who was expecting her death.

But when the trial eventually came off, the first witness, who was Marie's maid, a girl of only twelve, stated with great presence of mind that the man who had escaped was a Belgian, and that he was the lover of Madame Neusy, and stayed in the house when the master was away on business. As soon as Neusy heard this he jumped up in court and demanded a divorce, and acted the part of the wronged husband so well that as the Germans had no evidence to the contrary they had to accept the story. Marie was sentenced to one month's imprisonment for obstructing the police, and Neusy was charged the costs of the trial.

A few days later we were visited by D'Capiaux, the engineer from the hospital, and I learnt what happened there when we escaped. He said the Germans were furious, and fined everyone connected with the hospital, and removed all the prisoners into Germany. He then told us that he had made arrangements to get us away. He took our photographs, and presented us next day with a certificate of identity, which changed our nationality to Belgian. This certificate was an absolute forgery, but complete in every detail even to the police stamp. He had even gone so far as to append our signatures without ever having seen our handwriting.

In a few days a guide came for us and we left for Brussels, where we were taken to a hospital. The matron in charge of this hospital was Nurse Edith Cavell. I'm afraid I can't tell you much about Nurse Cavell. She was very busy all the time, and so we didn't see very much of her, but she seemed a very homely woman with a smile and a cheery word for everyone.

Brussels was teeming with Germans, and here under their noses were at least a score of helpless British Tommies waiting to be smuggled across the frontier.

We were only in the hospital for three days, and then there was a sudden alarm, and we were all cleared out in two's and three's, and conducted to the homes of various Belgians, who were all members of the same wonderful organisation. This organisation was linked up from Northern France, right across Belgium to the Dutch frontier, and existed solely for the purpose of helping British, French and Belgians out of the country.

In this sudden move I was separated from Heath, and left the hospital accompanied by Michael Carey, of the Munster Fusiliers. The Munsters were cut off during the retreat from Mons, and many of them had remained at large until picked up by the organisation.

A week later we left our house in the Avenue de Longchamps with a guide and made an attempt to reach the frontier. On the way we picked up four more Irishmen, which made our party seven, and we soon left Brussels behind, and reached the open country. The order of march was for the guide to go ahead and the remainder to follow in pairs at intervals of 200 yards.

We passed through Louvain and Aerschot, and in the late afternoon arrived at the Monastery of Averabode, where we received food and shelter for the night. There were over 200 monks in this monastery and only two could speak English.

The next morning our party was joined by a young Belgian who also wanted to get out of the country. We set off at daybreak, left the main road, and made our way across country. Our destination was Turnout, a town near the Dutch frontier. At about mid-day we came to a railway crossing, where a sentry examined our forged identity cards. He just compared the face with the photograph and allowed us to pass.

The two Belgians, the three Irishmen and myself got through without a hitch; but one of the Irishmen of the last pair could not for the moment find his identity card, and while he was fumbling in his pockets, he accidentally dropped a five-franc note. No sooner had it reached the ground than the sentry promptly put his foot on it, looked round at the guard house behind to see that no one was watching, and passed the Irishman on with a movement of the hand. That was accidental bribery.

Two hours later we struck the main road again, and here our guide gave instructions to the other Belgian and left us. Soon afterwards we entered Turnout, which was packed with Germans. We at once proceeded to the address which had been given us of the man who was the next link in the chain of the organisation. But when we got there we found, to our dismay, that the house was full of German soldiers. It had been taken over as a billet. This floored us: our guide had gone, and we had no other addresses so we retired to a café in a quiet part of the town to discuss the situation.

The Belgian made enquiries as to the possibility of our crossing the frontier by ourselves, but he was told that we should have to swim a canal and pass two chains of sentries, which was considered an impossibility without an experienced guide. It was very dangerous to remain in Turnout, so the only thing to do was to return to Brussels. But we were all footsore and weary after our two days' march, so we found an old woman with a horse and cart, and she agreed to take the risk and give us a lift back to the Monastery of Averabode for the sum of 12 francs 50 per head.

As soon as it was dark we set off, and got along all right until we were halted by a mounted patrol at about one o'clock. I was on the front seat, and the officer-in-charge of the patrol walked up to me with an electric torch and a revolver, both of which he pointed at me. He questioned me in Flemish, which I didn't understand, so I kept my mouth shut. The old woman and the Belgian butted in, with explanations, and we were ordered off the cart and lined up by the roadside, where our identity cards were examined. The officer seemed satisfied with these, and allowed us to pass on our way.

It was a narrow shave, for there were three things we should have been caught out on. Only two of the party had spoken at all; we were on the road during prohibited hours without a special permit, and we were many miles from the place of our registration.

We arrived at the convent four hours later, and when we had had some food turned in for a well needed rest. That evening the Belgian left us to return to Brussels, and promised to report our position to Nurse Cavell.

We were well treated by the monks. We slept in the laundry at night, and retired to a room at the top of the building by day, where we passed away the time by playing cards for buttons. We couldn't play for money as the cost of our journey back from Turnout had broke the lot of us.

Seven days passed and no word came from Brussels, so one of the monks volunteered to go in and find out what was to be done. He returned the next day with the guide who had conducted us to Turnout.

The following day we returned to Brussels. Michael Carey and myself were taken to another house in the Rue du Brasserie. The other four Irishmen went somewhere else, and I never saw them again.

Our hostess was a very wealthy woman. Her house was stocked with everything of the best, and for eight days we lived like lords. Then, with two Frenchmen who were already in the house when we arrived, we were picked up by the same old guide and made another attempt to reach the frontier. We passed up through Malines this time, and everything went smoothly until we reached an examining post at a bridge-head over a canal, about six miles south of Antwerp. There were two sentries, one on each side of the road. The guide had already passed and the Frenchmen were following behind Carey and myself. We looked at the two sentries as we approached, and weighed them up carefully. The fellow on the right looked less intelligent than the other, so we decided to give him the honour of inspecting our identity cards. He just compared the face with the photograph and allowed us to pass.

A little further on, round a bend in the road, we waited for the two Frenchmen to catch up. We waited ten minutes and then our guide became alarmed and went back to see what had happened. He learnt that the two Frenchmen had been arrested by the sentry on the left. They had identity cards the same as ourselves and we never knew the reason for their arrest or their fate. It was just luck that had made us choose the sentry on the right, instead of the one on the left.

When we reached Antwerp we found our next link, which was a Red Cross building which had been used during the siege. The building was empty, however, and the man-in-charge told us that it was being taken over by the Germans next day as a clearing station for the Belgian refugees who were returning from Holland. This was another disappointment. He allowed us to stay there that night and early next morning our guide took us to the Hotel d'Esperance, which soon belied its name.

This was on a Saturday towards the end of April, six months after I'd escaped from the hospital at Wasmes.

After we had some lunch our guide told us to remain where we were until he returned on Monday. He said we had nothing to worry about; that everything had been arranged and there was nothing to pay. On Sunday night the proprietress presented us with the bill, which included the cost of the guide's food for the day before. As this took place in the public dining room, and there were a good many Germans there, we couldn't argue the point, so we retired to our bedroom followed by the proprietress, and induced her to wait for her money until our friend returned on Monday. I needn't add we never saw him again. There were further arguments with the proprietress on the Monday and Tuesday, and the good lady informed us that if we didn't pay by 12 o'clock on Wednesday she'd inform the police. I'm pretty certain she'd have done this at once if she'd known who we were. Carey and I couldn't muster five francs between us and our position was serious. On the Wednesday morning I told her I was going out to find my friend. Where I really went to was a house nearby, which was tenanted by the American Commission for the relief of the Belgians, but there were too many Germans about the building for my liking and I returned to the hotel. About 11.30 Carey decided to go round and try his luck. I told him not to return if he was unsuccessful, and that I'd try and make a "get away" on my own, but he wouldn't agree to that. He returned just before twelve with a face wreathed in smiles and I knew he'd been successful. He'd gained audience with the Commissioner, who had given him enough cash to meet our immediate expenses, which we did without delay, and had promised to help us too in other ways. Half an hour later we were visited by a Belgian who owned a café in another part of the city. He said the Commissioner had sent him to look after us until such time that we could be passed over the frontier. The commission would allow us twenty francs a day, he said, but we were not to visit it again, and any communication was to be made through him.

After this, our prestige at the hotel went up by leaps and bounds; our meals were served in a private room, and there was no more trouble with the proprietress.

We roamed all over Antwerp for three weeks, and then, on 16 May 1915, we were introduced to the guide who was to take us over the frontier. He was a small withered old man over 60 years of age and almost a dwarf. The following night we met at the café of our friend who had been our link with the American Commission, and after cracking the best bottle of champagne in the house, Carey and I and the guide accompanied by the café proprietor boarded a tram for the outskirts of the city. Here our friend bid us God speed and returned to his home. It was now nine o'clock, pitch dark, and raining in torrents. We left the main road and soon realised that our guide was a marvel. In spite of his age he moved quickly, in fact we had difficulty in keeping pace with him. He could see like a cat, and appeared to know every inch of the country. After three hours of zig-zagging down railway tracks, wading ditches, and trespassing over private property, we emerged from some undergrowth by a deserted cottage, and saw the frontier barrier a few feet ahead. It was still raining heavily and we were soaked to the skin. The church clocks in Holland were striking midnight, and we could see the electric lights on the Dutch roads 500 yards away. Our guide motioned us to lay down, and left us for about ten minutes. When he returned he took off all his clothes except his shirt, under-pants and boots, and told us to do the same. This was to make it easier for us to crawl through the wire. We tied up our discarded clothes and threw them over the top of the barrier, which appeared to be fifteen to twenty feet in width. It was thickly meshed and very close to the ground. Each of us then selected a spot and commenced to crawl through. This could only be done by lying flat on the stomach, stretching the arms at full length, grasping the wire and pulling the body forward two or three inches at the time. It took us quite twenty minutes to reach the other side. My underclothes were ripped to ribbons and my body smarted from head to foot where it had been torn by the barbs. We rested a few moments, then grabbed our bundles and made a bolt towards the lights in the distance. Five hundred yards further we waded a ditch, stepped over a couple of strands of barbed wire, and saw a sentry in blue uniform a few yards away. We were in Holland. The sentry came up, patted us on the back and said: "Goot Engleesh." We put on our clothes and an hour later were being cared for at a Dutch inn.

The following morning our wonderful guide, who had taken us through without having seen or heard a German sentry, handed us over to the Belgian Consul at Roosendael and bid us goodbye. These guides were paid by the organisation at the rate of three pounds a head for everyone they got safely across. The same day we were sent to Flushing, and when I was signing my name in the Strand Hotel register I saw the signature of Arthur Heath, whom I'd left in Brussels. A day after I caught him up at Rotterdam and we both came home together on 21 May 1915. This was the end of my journey.

I had been told by the guide who took me from Nurse Cavell's hospital that I was known as No. 83 on her books; but out of that number I was only the thirteenth to get safely across the frontier.

You may like to know what eventually happened to some of the principals of this story.

D'Capiaux, who forged the identity cards, was sentenced to twenty years' imprisonment just after Nurse Cavell was shot. He was released at the Armistice.

Emil and Marie Neusy left the country and came to England as refugees in August 1915. They were afterwards compensated by the British Government. Marie Neusy and Madame Godart received special medals and illuminated addresses from both the British and Belgian Governments.

As for me I was officially reported by the War Office as killed in action on 24 August 1914, and when I reached England I found my wife a widow.

CHAPTER TWO

BEGINNERS

By H. A. Cartwright

It was early in 1915, when it had become quite evident that the war was not going to be a matter of a month or two, that a few of us first began to discuss the possibility of escape, and about the middle of February I began with another British officer seriously to work out a plan. We were then at Burg bei Magdeburg, which is six hundred kilometres from the Swiss frontier and four hundred from Holland. The camp had been hastily formed by throwing a fence round a group of gun-sheds and mobilisation store-rooms. We English – all bagged at Mons and Le Cateau – were a small minority in a large mob of Belgian, Russian and French officers. A few rank and file of all nations were kept in the camp for fatigue duties.

We decided that it would be quite possible, as soon as the weather became warmer, to walk to the Dutch frontier, travelling always by night and lying hidden in the forests by day. Neither of us could speak a word of German so a train journey was out of the question.

We bought, from a peddling bookseller who was allowed to visit the camp, a North German Baedeker which contained a few maps, and, from a study of these, though they did not cover the whole route, it seemed that the road was not too difficult. There appeared to be plenty of woods and forests.

We decided to collect a store of chocolate, biscuits, oxo and other portable forms of food from the parcels which were then beginning to arrive, believing that we could carry enough of such concentrated foods for a month's walk. We counted on being able to steal a certain amount of roots, etc., to give the necessary bulk. We thought that we should be able, without much risk, to light fires for cooking purposes in the woods.

The camp was a strong one and we had great difficulty in hitting on a plan to break out of it which offered a reasonable chance of success and before we found one our first schemings were ended by my being sent to the local civil jail, with several other British officers, by way of reprisal for the internment of German submarine crews in detention barracks in England. Solitary confinement, after several months in a very small room in which three Russians, three Frenchmen, three Belgians and only one other Englishman slept, cooked, ate, quarrelled, spat and sometimes washed their feet, was the purest bliss. I came out of prison in June 1915 and returned to Burg camp, which I found much enlarged. All the prisoners whom I had known had gone to other camps, and a new batch, of whom only three were English, had been brought in. Among them was Charles Harrison, of the Royal Irish Regiment, whom I had never previously met, although we had been at school and Sandhurst together and our battalions had occupied and mobilised in the same barracks at Devonport.

Harrison one day found me making a copy of a "camp permit", a small printed ticket which was given to contractors and workmen who visited the camp and which was supposed to be given up to the guard on their leaving. I was making the permit without having any definite idea as to how it might be used, but I had always at the back of my mind the feeling that the easiest way out was through the front door. Harrison told me that he meant to try to escape, and we decided to work together. As later events showed, he was by far the most ingenious, resourceful and determined trier of all those who eventually turned their hands to the business.

The camp (see plan on page 15) was bounded all round by a fence of solid boarding about eight feet high with six strands of overhung barbed wire on the top. Outside this was a twenty-strand barbed wire fence about ten feet high – in all about thirty-one miles of wire were used for a perimeter of six hundred yards. There was one sentry – or more – at every angle outside, and sentries inside at every point where buildings stood close to the board fence. There were big arc lights dotted about all over the inside and small electric lamps at about twenty-yard intervals along the board fence.

BURG

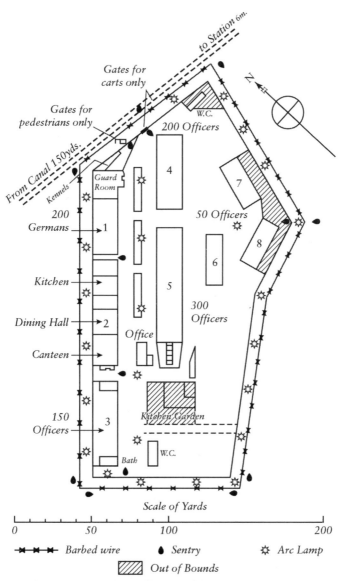

MAP OF INTERNMENT CAMP AT BURG BEI MAGDEBURG

The exits were, firstly, a small gate giving on to the road just by the guard-room, where a lot of idle German soldiers were always loafing; and, secondly, close to it, a big double gate for wagons. All civilians had to pass through the small gate, showing a pass, and all soldiers were supposed to do the same, but there was a good deal of slackness in the carrying out of these rules.

We decided that the only way out was through one of the gates, and accordingly we began to work on two alternative plans so as to have something to fall back upon if anything should occur to upset one of them.

One plan was to wait for a wet day, when the guard and loafers would be inside the guard-room, disguise ourselves as workmen and try to shuffle out with sacks over our heads (a common practice in wet weather), carrying a stove between us with several lengths of stove-piping. We would show the permits, which I was making, as we passed the gate. The advantage of this plan was that we could stow any amount of food, extra clothing, rucksacks, etc., in the stove and pipes and re-pack at leisure when we got into cover outside the camp. The attempt was to be made just before dusk, and we knew of cover within a few hundred yards of the gate.

The other plan was to disguise ourselves as German officers and walk straight out of the gate. This also would have to be just at dusk, so that we should soon have darkness to cover our change of clothes; but it must be light enough for us to be easily recognised as officers.

We were prepared to gamble on no Hun soldier daring to address an officer who failed to show a pass, no matter how strict or intricate the rules on the subject might be.

For this plan we needed German officers' great-coats, caps, leggings and swords – or something that looked very like them. I apologise for the following long description of our uniform, but to us the matter was of the first importance.

Harrison wrote to his tailor, told him that he was being transferred to the Grenadiers and ordered the great-coat of that regiment, which is of a blue-grey colour instead of the universal drab. I asked a Grenadier of about my own build to order a coat for me. Harrison also ordered from his tailor two blue caps with red bands – the undress cap of his regiment – which, with a little cardboard stuffing, could be made to look exactly like the German home-service cap.

The German wears two small badges on his cap; they consist, in Prussia, of small silver rings with, in the top one, a red spot in the middle and, in the bottom one, a silver Maltese cross on a black ground. Each is mounted on a rosette of patent leather. With buttons and silver paper I made badges which would have passed any inspection, notwithstanding the fact that the red spots were really minute Union Jacks and the Maltese crosses were spread-eagle angels of peace. We made this little variation because we were not too happy as to how the Germans might view the wearing of their uniform by enemies in the event of our recapture, and preferred to be able to deny that what we were wearing was their uniform at all.

The shoulder-straps were more difficult. They consist each of two pieces of silver braid, curled round a button and mounted on cloth of various colours, according to the corps, regiment, etc. They carry badges of rank, numerals and sometimes regimental badges. I made the braid by weaving blue, grey and white silk on a kind of Heath Robinson loom, and the effect was a good enough imitation of silver. Later the German took to making his shoulder-straps, for active service, of silk instead of silver, so ours were not only effective but correct. We bought stars (they were much like our own pattern) and numerals and plain gilt buttons (as worn by all ranks) at the camp canteen. On a show of worn-out boots borrowed without leave from a Belgian private, we were allowed to buy new yellow boots, and we bought yellow leggings from the merchant who came to supply them. Harrison carved the swords very artistically out of bits of packing-case. The German service-dress scabbard is of black metal, so we blackened the last eighteen inches of them, which was as much as would show below our great-coats, and polished them with boot-blacking.

While waiting for our great-coats we began to work out a route.

The Swiss frontier was ruled out by distance.

At this time nothing was known of the Dutch frontier by anyone in the camp, but we imagined that it was very closely guarded, and possibly wired, and we thought it probable that the whole frontier district would be very carefully supervised and controlled.

We knew, from watching the comic "alarms" which the Commandant was in the habit of staging, that cyclist patrols would be sent out on all likely roads as soon as any prisoner was missed, and we thought it likely that towns and villages lying west of the camp would be on the look-out. For these reasons, and on account of many other difficulties, possibly quite imaginary, which our complete ignorance of conditions in Germany may have made us exaggerate, we decided to go north to the Baltic.

Not till daylight on the morning after we were missed was the "alarm" given a genuine trial. Then with all the prisoners craning from the windows of their rooms, the Commandant himself dispatched his patrols, giving them suitable advice in a loud harangue. Police dogs, the things now called Alsatians, were produced, our bedding was brought out, and they were invited to take up the trail from it. They were interested in the bedding neither more nor less than they would have been in a lamp-post.

We decided to go first to Rostock, whence we believed there was a daily service of ferry-boats into Denmark. As a matter of fact we were wrong; the ferries ran from Warnemünde, at the mouth of the Warne, fifteen kilometres north of Rostock.

We thought it might be possible to board a ferry at night, stow ourselves away and so cross into Denmark. Failing this, rumour had it that there were many small sailing-boats about the Baltic coast engaged in smuggling cheese, butter, etc., into Germany. We thought we might find one of these and persuade the skipper to take us across. If we found a Dane all would probably go smoothly; if a German, ten months in the Fatherland had shown us that the conscience-price of the average working-class German was very dear at fifty marks, and we had about two hundred between us. Thirdly, there was always the possibility of finding a boat on the beach and rowing or sailing it across. We were neither of us experienced sailors, but the distance was not much over twenty miles, and we had only to steer approximately northwards and we could not fail to hit Denmark somewhere. We gathered that, owing to the shortage of food, which was beginning to be seriously felt, and the consequent desirability of getting as much Danish produce as possible into the country, the customs officers did not unnecessarily worry the masters of fishing or small trading vessels, and were not too severe in their visits to the ferries and other small steamers, though they kept, of course, a very strict watch for spies on the docks and in the town.

Rostock was due north of us and distant a little more than two hundred kilometres (a hundred and twenty-five miles) as the crow flies – to which must be added about 25 per cent to get the distance as the prisoner treks. The road, as far as we could tell from Baedeker, was nearly straight, and one of the Baedeker maps covered a little more than half the distance. We got the names of a couple of small towns which lay on our line, beyond the limits of the map, from a small-scale map of Europe which was sold as a war map. We stole a compass from a brother officer, who, by some oversight, had not been deprived of it on his capture. We must give him new one some day.

We hoped to start about the last week in September, the nights would be fairly long and the weather not too cold.

We did not reckon, however, on the imbecility of tailors.

Since June we had been walking ten or twelve miles very fast round and round the exercise ground. Early in September our "workmen" scheme was hit on the head by the Germans wiring off the small gate so no one could approach it without passing through the room (see plan on page 15). This was more than we could face. At the same time the rule that no civilian might pass out by the wagon gate was strictly enforced.

There remained the "officer" scheme.

The first hitch in this took the shape of a postcard from Harrison's tailor saying that he was sending off the great-coat, but suggesting that Harrison had made a mistake in asking for the caps of his old regiment when he must have meant Grenadiers' cap.

Harrison, however, managed to bluff the censors into allowing him to send off a post card immediately – without the usual fourteen days' delay which was the rule in all the camps – asking his tailor not to try to think but to do what he was told. The delay in the censor's office was intended to ensure that any secret information sent by prisoners' post should arrive stale. It also gave the censors time to test at leisure for all kinds of invisible ink. Harrison was allowed to dispatch this card at once, as the camp rule was: "Prisoners must always wear headgear so as to be able to salute German officers." He always went about bare-headed, claiming he had no head-dress, and had been ordered to write home for a uniform cap. The reply from the tailor was sufficient to justify an extra card to expedite dispatch.

Then the Grenadier who had ordered a coat for me was transferred to another camp and, although he tried to arrange for me to have the opening of the parcel containing the coat when it came to Burg, the censors somehow muddled things and I never got it.

I therefore began to negotiate with an old Russian colonel for a cape which he had had made by a German tailor, and which, while it was, presumably, something like the cape of his regiment, was exactly the cut and colour of the German article in all respects, except that it had no red-lined collar. After weeks of haggling I persuaded the old man to part with the garment in exchange for a "British Warm", a large sum of money and a promise that, if I were caught and the cape traced to him, I would swear that I had stolen it. He was a confirmed drunkard, and we hated his knowing anything about the scheme, but I had to have his cape.

Harrison's great-coat and the caps arrived together on 5th November. Everything else had been ready for some weeks.

Having had no sample in the camp from which to judge, we had rather banked on the Grenadier great-coat bearing a strong resemblance to the German article, but we found to our horror that it was entirely different both in cut and colour. The former is a thoroughly serviceable, comfortable garment of a dark slatey-blue grey, while the latter is almost as tight as a frock-coat, of a lightish blue colour, and is covered with flaps and buttons. We had been quite prepared to add the flaps buttons, and we had hoped that the difference in colour would be so slight as hardly to matter in a bad light, but we had not contemplated any dyeing or extensive and complicated tailoring. However, there was nothing for it but to start in on the job.

The tailoring which we had to do could not be done with any sort of secrecy in the crowded room in which Harrison and I lived, but Elliot, of Harrison's regiment, who had a small room to himself in a hut barrack (Block 7 on plan), very kindly allowed us to use it as a workshop, and here for a time we worked undisturbed. But, just as the coat and cape began to look unmistakably German, the room was suddenly raided by a gang of under-officers, who arrested Elliot on some trumped-up charge of bribery, and proceeded to search the room. We managed to shuffle our gear out of the window, which fortunately opened and, not being ourselves "wanted," got clear of the room in the general mess-up and retrieved unharmed. Elliot's arrest was the work of the *provocateur* and informer, mentioned elsewhere, who been hanging around the room for some days without, however, being able to discover what was going on. He had been assisted by a Polish Jew, in the uniform of a Russian Red Cross orderly, who had offered to supply Elliot with anything from brandy to machine-guns, and had been very unkindly rebuffed.

We went on with the work in another small room in a similar hut.

Three or four days after the arrival of the coat the tailoring was complete. We then laid it on the floor and poured it about a pound of boracic powder, the only white available, which we beat into the cloth with brushes. This rather crude treatment had the desired effect of raising the shade of the coat to a much lighter blue – a bit patchy, but good enough in a bad light.

We first dressed for the attempt on 10 November. We wore double or treble the usual allowance of underclothes and numerous sweaters, cardigans, etc. I had an old Norfolk jacket, acquired in hospital by a British officer who had lost his uniform. Harrison had a uniform jacket, dipped in ink, from which the pockets, flaps, shoulder-straps, etc., had been removed. We both wore corduroy trousers with thin red stripes down the seams, this being the only kind of nether garment which we were allowed to buy to replace our worn-out uniforms. We painted out the stripes with water-colour.

Our food, which consisted of chocolate, biscuits, potted meat, "Bivouac" cocoa, beef tabloids, malted milk, oxo, etc., with a "Tommy's Cooker" and supply of solid spirit (all from home parcels) was packed all over our bodies. Some was in pockets and some down trouser legs, some in rucksacks hung over our stomachs and some in sacks hung on our backsides. The latter two loads gave the correct Prussian figure.

I had for months past worn a long, straggling moustache; I hogged this closely and mounted a pair of enormous round gold-rimmed spectacles. Harrison is very fair, so his moustache, eyebrows and back hair were blackened with grease-paint (the kindly Hun provided this for a purely imaginary dramatic club) and his face was washed in a strong solution of coffee. These alterations changed our appearance enough to make recognition unlikely in a bad light, but they were, as things turned out, quite wasted.

Our outer garments consisted of the uniform caps, the great-coat in Harrison's case, the cape in mine, yellow boots and leggings, and the correct brown leather gloves. We wore wooden swords. Since I should have to discard my cape when we were safely out of the camp, I wore beneath it a Belgian army great-coat (dark blue) deprived of its frills and with civilian buttons. I had to pin up the skirts to prevent them from showing beneath the cape.

Harrison's German overcoat could be hastily converted into a seedy-looking civilian garment – most of the powder would soon wear out of it and we did not intend to be seen, as civilians, by daylight.

We intended to loiter in the darkness of a doorway near the wagon gate, until the departure of a kitchen refuse wagon which went out nearly every evening at about the right time. Then, when the gate was opened we hoped to be able to strut it without attracting undue attention. Strange German officers often visited the camp on mysterious missions to Russians, so that, if they accepted us at all as officers, the guard were not likely to pay much attention to us.

The German officer's collar, when turned up, shows a deep lining of scarlet cloth. This splash of red marks out the officer very clearly at any distance at which the colour can be seen, and the German soldier who sees it coming either bolts for cover or, if too late, shakes himself together for a terrific salute.

Lieutenant Edmond Terlinden, a Belgian officer of Guides, who afterwards brought off a particularly neat escape and sent me a lot of valuable information and material from Holland, sacrificed his breeches to provide our red collars.

We reached our doorway (in Block 4 – see plan on page 15) safely, wearing English great-coats on top of all the rest. One British officer carried our caps while another lounged outside reporting German movements and watching for the wagon.

Just as the wagon hove in sight and our quick change being effected, two German under-officers elected to loaf into our particular doorway, where they stood, talking about food, but not for the moment taking any great interest in us. This was not on the programme. Our group broke up in some disorder but, after dodging all over the camp and meeting an unexpected German (all of them, fortunately, stone-blind) at every turn, we eventually reached our rooms with the loss of only one cap-badge.

After this fiasco we had to change our tactics. Secrecy was no longer possible, since half the officers in the camp knew now what we were at, and any unusual movement of Britishers attracted a mob of chattering allies. We decided to wait in my room (in Block 5 – see plan on page 15), which I shared with five other British officers, until the wagon was signalled, when we would walk out of it, along a corridor, down a staircase and across about a hundred yards of exercise ground to the gate. We hoped to time our start so as to reach the gate just as it was being opened. We took the precaution of smashing the electric lamps in the corridor and on the stairs, in case we should meet a German on our way down.

We dressed for an attempt on 11 November, but it was dark before the wagon appeared. The same thing happened on 12th and 13th. On 13th a German officer came into the room while we were waiting, and we had to dive into very insufficient cover under a bed and a table while he stood within a few inches of Harrison asking silly questions about Irish politics. This sort of thing was more than I had bargained for and, although Harrison was quite willing to dress up every night until our chance came, the thing was getting on my nerves and I was afraid of doing something idiotic and spoiling the whole business. We therefore decided not to dress again until there was reason to expect a wagon to be going out at exactly the right time. We had smashed the lamps on the stairs on 11th, 12th, and 13th – the German was very keen on light and always replaced them – but for some reason which we never discovered he posted no sentry to watch them and took no apparent notice of the damage. He must have been playing some very deep game, but, since the lamp-smashing stopped after our departure and he could not connect us with it, it was never played out.

On the afternoon of 18 November a small party of British soldiers was told off to gather up the paper, straw, etc., from the room in which our parcels were unpacked and censored. They were to have it baled up and ready for loading on to a wagon at 5.30 p.m. This was just what we were waiting for. The oldest soldier was let into the conspiracy and asked to arrange for the loading to be completed at exactly 5:30 – and he carried out his instructions almost to the second.

We had a big feed, with exactly the right quantity of German brandy, and were dressed and ready a few minutes before the hour.

On the stroke of the half-hour the wagon was signalled. We left our room and the building and walked down the yard towards the gate, accompanied by an English officer – dressed as a Russian to make the party look more commonplace – who was talking bad German to us at the top of his voice. We were very much encouraged by meeting some French and Russian officers who, in all innocence, gave us the grudging salute on which the German always insisted. We carried in our hands the bunches of papers which seemed to be part of the dress of the German staff officer, and each smoked the customary foul cigar.

While the gate was being unlocked we stopped and exchanged the customary series of salutes and bows with our imitation Russian and, that over, turned and walked out by the side of the wagon. The gate sentry jerked himself to attention, the sergeant of the guard dropped his keys and saluted, and the worst was over. We politely returned the salutes and walked ahead of the wagon towards the gate in the outer fence. Here the sentry, whose job it was to unlock it, remained at ease, staring with open mouth at the two strange officers and apparently trying to screw himself up to draw their attention to the regulations by which no pedestrian might pass through his gate. Possibly he was expecting an order from us, but this was something we were quite unable to give him.

We were brought up short by the gate, and were both of us silently wondering what on earth to do next, the situation for a moment looking desperate, when, in despair, I raised a finger in the salute which he had so far forgotten himself and must have realised that he, a private soldier, at ease within a yard of two officers – than which, it would be hard to imagine a more appalling situation. Seized with remorse he hurled himself at the gate, threw it open, clicked his heels and froze to attention. We walked out, acknowledged some jerks from the sentry on the fence and down the road towards the town. We had to walk some hundreds of yards of main road – Harrison going dead lame and rattling like a cheap-jack, a tin of biscuits having come adrift in his trousers – before we came to the turning where we hoped to get into cover. I had made several visits, under escort, to a dentist, for the purpose of reconnoitring the camp, and knew of cover close by if we could get to it unobserved. We were lucky, and within minutes of leaving my room we were hidden between a couple of greenhouses in a large garden.

We hastily peeled off our caps, coats, leggings, etc., and stuffed them, with the rucksacks and food, into the sacks, put on caps and emerged as heavily laden workmen.

Harrison wore a service-dress cap, deprived of its stuffing and dyed in ink. I wore one which had been given to a British solider in a soldiers' camp. The playful Hun had decorated it with an identification patch of yellow paint, but this was easily removed.

It was only when we emerged from the garden that Harrison, who is a complete non-smoker, discovered that he had smoked his cigar right through and that it was singeing his moustache.

We passed the camp again at a little distance, and were relieved to see that all was quiet and that no suggestion of an escape had reached the sergeant of the guard.

'According to plan' we made our first night's march due east along a canal bank – the direction in which we least wanted to go but also the one in which the Germans were least likely to look for us. After going at top speed for five or six miles we stopped, got rid of most of the traces of our disguise, and removed the surplus clothing, which was only needed for the daily hide. The caps, Harrison's red collar, his shoulder-straps, patches, buttons and other frills were done up in my cape, which was weighted with stones and sunk in the canal. We had broken up and thrown away the swords at our first quick change.

After this we got on much more comfortably, with our baggage properly stowed in rucksacks. A good deal of rain and sleet was falling and we only met two or three men, with whom we exchanged the customary "*n'Abend*" – the only German to which we were prepared to commit ourselves. We roused a good many dogs on barges and in cottages, which alarmed us horribly at first, but we soon learnt that no one took any notice of them. We made detours round all the locks, hamlets and other places where more than a few solitary natives were likely to be met.

At the first streak of dawn we began to look for cover and were lucky in finding, without much searching, a large Dutch barn, full of straw and with no habitation near it. We climbed to the top of the straw, dug down between it and the end of the roof, put on all our extra clothing, and made ourselves as comfortable as we could. We had lost our water-bottle (a rubber air-cushion, with a funnel as filler) while collecting water from a ditch during the night, so had to carry up the day's supply in tins. We did this, of course, in the early morning before digging ourselves in. It was rather cold, but we spent a quiet day without any interruptions. During the day we got rid of the last traces of Prussian glory from Harrison's coat.

We allowed ourselves two hot drinks during the day, one of oxo and one of "Bivouac" cocoa. The daily ration worked out at about eight ounces of chocolate, four small Plasmon biscuits and half a tin of potted meat each, and the two hot drinks. We had a lot of malted milk and beef tabloids which we sucked on the march. This unpleasant diet provided plenty of nourishment but precious little bulk, and we soon learnt the value of tight belts. We had reckoned on reaching the coast in fourteen nights but we did it in nine, so were able to increase our rations towards the end.

This first day was typical of the next nine. We always hid in barns, in spite of the rather greater risk of discovery, because we did not care to face the cold and damp of the woods with such a long walk before us. Only twice more were we lucky enough to find isolated barns; the other days we had to spend in villages, in barns which were close to their owners' home-steads, often communicated directly with the kitchen. The barns were mostly very big and contained large stacks of corn or straw. Dug well in to the top of a stack, at the end farthest from the ladder, we felt fairly safe. The farm people often came into the barns, and sometimes worked in them all day, but only once were we in real danger of discovery. This was when we were in a small barn and lying in hay instead of the more usual straw (it was much warmer) and a farm hand came up to three times during the day to get food for the beasts. The first time we were not expecting him and he nearly walked right on to us, and came much too close with his pitchfork. After that we dug down about six feet into the hay, and he might have stood on us without spotting us.

Harrison used to sleep like a babe nearly all day and could hardly keep awake long enough to have his hot drinks. I felt the cold and could not sleep, except for the first hour after we got in, when I slept from sheer fatigue.

It began to snow a little on the sixth night of our walk and at the same time a very hard frost set in and held to the end of the trek. For the last day and night it snowed hard and continuously.

We generally marched from dusk, about 5.30 p.m., till the first signs of dawn at about 4.30 a.m. Sometimes our start was delayed by the farm people working later than usual and preventing our breaking out. One Sunday morning we stayed out until 5 a.m., thinking the natives would lie in bed a little longer than usual, but we were nearly caught out by the farmer, who came in just as we got to the top of our stack, and we had to lie doggo for an hour or more before he left us to dig in in peace.

We generally halted for an hour or an hour and a half, if we could find some sort of shelter, at about 11 p.m., but it was too cold for us to get much rest.

We drank, if possible, from ditches and ponds, but sometimes had to tackle a pump in the small hours of the morning. We were often chased away from one farm after another by barking dogs when in search of a good barn.

All the barns which we used had big double doors of thin match-boarding. To open them, I used to lie down on my back and pull one flap with my hands while I pushed the other with my feet. In this way I could bend the boards and make a gap through which Harrison could crawl; he then lit a candle, found the fastening bar and let me in.

During one lie-up Harrison crept down during the day, armed with a chocolate tin, to rob a cow which we thought we could hear moving about in a stall somewhere below us. He did a long and careful stalk, practically in darkness, and found – a bull.

After the first night's march we went north-west, on a compass bearing across country, to hit off the Rostock road about thirty kilometres north of Burg. We had made up our minds not to pass through a single village until we had crossed the river Havel (about seventy kilometres north of Burg), and we made detours through the fields round every one. There was a village every three or four kilometres. There was, however, a light railway which circled round the outsides of the villages, and by following this we saved a good deal of time, though the going was far from good. We thought there might be some kind of organised look-out for us on the bridge or bank some distance below where our road crossed the river, so made for the bank some distance below the town in the hope of finding a boat. We found ourselves in a marsh cut up by innumerable channels, and, being unable to find any sort of boat, had to go back to the road. There was a strong light on the bridge, thrown from some kind of engine-house which stood at the far side of it, and we could see several people moving about. As we approached the road from the marsh we passed through some gardens in which was a large pile of faggots. We took some of the biggest of these on our heads and staggered wearily across the bridge, exchanging the usual greetings with one or two men of whom, on account of our loads, we could see nothing except the feet. We left the faggots in the first yard which we passed. Probably some one had to do time for stealing them.

The road was nearly straight most of the way and fairly easy to follow, the greatest difficulty being to hit off the right one when emerging from big villages and small towns. We never hesitated in towns, but always walked straight through and, if we came out on the wrong road, we never turned back but went across country until we struck the right one. This sometimes lost us an hour or more, since the country close to the towns was very much enclosed. In the open country the roads are always flanked on both sides by trees, and are, therefore, easy to find even on a very dark night. We did not have to use the compass much – always a slow process at night – since, until the last three nights, the sky was fairly clear, and as long as we could see the pole-star ahead of us we knew that we could not be far out of the right direction.

We put into one sack everything which would not stow comfortably into our rucksacks and took it in turns to carry it for half-hour spells. We walked about four miles an hour.

Three nights from the finish I acquired a very warm blanket-lined coat, which was a great comfort. Its owner, who had made a nuisance of himself by working in our barn all day, was thoughtful enough to leave it there when he knocked off for the German equivalent of tea just when it was time for us to be moving. When we were brought back to Burg the Commandant seized on this coat as conclusive evidence that we had been helped to escape by a German. (In civil life he was a judge.)

On the last night we nearly blundered into two women who had come to steal straw from our barn and, supposing that they had spotted us, we made off in the direction opposite to the road – a change of plan for which we paid very heavily – meaning to circle round and get back to it about a mile farther on.

For this last march we had no map, but we knew there was a choice of two roads, one running north-east through a place called Lage and the other north-west through Schwaan. We found neither place, nor did we get back to the main road until we were within two or three miles of Rostock. Between 6 p.m. on 26 November and 1.30 a.m. on 27th we covered about twenty-three miles, all either across country or on the worst of country roads – under a foot of snow. The result was that we arrived in Rostock completely tired out – a great mistake. In our later attempts we always planned to have a very short march on the last night so as to arrive at or near the frontier fresh and fit for any unforeseen emergency.

The going on those country lanes was very bad; they had been cut into deep ruts the mud of which was frozen as hard as stone and the snow was so deep that in the dark the surface appeared to be quite smooth. The consequence was that we trod on a ridge and twisted an ankle more or less at every step. It snowed hard almost the whole night and was so cold that we only tried once to rest and gave it up after a few minutes. We found no water, every ditch, stream or pond being frozen hard (the thermometer marked – 20° centigrade, they told us afterwards in Rostock), and we were forced to quench our thirst by sucking handfuls of snow – anyone who has ever tried this will know that it causes the tongue to break into a mass of small blisters, a most painful condition.

We came into the outskirts of Rostock at about 1.30 a.m, and there made the acquaintance of a most amazingly stupid German sergeant-major.

We were following the main road towards the docks when he stepped out from the shadow of some trees and called on us to halt. We shuffled on a few paces, but he roared again and, not having a run left in us, we could only adopt the tactics on which we had agreed for this sort of emergency and pretend to be slightly drunk. We halted and stood swaying slightly and looking stupidly at the German.

I think I have said that we spoke no German; to be more exact, I had a very, very thin smattering of the language, and Harrison an even thinner one, but we could both understand the gist of anything likely to be said to us in such circumstances as these.

The German stood under a lamp and ordered one of us to advance. I staggered forward and he began to bellow at me: "Who are you?" "What are you?" "Where do you come from?" "Where are you going and why?" etc., etc. I looked drunkenly at him, but did not venture on an answer. He followed up with the inevitable: "What nationality are you, and have you got papers?" – his voice getting louder and he began to revel in the certainty of having found something really easy to bully. I began, between hiccoughs, to deliver a sentence in a mixture of languages which was meant to explain that we were Danish sailors from a ship in the docks, that we did not speak German, that we had left our papers in the ship, that we had been drinking with friends at the canal docks (we had just passed them and heard sounds of carousal), that German beer was very good and we were only poor sailors, and he was a dear, good, kind Prussian officer of very high rank and it was very cold. Good-night!

He seemed to follow my meaning, for he kept repeating my words, with corrections, at the top of his voice.

He tore open my coat and examined my clothes, finally running his finger down the seam of my trousers to feel for a stripe – which was there! Then he pushed me back against a wall and called up Harrison, who, during this performance, had been giving a wonderfully realistic imitation of a drunken man being sick in the gutter. Harrison let him roar half a dozen times, each roar angrier than the last, then staggered towards him, and, when he was right up against him, let go, with appropriate music, a full mouthful of chewed snow and chocolate all over the hero's manly breast. He was wearing a brand-new great-coat of the expensive pale blue kind which German under-officers were allowed to have made at their own expense. He screamed with rage, and, hurling Harrison violently away from him, treated us for three minutes to the choicest flow of obscenities to which he could lay his tongue while he scraped his chest with a piece of stick.

Then, to our utter amazement, he said something about having thought at first that we were prisoners of war and we could (not very politely) get out of his sight for a couple of blank, blank foreigners.

From start to finish we neither of us thought for a moment that we had the slightest chance of bluffing that Hun – or any other – and had always agreed that, once fairly suspected, our only hope lay in running. Had our friend thought of looking in our packs he could not have failed to realise what we were. We learnt later at the police station that he was on the look-out for a couple of Russian privates who had bolted from a working party at Stralsund, but he actually knew that two British officers were reported escaped and that the Magdeburg Command had offered two hundred marks for the recapture of either.

After this incident we continued to walk drunkenly whenever there was anyone in sight. We often found the drunken walk useful during later attempts.

We made straight for the docks, and soon found a road which ran the whole length and quite close to the water-side. We had originally intended to have only a preliminary look at the docks that night and, unless we hit on the ferry-steamer at once and it seemed fairly easy to board to push right on to the open coast and try for something in the way of a small boat the next night. But our cross-country trek had taken so much out of us that we decided to try there and then to get on board some kind of neutral steamer. We walked the whole length of the docks, meeting only one policeman, who was not interested in us, and seeing a great many steamers, several of which appeared to be neutrals.

It was an ideal night for our purpose, snowing and freezing hard, with a biting wind, and we knew quite well that any watchmen who might be posted about the docks would be in their huts with the door closed and braziers going full blast. We moved without a sound over the snow. The docks were fairly well lit.

Eventually we hit on a small steamer lying alongside the quay, with a little smoke coming from her funnel. She had the Danish flag painted on her side and an obviously Scandinavian name under her counter. We looked her over from end to end, saw that there was no sign of a watch on deck and were on the point of creeping up her gangway when a big police-dog rushed up from behind and jumped around us, barking noisily.

The door of a shed opened and a policeman walked up to us holding a whistle to his mouth. We tried the drunkard business, but we were up against a man of very different type to our sergeant-major friend. We were on enclosed premises, and in any case we could not run, so that was the end of first attempt.

We were taken to the police station, where we shared remains of our condensed rations with the police, who, for a small consideration, agreed to forget all about them. Consequently, when we were searched at Burg nothing was found to show how we had lived, and the Germans flatly refused to believe that we had walked from Burg or fed from our pockets. Moreover, no suspicion fell at that time on the concentrated foods which continued to arrive in every parcel from home.

The police treated us very civilly. We spent the rest of night together in a rather lousy cell and, after a hearty breakfast of mangold soup next morning, were ordered to prepare for the journey back to Burg. This instruction was given to us by a handcuffed prisoner, who was produced to act as interpreter. He told us incidentally that he was a Swedish sailor and had been condemned to death the day before on espionage.

We were taken over at the police station by an escort consisting of two of the most ferocious-looking sergeants I ever set eyes on – enormous men with fat, pink necks, bulging pink eyes and ginger moustaches on the model of the All Highest. They came to our cell, after we had been told to dress for the journey, and peremptorily ordered us out of it. Then each produced a firearm – one a revolver, the other an automatic pistol – which they ostentatiously loaded, cocked and waved in our faces with the customary blood-curdling threats.

We arrived at Magdeburg at 10 p.m. and Hauptmann Chessmann, the Burg Commandant, was so overjoyed at the thought of seeing us again after mourning us as lost forever (and probably having been severely "strafed") that he came in person to meet us and held a preliminary inquiry on the spot while we waited for our connection.

We were rather roughly handled by the guard which took us on from Magdeburg to Burg – probably they had had a pretty thin time in consequence of our escape.

I should mention here that, when we were preparing to quit the camp, we wanted to make the Germans think, if we succeeded in getting out, that we had gone by train to Holland so that the look-out in the other directions might be less strict. Harrison therefore wrote a note which he addressed to an English officer, Templer, who was doing time for some trivial offence in Burg prison. In the note (which he mentioned would be smuggled into prison by a corrupted German) he said: "If we are not with you by the day after to-morrow we shall be in Holland. The Germans do not know that Cartwright speaks German so will never dream that we are going by train." He left the note among his belongings, where it was found as soon as we were missed. The Commandant swallowed it whole. It was dramatically produced at the official inquiry to prove me a liar when I denied that I knew the language. When I left Germany the following entry still stood in my "conduct sheet": "Speaks German perfectly, but will not admit it." This has been brought up at every court martial or court of inquiry at which I have had the pleasure of assisting since that date.

At the inquiry after our recapture, a pair of English gloves and a tin-opener were produced as evidence against us. They were supposed to support a trumped-up charge of burglary. The things had been found in the garden where we did our first quick change – which, by a curious coincidence, happened to be the Commandant's own garden – and a broken board in the fence was the basis of the burglary charge. Harrison said he wanted the post office parcels register produced as evidence for us. Asked by the Commandant what he meant, he replied: "To prove that enough prisoners' parcels have arrived at the post office, and have not been signed for by the addressees, to outfit the whole population of Burg with English goods." We heard no more of the burglary charge.

The glove question was the only one which we would answer at all, so that, since the Germans had not the slightest idea how we really got out, the inquiry was not a success. In subsequent interrogations and inquiries of the same kind we both always declined to answer a single question. This made the German very angry, since, failing evidence, he always charged a prisoner on "his own confession" if he had opened his mouth at all. Even if he had not he got no peace until he had signed a long statement, in German, alleged to be a verbatim report of the inquiry. I always willingly signed these novels, writing over my signature: "I do not understand the above." This too seemed to make them angry.

After we had left the camp the officers in our room – all British – had tried to fake the 9 p.m. roll-call for us, so as to give us a longer start. The evening roll-call was a hasty run round the rooms by an officer and two or three underlings. They made dummies to represent us and stood them in darkest corners of the rooms. Unfortunately the man whose job it was to stand so as almost to obscure the view of the first dummy stood a little too close to it, with the result that, just as the German officer turned to leave the room, some movement caused the dummy to fall and its head rolled out at his feet. The subsequent proceedings were rather sultry and very Prussian.

It is perhaps worth mentioning that we had had to make all our preparations in the knowledge that the Germans might at any moment descend in mass and search the whole or any part of a camp. They would suddenly surround one or more buildings with sentries and systematically search every room, finally stripping the occupants naked and searching their clothing. At Burg the soldiers who conducted the searches sometimes had the help of two or three dozen Magdeburg detectives – if they were a fair sample the Magdeburg criminal should lead a care-free life. One of these searches took place soon after Harrison and I had begun our preparations and when our uniforms were more than half-made; every stitch of our clothing was examined but nothing suspicious was noticed except the half-made swords. The officer to whom these were triumphantly brought by the finder remarked that he saw no harm in the English amateurs playing at soldiers if it amused them.

We were five weeks in the civil prison but since, in spite of continual interrogations we refused to convict ourselves, and the Germans had no evidence at all and could not think up any which would fit the facts, we were never brought to trial. In the last week someone in the camp did describe to the Germans exactly how we had escaped, and the assistant Commandant (known to his flock as Rumblebelly, but he probably had another name) had the whole story beautifully typed out in English for us to sign. Of course we refused, and when we pointed to our various articles of clothing – in particular my beautiful yellow boots, which I had converted into shoes – he had to admit that the story was an impossible one. The informer, whoever he was, probably had a rough passage for putting up such a ridiculous yarn. They had previously put up three or four other accounts for our approval, all of which, they had said in turn, could be proved by overwhelming evidence. They do not know to this day how we got out.

I hinted above that the Germans were not always clever searchers but perhaps it is only fair to say that a crowd of British officers, herded together in a very small space, was not the easiest thing to search. For one thing, they simply would not stay put, but insisted on circulating in spite of every kind of abuse and the oft-repeated and sometimes executed threat of instant arrest. Thus I have seen a really keen officer searched three times in the course of a single visit while a more retiring and bashful brother-officer was not searched at all – but the number of *Herren* searched apparently tallied with the number of beds in the room, so what could be wrong? Again, they were apt to be insistent, not to say officious, in their efforts to help the searchers in their disagreeable and difficult job. For instance, when a German had made a heap, on the table perhaps, of properties from one corner of the room and was about to go through them, an over-zealous British helper would add twice the volume of already searched properties from another corner – and vice versa – and in the ensuing dash to separate the two lots quite possibly the whole bunch, and the table, would collapse on the floor. It was all very difficult and confusing for the German, who was really doing his best, and sometimes he got quite irritable.

Then the German is a shocking bad counter, and he cannot live without lists and the checking of lists, and the lists are hardly ever quite right. At Küstrin once he searched a room and at the first dart unearthed a forbidden felt hat. One of his assistants placed the hat on a table while another licked his pencil and wrote "*Ein Hut*" in a notebook. The search continued. Presently the hat vanished from the table, unnoticed by the searchers, but the same one was discovered soon afterwards stuffed into someone's mattress, whence it was dragged in triumph and again placed on the table with the bag. (We always provided a lot of useless but forbidden trash, hidden in the most obvious places; they liked finding it and it prevented them from becoming despondent and gave the tally-clerk a job to keep him quiet.) Again "*Ein Hut*" was written in the note-book and the work proceeded. Again the hat, unnoticed, vanished from the table and again it was found, this time hanging by a string outside the window. For the third time "*Ein Hut*" was written in the book, and still the good work went on. Finally, when all was over, the bag was laid out to be checked and each article was ticked off by the tally-clerk as it was dropped into a basket for removal. There remained three items unticked in the note-book, each of them reading "*Ein Hut*," and this by simple addition makes "*Drei Hute*" but not a single hat could be found in the bag.

One can imagine what would have happened had this game been tried by German prisoners in an English camp, but it was just the sort of situation with which the German, for all his ferocious discipline – at all events the second-rate kind of German – which was found in and about prison camps – could not compete. They pretended there was nothing wrong, withdrew noisily and left that room severely alone in the next search.

On 29 December 1915, the Commandant and Rumblebelly came to our cells and informed us that we need not waste time on any further plans, since we were to be separated and would not meet again in Germany. The same day Harrison was sent to Torgau and I to Halle.

CHAPTER THREE

TUNNELLING TO FREEDOM

By Hugh Durnford

I will begin with an incident. When the bubble was just about to burst at Holzminden in July 1918, there was a theatrical show in one of the camp dining rooms. Two German interpreters were present to stop the libretto containing anything too disrespectful to the German Reich. During a lull in the proceedings, a very newly captured officer (who was, however, old enough to have known better) addressed this devastating question to one of his neighbours in the immediate vicinity of an interpreter: "Are you in the tunnel?"

What electric memories – even to-day and in its most ordinary and work-a-day context – that word stirs! Tunnel! It is common to the two languages of English and German, and pronounced exactly the same. It was, therefore, so pregnant a word, that it simply mustn't be used. Hole, excavation or even tube, if you liked, but not, where the very walls had ears – not tunnel.

That one remark might have crashed the continuous work of nine months. Our Commandant was naturally suspicious, and clever, and more than once he'd been badly rattled. But at last he had been systematically lulled into a feeling of security against any attempt to escape on the grand scale. "You see, gentlemen," he would say, in his Americanised English, "you see, gentlemen, you cannot get out now, I should not try. It will be bad for your health," and we allowed him to think that we agreed. So you can understand that such an unwise remark could easily have bridged the narrow margin between safety and discovery. And this was an all-British camp, remember, starting from scratch, without racial jealousies, the clash of national temperaments or the possibility of spying and betrayal by other prisoners.

I am writing here not as author or part-author of the "Holzminden Tunnel," but as chronicler. I wasn't one of the tunnellers myself. I can describe near enough, at second hand, what it was like, how it was dug, and Walter Butler's sensations as he emerged, the first man through, on that fateful July night. But there were many difficulties and risks besides those which were encountered underground. I was adjutant, and it was my job to try to get to know what was in the German mind and to sense whether there was any fresh trouble afoot. Then, in the later stages, I had to keep the peace of the camp at all costs and make everything take second place to the completion of the tunnel, and when the bubble burst I had a good deal to do, so perhaps I'm in the best position to tell you the whole story.

I do not claim a record for the Holzminden Tunnel. It measured over sixty yards, and it took nine months to complete. It may not have been the biggest tunnel, but it was certainly the most successful in the war. But its main interest is as a monument of teamwork and resource, and for the fact that it was dug under the nose of a Commandant who openly boasted that he had made his camp escape proof, and that no one could possibly get out of it. I must say just one word about this Commandant. Perhaps what jarred most in him was that he was so hopelessly *infra dig* and behaved more like a tiresome camp feldwebel than a Commandant. He was a busybody. He prowled and pounced. He burst into our rooms in the morning to roust us out of bed. He kept us all on the jump, including his own people. No one trusted him, and he was so cocksure and blatant that he wasn't even an object of pity in his solitude. Even his own puppy didn't like him. He used to walk round the camp, and the only time he was ever seen to bend down was when he stooped to coax the puppy away from English officers, with whom it was always making friends.

The small town of Holzminden on the Weser was near Hanover, and about 100 miles from Holland. The camp was a cavalry barracks – two large buildings – just on the outskirts. There was open country between the camp and the river.

You entered through the main gate, leaving Barrack A on your left, and went straight on for another seventy yards or so to Barrack B. Imagine a large letter D with a total perimeter of about 400 yards. The main gate and Barrack A are the bottom of the straight part of the D, and Barrack B is the top point. Barrack B was 50 yards long, and held about 250 officers and 20 British orderlies, who were privates or N.C.O. prisoners of war. All round the camp were either iron railings with barbed wire at the top, or else a double line of posts and barbed wire. And now a brief description of this further building, Barrack B – the scene of the crime – for the difficulties which met the tunnellers at every turn can hardly be appreciated without some topographical sense of the place. Remember that in this game, you had not only to get below ground, but you also had not to be seen getting there. You couldn't say one morning, "Hullo chaps, let's do a bit of tunnelling to-day." You had to be as secret as the grave even from the rest of your compatriots, and think out all your moves well ahead.

Barrack B was a four-storied building with an entrance and a staircase at each end – the near one for the officers, and the far one for the orderlies. Also there was a basement floor with cellars and a flight leading down to them. The ground floor, the first floor and the second floor were all much the same, officers' rooms opening out on to a corridor. On the attic floor there were two or three officers' rooms at our end, then (partitioned off) the English orderlies' quarters, the luggage room, and finally the orderlies' staircase. This part of the attic floor – the orderlies' quarters and luggage room – was out of bounds to British officers; hence the partition. The whole of the basement floor was also out of bounds: so was the orderlies' staircase. It was barricaded off at the end of each of the other three corridors, and we were not allowed to use the only other means of getting to it – the orderlies' entrance. We couldn't therefore reach it from the inside or from the outside.

Why were we excluded in this way from this end of building? The reason wasn't difficult. The orderlies' end of Barrack B was closest to the confines of the camp, the shortest way to freedom. From somewhere underneath this, through the wall of the building and so under the outside wall, wasn't more than about sixteen yards in all, and the Commandant had *foreseen our interest* in this. Hence the partition on the attic floor, the barricades at the end of the three lower corridors, the ruling that the orderlies' entrance was out of bounds officers. To enforce this rule a sentry had been posted between the camp wall and the barracks, exactly opposite the orderlies' entrance.

I must mention at this point the name of the founder of the tunnel, Major Colquhoun, a Canadian. With two other officers and an orderly, he broke through the partition on attic floor between their own quarters and the orderlies' quarters, and came down to the forbidden ground at the foot of the orderlies' staircase to reconnoitre.

Now try to imagine their problem as they stood there at the orderlies' entrance. Their most obvious course was to pick the lock of the door leading down to the basement corridor, and they had come prepared to do this. But there were disadvantages, for the punishment cells reserved for officers under arrest were in the basement corridor, and these cells were always pretty full. "I give you three days right away, cost price," was the familiar formula, after the Commandant had raided some room at an unseasonable hour and found something quite to his liking. So a German was likely to come along any moment to visit these officers, and if he did so the tunnellers would be caught red-handed. So rather desperately, as you will imagine, for they were very exposed there at the foot of the stairs, they cast about for alternatives. And then one of them had a brainwave. The space on the *underneath* side of the flight of steps *up* – that's to say between this flight and the flight down to the basement – had been boarded up with yet another palisade of stout upright planks. If they could get through this palisade they judged they would find themselves in a hollow chamber, out of sight, below ground level, and right up against the outer wall of the barrack. There should, moreover, be plenty of room there for disposing of the excavated earth. They decided to try.

It was a ticklish job – with a sentry almost in the offing – but they did it a day or so later. They took out the whole of the palisade, loosened two of its planks, hinged them so that they could be moved in and out of position, and fixed them with a bolt which wouldn't show *on* the outside, but could be worked *from* the outside. This bolt was so skilfully concealed at the top of the boarding that it kept its secret to the end. The hole through which it was worked was so small that only one or two of the tunnellers could put his hand inside to slide it and let the working shifts in and out.

The chamber they found down below was ideal, some four yards by five, and all seemed favourable then – in November 1917 – for starting this tunnel of only sixteen yards. Work began. Then someone was spotted; the alarm was raised; the Commandant and all his myrmydons got on the warpath and the secret of the tunnel entrance hung in the balance. But though the tell-tale hole in the planks was literally under his nose for many minutes at a time and he became very warm, indeed, the Commandant missed it: and with it, his great chance of scorching tunnelling at Holzminden for good and all. However, he managed to make it much more difficult all the same. He closed the officers' rooms in the attic, posted a permanent sentry outside the outer wall and strengthened the orderlies' partition and the corridor barricades with sheet iron. It seemed clear, in fact, that the tunnellers couldn't any longer get into the chamber from inside the building; and all this meant three things. Firstly, that the tunnel would have to be greatly lengthened so as to clear the new sentry's range, which was pretty good considering that the camp was brilliantly lighted by arc lamps: secondly, that since the conspirators couldn't any longer get into the orderlies' quarters from inside the barracks, they would have to get there from outside – through the orderlies' entrance – which would mean disguising themselves as orderlies; and thirdly, that the work to be done during the daytime since no officer could be outside the building after dusk when the entrance doors locked.

So a new chapter in the tunnel making began.

Each shift consisted of three men. They entered and left the chamber in the garb of orderlies, which consisted of civilian coats and trousers with a band sewn into the arm and a stripe sewn into the trouser seam. This was the distinctive badge of prisoners at large on the land or in the mines or elsewhere. Their working clothes were kept in the chamber. Now, obviously, the one moment at which they could not afford to be caught was when coming through the trap-door. If they were spotted at any other moment, the worst might still, possibly, be averted. Of course if they were detected as orderlies' clothes there would be alarums and excursions, and almost certainly a search. And if the Commandant got a second scare, would he overlook that tell-tale hole in the planks again? So the risk was great either way. But as it happened the luck held. The working party was never spotted and never challenged as they made their chancy passage from door to door, back to their own rooms. The patrols were too wide awake. This was the sort of thing. When the relief hour was due, the patrols, loafing at the orderlies' entrance, waited till the sentry had turned his back and then gave the "all-clear" signal, which might be some snatch of a song or a password. The workers slipped the bolt, squirmed through the trap-door and came out into the open with the quick military step of three orderlies walking abreast. Once they had gained their own door there were many bolt-holes and they were fairly safe. Remember that the hours of work were limited by daylight and by the periodic rollcalls or "appells." Remember too that each shift worked to the last possible moment and that any hold-up in the tunnel or base-chamber might have meant three officers missing on "appell": and that this routine went on day after day for three or four months without intermission. You will then get a clearer idea of the team-work. The average sentry wasn't a bright lad and was unlikely to recognise any particular officers out of 500. But the German personnel included many who were good at faces. A collision often seemed inevitable and only by skilful diversion on the part of the flanking patrol – after the manner of matadors in a bull fight – was the German attention persuaded to wander.

Now let us follow one of the shifts behind the trap-door and see them actually at work. The tunnel is progressing steadily if slowly. A stratum of very hard, large stones has been encountered, much worse than that earlier stratum of yellow clay. The man on the job at the tunnel face lies on his stomach in a strained and cramped position. The tunnel is only eighteen inches in diameter. He has two tools – a trowel and a cold chisel – within reach of his hand and a candle in the wall beside him. He prods, levers, and finally wrenches out the big stones till they lie in a heap up to his chin, large enough to be removed. He pulls in a rope which is attached to him. At the other end of the rope is a basin which he gets past and in front of him and fills up with the stones. Then with incredible difficulty he gets the full basin somehow behind his body again. Now one of his mates who is working the pump at the tunnel mouth does his share. He also has hold of another length of rope attached to the basin and at the signalling jerk from the excavator, he pulls the basin towards him. And so backwards and forwards, while the third man packs away the stones in the rapidly filling chamber.

The pump consists of bellows home-made from wood and the leather of a flying officer's coat. It has to keep the air tolerably clean at the tunnel face so that the tunnellers can breathe and the candle can stay alight. It is fixed on wooden uprights and discharges its blast into a pipe of tin tubes made out of biscuit boxes which have come in parcels from home. The pipe is sunk in the tunnel floor and grows, of course, with the tunnel. Later on – as the twists and irregularities of tunnel increased – the rope and basin method gave place to merely filling sacks with the earth and stones and pulling them out from the face. It isn't a popular pastime to wriggle fifty yards back, fifty yards forward, on elbows and toes in clean air in the open. In foul air, in a tortuous and uneven hole, pulling a heavy sack out behind you, it is still less so.

So the tunnel nosed its crinkly and unlevel course along, hollowed out and rivetted with constantly and mysteriously disappearing bed-boards, till the end of June was reached and the time question became serious. The nearest decent cover was a crop of rye. Was the tunnel long enough yet to reach the rye? You might guess the length of the tunnel underground, and you might from an upper window guess the distance of the rye and make the two about the same. But would the lengths tally in practice? Would the rye be cut before the tunnel was ready? Would the chamber hold all the earth? One day Butler gingerly pushed out a white rag on a bit of stick, to make sure of the actual position of the tunnel face, and the anxious watchers from the building saw that he was still *eight or nine yards* short of the rye. That was bad; and then we suffered a second blow, which was entirely unforeseen either by the German camp personnel or by ourselves, and came from the Army Corps Headquarters. Reprisals. Because of some alleged injustice to German prisoners in England, we were now to be cut off games, walks and exercise. What was worse, we were to be subjected to four "appells" a day instead of two. This was depressing for the tunnellers, as of course it meant a much greater restriction of working hours. So they took two desperation decisions. Henceforth they would work from indoors again and through the night. A new way via the eaves of the building was found to the orderlies' quarters. And they would break surface as soon as they judged the tunnel had reached to some beans, which were at any rate better cover than the bare earth.

By now the camp was agog. There could be no more secrecy amongst ourselves. The tunnelling party settled its own order of departure and that of its favoured band of helpers. There were some twenty in these two parties. Applications for places in the queue to follow them came from all sorts of officers, qualified or unqualified to attempt a serious escape. I remember I had my own regrets. The so distantly realisable thing was apparently coming off after all. Perhaps this feeling of mine (which was shared by many others) shows the merit of the tunnel performance more clearly than anything else. We had in our hearts, in the earlier stages, doubted the possibility of its success in the face of such tremendous obstacles: and by the time that the odds had shortened, we found ourselves unprepared in equipment to take our great chance.

The one qualification for a place insisted on by the tunnellers was that every starter should be a *bona fide* inhabitant of Barrack B. The risk of an eleventh hour leakage was obviously very great, as I have shown. We couldn't have people from Barrack A concealing themselves in Barrack B and so risking being missed. Owing to fears of a general search, the senior officer put an official embargo on any individual attempt to escape until the tunnel had been tried out. He didn't pretend to be entirely disinterested for he spoke admirable German and had been offered a place immediately behind working party!

We will pass over the next few hectic days and come to zero night, 24 July. As soon as lights are out and the last sentry has left the building – about 10.15 – the tunnellers penetrate the top floor, pass through the orderlies' quarters and go down in small, successive parties of two or three to the tunnel mouth. Butler, who had done the lion's share and who had remained for so many months a constant member in a changing crew, had been chosen to go down first and cut out. This he did, and you can imagine with what relief he wriggled and bumped his way for the last time over that unfriendly floor. He cut out with a large bread knife. He pushed his kit through first and then crawled up, to much satisfaction – in the beans. Though the sentry was quite near and the arc light appeared to be throwing everything into strong relief, he was aided by rain, and he and his companions got safely into the rye: shortly after, they had crossed the river and were well away. The others followed and all was going according to plan. Now back to the building. It was my job to regulate the departure of all those after the first twenty, so as to avoid unnecessary noise and movement. All the escapers were lying ready dressed on their beds, and I summoned each as his turn came, and sent him through to the orderlies' quarters where he was taken in tow and escorted to the tunnel mouth. All went well till at two o'clock there was a reported hold-up. At four o'clock someone went through on his own and found the tunnel to be empty: during all this time traffic had stopped. Now the stream got going again and twenty-nine had actually got out when the tunnel caved in beyond reparation. There were three or four officers in the tunnel at the time, and though the first man knew he couldn't get on, the others didn't know. It was a little comic. You remember in Macaulay's lay how:

> "Those behind cried forward,
> And those before cried back."

Well, it was like that in the tunnel, and even when the rear-guard were resigned to retreat, they couldn't. Back they all had to be pulled by the legs, packs and all. One very strong officer whose turn hadn't yet come and who was quite fresh offered to do all the retrieving work; and he did it, but it took him a long time. It was getting light when the last of them emerged. With ordinary luck – if they had all succeeded in getting safely back to their rooms, the secret would have been kept from the Germans until morning "appell" several hours later: which would have meant, of course, so many more hours grace to the successful escapers. But just then, if you please, the Commandant of all people, put in one of his unadvertised appearances – out for an early morning stroll. He ran into two mudstained officers at the staircase entrance and the secret was out.

But the extent of the escape did not dawn upon the Germans until the roll had been called. It was a delicious moment when the fat and good-natured feldwebel in charge of Barrack B reported to the Commandant that no fewer than twenty-nine officers including the senior British officer were missing. That moment repaid many an old score. The air was charged. We who had held ourselves in for many weeks now laughed loud and long. Loud and long laughter was always the most certain method to annoy. And you may be sure the Commandant responded. We were all shut up at once in the barracks and the place became alive with secretly amused and delighted sentries. Emergency rules were posted up and recited forbidding any officers to do practically anything except breathe, under penalty of the cells – which were, of course, at once filled. Several shots were also fired. We organised a sort of passive resistance mutiny in the hope that there might be an enquiry from headquarters and the Commandant would be discredited as a gaoler and as a keeper of order: but it didn't come to that, and after a hectic week things got back more or less to normal.

If the tunnel had been fully occupied for every minute between 10.15 (when Butler went through) and 6 a.m when the last entombed officer had been pulled out, feet foremost, from the ruins – there is no doubt that many more than twenty-nine would have at least got clear of the camp. Whether a larger number would have finally escaped is a different question. We never succeeded in solving the mystery of the block. The orderlies kept their own counsel about this. The most likely explanation is that they purposely left the tunnel clear for longer than the scheduled time so as to give the better chance to the first twenty who were the real tunnellers. It was for these, after all, that they had worked so loyally and ungrudgingly for many months – without any hope of ulterior benefit for themselves – and not for any Tom, Dick or Harry who pressed for a free passage at the end. It must be left at that.

In the end, ten of the twenty-nine reached freedom. Butler, alas, was recaptured. But Rathborne, the senior British officer of the camp – whose escape had particularly agitated the Commandant – rubbed it in by sending us a telegram from Holland. I showed this to the Commandant just as I was myself about to be removed as a suspected character to another camp: and when I was lucky enough to escape myself into Denmark a few weeks later, I too could not resist the temptation of sending him one myself.

CHAPTER FOUR

EXPLOITS OF THE ESCAPING CLUB

By A. J. Evans

In the early days of the war Fort 9, Ingolstadt, had been a quiet, well-behaved sort of place according to its oldest inmates. But for the six months previous to my arrival before its forbidding gates at the end of 1916, the Germans had collected into it all the naughty boys who had tried to escape from other camps. There were about 150 officer prisoners of different nationalities in the place, and at least 130 of these had successfully broken out of other camps, and had only been recaught after from three days' to three weeks' temporary freedom. I myself had escaped from Clausthal in the Harz Mountains – but had been recaptured on the Dutch frontier after I'd been at large for a few days.

When I arrived at Fort 9, Ingolstadt, 75 per cent of the prisoners were scheming and working continually to escape again. Escaping, and how it should be done, was the most frequent subject of conversation. In fact the camp was nothing less than an escaping club. We pooled our knowledge and each man was ready to help anyone who wished to escape, quite regardless of his own risk or the punishment he might bring upon himself. No one cared twopence for court-martials and nearly everyone in the fort had done considerable spells of solitary confinement.

It is scarcely necessary to say that the Germans, having herded some 150 officers with the blackest characters into one camp, took considerable precautions to keep them there. But there were some of the most ingenious people in Fort 9 that I've ever met – particularly among the French – and attempts to escape took place at least once a week.

Fort 9 had been built in 1866 after the Austrian wars. There was a wide moat, about fifteen yards broad and five feet deep, round the whole fort and inside the moat the ramparts rose to a height of forty feet. Our living rooms were actually in the ramparts and the barred windows looked down upon the moat, across a grass path along which a number of sentries were posted. It looked as though there were only two possible ways of getting out: to go out the way we'd come in, past three sentries, three gates and a guardhouse; or to swim the moat. It was impossible to tunnel under the moat. It had been tried, and the water came into the tunnel as soon as it got below the water level. An aeroplane seemed the only other solution. That was the problem we were up against, and however you looked at it, it always boiled down to a nasty cold swim or a colossal piece of bluff. We came to the conclusion that we must have more accurate knowledge of the numbers, positions and movements of the sentries on the ramparts and round the moat at night, so we decided that one of us must spend the night out. It would be a rotten job; fifteen hours' wait on a freezing night, for it was now winter. For the first three and last three hours of this time it would be almost impossible to move a muscle without discovery, and discovery probably meant getting bayoneted. We cast lots for this job – and it fell to a man named Oliphant. I owned I breathed a sigh of relief. There would be two roll calls to be faked, the roll call just before sunset and the early morning one. How was this to be done? Our room was separated from the one next door, which was occupied by Frenchmen, by a three foot thick wall, and in the wall was an archway. This archway was boarded up and formed a recess which was used as a hanging cupboard for clothes. Under cover of these clothes we cut a hole in the boarding big enough for a man to slip quickly through, from one room to the other. The planks which we took out could be put back easily and we pasted pictures over the cracks to conceal them. It was rather difficult work. We had only a heated table knife to cut the first plank with, but later on we managed to steal a saw from a German carpenter who was doing some work in one of the rooms, and return it before he missed it. You must remember that there was absolutely no privacy in the fort, and a sentry passed the window and probably stared into the room every minute or two. We then rehearsed the faking of the roll calls. One of us pretended to be the German N.C.O. taking the roll. First he tapped at the Frenchmen's door and counted the men in the room, shut the door and walked about seven paces to our door, tapped and entered. Between the time he shut the first door till he opened ours only six or eight seconds elapsed, but during these seconds one of the Frenchmen had to slip through the hole, put on a British warm and pretend to be Oliphant! The German N.C.O.s knew every man by sight in every room, but so long as the numbers were correct they often didn't bother to examine our faces. That accounted for the evening roll call. The early morning one was really easier. For several mornings the fellow in bed nearest the hole in our room made a habit of covering his face with the bedclothes. The German N.C.O. soon got used to seeing him like that, and if he saw him breathing or moving didn't bother to pull the clothes off his face. So the Frenchman next door had simply to jump out of bed as soon as he had been counted, slip through the hole, and into the bed in our room and cover up his face. We practised this until we got it perfect, and the rehearsals were great fun.

The next thing to do was to hide Oliphant on the ramparts. Two of us dug a grave for him there while the others kept watch. Then just before the roll call went we buried him and covered him with sods of grass. It was freezing at the time. It was about 4.30 p.m. when we buried him and he wouldn't be able to return to our room till 8.15 the next morning, when the doors were open. The faking of the evening roll call went off splendidly, but the morning one was a little ticklish, as we couldn't be quite sure which room the N.C.O. would enter first. However, we listened carefully, and fixed it all right, and when he poked our substitute, who groaned and moved in the rehearsed manner, we nearly died with suppressed laughter. About an hour later Oliphant walked in very cold and hungry but otherwise cheerful. He had had quite a successful night. A bright moon had prevented him from crawling about much, but he had seen enough to show that it would be a pretty difficult job to get through the sentries and swim the moat on a dark night. However, Providence came to our help.

The winter of 1916 was a hard one; and the moat froze over, and although the Germans went round in a boat every day and tried to keep the ice broken, they eventually had to give it up. It was difficult to know whether the ice would bear or not, but I tested it as well as I could by throwing stones on to it, and decided one morning that I would risk it and make a dash across the moat that evening. A man named Wilkin, and Kicq, a little Belgian officer who had accompanied me on my previous attempt to escape, agreed to come with me.

Our plan was to start when the "appell" or roll-call bell went at 5 p.m., for it got dark soon afterwards, and I trusted that this would cover our flight. We had to run down a steep bank on to the ice, about forty yards across the ice and then another two hundred yards or so before we could put a cottage between ourselves and the sentries. There was sure to be some shooting, but we reckoned the men's hands would be very cold, for they would already have been two hours at their posts. Moreover they were only armed with old French rifles, which they handled badly. We arranged with some of the officers to create a diversion when the roll-call bell went, yelling and throwing stones on to the ice to distract the attention of the two nearest sentries. Our main anxiety was: would the ice bear? I felt confident it would. Wilkin said he was awfully frightened, but would go on with it. Kicq said that if I was confident, so was he. It would be extremely unpleasant if the ice broke for we would be wearing a lot of very heavy clothes. Still anyone who thinks too much of what may happen will never escape from prison. We filled our rucksacks with rations for a ten days' march and enough solidified alcohol for at least one hot drink a day. We then concealed them and our coats at the jumping-off place.

A few minutes before the bell went we were all three dressed and in our places. It was a bad few minutes. At last it rang and almost immediately I heard laughter and shouting and the sound of stones falling on the ice. We jumped up and bolted over the path and down the slope. I was slightly ahead of the others, and when I got to the moat I gave a little jump on to the ice thinking that if it was going to break at all, it would break at the edge instead of in the middle. It didn't break, and I shuffled across at good speed. When I was about half-way over I heard furious yells of "Halt!" behind me, followed by a fair amount of shooting; but I was soon up the bank on the far side and through a few scattered trees. Then I looked back.

The others were only just clambering up the bank from the moat, and were a good hundred yards behind me. It turned out that instead of taking a little jump on to the ice as I had done they'd stepped carefully on to the edge, which had broken under their weight, and they had fallen flat on their faces. Wilkin had somehow got upside down, his heavy rucksack falling over his head so that he couldn't move but Kicq had freed himself and pulled Wilkin out.

The covering parties had done their job well. They'd managed to divert the attention of the most formidable sentry until I was well on the ice. He had then noticed me, yelled "Halt!" loaded his rifle as fast as possible, dropped on one knee, fired and missed. Cold fingers, abuse and some stones hurled at him by the party on the ramparts above had not helped to steady his aim. After one or two shots his rifle jammed. Yells and cheers from the spectators. He tore at the bolt, cursing and swearing, and then put up his rifle at the crowd of jeering prisoners above him, but they could see that the bolt hadn't gone home, and only yelled louder.

Meanwhile I'd nearly reached the cottage, when I saw a large, four-horse waggon on the main road on my right with a number of civilians by it. They were only about 150 yards away, and they started after us, led by a strong, healthy-looking fellow with a cart whip. The going through the snow was heavy, especially with the weight we were carrying; so the carter quickly overtook me and slashed me across the shoulders with his whip. I turned and rushed at him, but he was just out of my reach. His companions then arrived, and I saw, too, some armed soldiers coming on bicycles along the road from the fort. The game was up, and the next thing to do was to avoid being shot in the excitement of re-capture. So I beckoned the smallest man and said in German: "Come here and I'll give myself up to you." The chap with the whip immediately came forward. "No, not to you," I said, "you hit me with that whip." The little fellow was very pleased, for there was a hundred marks reward for the capture of an officer, so he hung on to my coat-tails as we started back to the fort. I tore up my map and dropped it into a stream as we went.

The scene in the Commandant's office was quite amusing. We were stripped and searched. I had nothing more to hide, but both Kicq and Wilkin had compasses, which they smuggled through with great skill. Kicq's was hidden in the lining of his great coat, and Wilkin had his in his handkerchief, which he pulled out of his pocket and waved to show that there was nothing in it. All our food stuffs and clothes were returned to us, except my tin of solidified alcohol. I protested, but in vain. I was given a receipt for it and told I could have it back at the end of the war. As we left the office I saw it standing almost within my reach, and nearly managed to pocket it as I went out. However, I found a friend of mine – a French officer – outside and explained to him the position of the tin and suggested that he should go in with a few pals and steal it back for me under the cover of a row. This was the kind of joke that the Frenchmen loved, and they were past-masters at it. They were always rushing off to the Commandant's office with frivolous complaints about one thing and another, just for a rag, which never failed to reduce the Commandant and his officers to a state of dithering rage. Within ten minutes I had my solid alcohol back all right, and kept my receipt for it as well.

Compasses and maps were of course forbidden, but we managed to get them smuggled out in parcels all the same and watching a German open a parcel in which you knew there was a concealed compass was one of the most exciting things I've ever done.

For the next six weeks life was rather hard. It froze continuously, even in the daytime, and at night the thermometer registered more than 27° of frost. Fuel and light shortage became very serious. We stole wood and coal freely from the Germans, and although the sentries had strict orders to shoot at sight anyone seen taking wood, nearly all the wood work in the fort was eventually torn down and burnt.

The Germans didn't allow us much oil for our lamps, so we used to steal the oil out of the lamps in the passage, until the Germans realised that they were being robbed and substituted acetylene for oil. However this didn't deter us, for now, instead of taking the oil out of the lamps, we took the lamps themselves, and lamp-stealing became one of the recognised sports of the camp. How it was done has nothing to do with escaping, but was amusing. Outside our living rooms there was a passage seventy yards long, in which were two acetylene lamps. The sentry in the passage had special orders, a loaded rifle and fixed bayonet, to see that these lamps weren't stolen, and since the feldwebel, or sergeant-major, had stuffed the sentries with horrible stories about our murderous characters, it isn't surprising that each sentry was very keen to prevent us stealing the lamps and leaving him – an isolated German – in total darkness and at our mercy. So whenever a prisoner came out of his room and passed one of the lamps, the sentry would eye him anxiously and get ready to charge at him. The lamps were about thirty yards apart, and this is how we got them. One of us would come out, walk to a lamp and stop beneath it. This would unnerve the sentry, who would advance upon him. The prisoner would then take out his watch and look at it by the light of the lamp, as if that were all he had stopped for. Meanwhile a second officer would come quickly out of a room further down the passage and take down the other lamp behind the sentry's back. The sentry would immediately turn and charge with loud yells of "Halt! Halt!" whereupon the first would also be grabbed, both would be blown out simultaneously and the prisoners would disappear into their respective rooms leaving the passage in total darkness. The amusing part was that this used to happen every night, and the sentries *knew* it was going to happen, but they were quite powerless against tactics of this kind.

At about this time an officer named Medlicott and I learnt that some Frenchmen were trying to escape across the moat by cutting a window-bar in the latrines which overlooked it. The Germans, however, smelt a rat, but though they inspected the bars carefully they couldn't find the cuts which had been artfully sealed up with a mixture of flour and ashes. Then the feldwebel went round and shook each bar violently in turn until the fourth one came off in his hands and he fell down flat on his back. They then wired up the hole, but Medlicott and I saw a chance of cutting the wire and making another bolt for it about a week later, and we took it. We were only at large however for about two hours. The snow on the ground gave our tracks away; we were pursued, surrounded, and eventually had to surrender again. This time we had a somewhat hostile reception when we got back to the fort.

They searched us and took away my tin of solidified alcohol again. They recognised it. "I know how you stole this back," said the senior clerk as he gave me another receipt for it, "but you shan't have it any more." We both laughed over it. I laughed last, however, as I stole it back again in about a week's time, and kept my two receipts for it as well.

It may seem extraordinary that we weren't punished severely for these attempts to escape, but there were no convenient cells in which to punish us. All the cells at Fort 9 were always full and there was a very long waiting list besides.

After this failure I joined some Frenchmen who were making a tunnel. The shaft was sunk in the corner of one of their rooms close under the window, and the idea was to come out in the steep bank of the moat on a level with the ice and crawl over on a dark night. It was all very unpleasant. Most of the time one lay in a pool of water and in an extremely confined space and worked in pitch darkness, as the air was so bad that no candle would keep alight. Moreover, when we got close to the frozen surface of the ground it was always a question whether the sentry outside wouldn't put his foot through the tunnel, and if he did so whether one would be suffocated or stuck with a bayonet. It was most unpleasant lying there and waiting for him to pass within six inches of your head. All the earth had to be carried in bags along the passage and emptied down the latrines.

Unfortunately, just before the work was finished the thaw set in, and it was generally agreed that we couldn't afford to get our clothes wet swimming the moat. However, the Frenchmen were undaunted and determined to wade through the moat naked, carrying two bundles of kit sewn in waterproof cloths. The rest of us disliked the idea of being chased naked in the middle of winter carrying two twenty-pound bundles, so we decided to make ourselves diving suits out of mackintoshes. We waterproofed the worn patches of these with candle grease, and sewed them up in various places. The Frenchmen would have to fake roll call, so they made most life-like dummies, which breathed when you pulled a string, to put in their beds. Whether this attempt to escape would have been successful I can't say, for, thank Heaven, we never tried it. When we were all ready and the French colonel, who was going first, had stripped naked and greased himself from head to foot, we learnt that the trap door which we had made at the exit of the tunnel couldn't be opened under two hours owing to unexpected roots and stones. We had to put off the attempt for that night, and we were unable to make another as the end of the tunnel suddenly fell in, and the cavity was noticed by the sentry.

This was practically the end of my residence in Fort 9 for soon after the Germans decided to send the more unruly of us to other camps. We learnt that we were to be transferred to Zorndorf, in East Prussia, an intolerable spot from all accounts, and a man named Buckley and myself decided to get off the train at the first opportunity and make another bid for freedom. The train would be taking us directly away from the Swiss frontier, so it behoved us to leave it as soon as possible. We equipped ourselves as well as we could with condensed foods before starting, and wore Burberrys to cover our uniforms. Although there were only thirty of us going we had a guard of an officer and fifteen men, which *we* thought a little excessive. We had two hours' wait at the station and amused ourselves by talking as little notice as possible of the officer's orders, which annoyed him and made him shout. Six of us and a sentry were then packed rather tightly into a second-class carriage. We gave him the corner seat next to the corridor, and another sentry marched up and down the corridor outside. Buckley and I took the seats by the window, which we were compelled to keep closed, and there was no door in that side of the carriage. The position didn't look very hopeful, for there wasn't much chance of our sentry going to sleep with the other one outside continually looking in. Just before we started the officer came fussing in: he was obviously very anxious and nervous, and said he hoped that we would have a comfortable quiet journey and no more trouble. The train started, night fell, and the frontier was left further and further behind. We shut our eyes for an hour to try to induce the sentry to go to sleep, but this didn't work.

The carriage was crowded, and both racks were full of small luggage, and, noticing this, I had an idea. I arranged with the others to act in a certain way when the train next went slowly, and I gave the word by saying to the sentry, in German: "Will you have some food? We are going to eat." Five or ten minutes of tense excitement followed. Suddenly the train began to slow up. I leant across and said to the sentry, "Will you have some food? We are going to eat." Immediately everyone in the carriage stood up with one accord and pulled their stuff off the racks. The sentry also stood up, but was almost completely hidden from the window by a confused mass of men and bags. Under cover of this confusion, Buckley and I stood up on our seats. I slipped the strap of my haversack over my shoulder, pushed down the window, put my leg over, and jumped into the night. I fell – not very heavily – on the wires at the side of the track, and lay still in the dark shadow. Three seconds later Buckley came flying out after me, and seemed to take rather a heavy toss. The end of the train wasn't yet past me, and we knew there was a man with a rifle in the last carriage; so when Buckley came running along the track calling out to me, I caught him and pulled him into the ditch at the side. The train went by, and its tail lights vanished round a corner and apparently no one saw or heard us.

I have not space to say much about our walk to the German-Swiss frontier, about 200 miles away. We only walked by night, and lay up in hiding all through the hours of daylight – which was, I think, the worst part of the business and wore out our nerves and physical strength far more than the six or seven hours marching at night, for the day seemed intolerably long from 4.30 a.m. to 9.30 p.m. – seventeen hours – the sun was very hot, and there was little shade, and we were consumed with impatience to get on. Moreover, we could never be free from anxiety at any moment of those seventeen hours. The strain at night of passing through a village when a few lights still burnt and dogs seemed to wake and bark at us in every house, or of crossing a bridge when one expected to be challenged at any moment never worried me so much as a cart passing or men talking near our daytime hiding places.

We went into hiding at dawn or soon after, and when we'd taken off our boots and put on clean socks we would both drop asleep at once. It was a bit of a risk – perhaps one of us ought to have stayed awake, but we took it deliberately since we got great benefit from a sound sleep while we were still warm from walking. And it was only for about an hour, before we woke again shivering, for the mornings were very cold and we were usually soaked with dew up to our waists. Then we had breakfast – the great moment of the day – and rations were pretty good at first, as we underestimated the time we would take by about four days. But later on we had to help things out with raw potatoes from the fields, which eventually became our mainstay. All day long we were pestered with stinging insects. Our hands and faces became swollen all over, and the bites on my feet came up in blisters which broke and left raw places when I put on my boots again.

On the fifteenth day our impatience got the better of us, and we started out before it was properly dark, and suddenly came upon a man in soldier's uniform scything grass at the side of the road. We were filthily dirty and unshaven and must have looked the most villainous tramps; it was stupid of us to have risked being seen; but it would have aroused his suspicion if we'd turned back, so we walked on past him. He looked up and said something we didn't catch. We answered "Good evening" as usual. But he called after us, and then when we took no notice, shouted "Halt! Halt!" and ran after us with his scythe.

We were both too weak to run fast or far, and moreover we saw at that moment a man with a gun about fifty yards to our right. There was only one thing to be done, and we did it.

We turned haughtily and waited for our pursuer, and when he was a few yards away Buckley demanded in a voice quivering with indignant German what the devil he meant by shouting at us. He almost dropped his scythe with astonishment, then turned round and went slowly back to his work. Buckley had saved the day.

The end of our march on the following night brought us within fifteen kilometres of the Swiss frontier, and we decided to eat the rest of our food and cross the next night. However, I kept back a few small meat lozenges. We learnt the map by heart so as to avoid having to strike matches later on, and left all our spare kit behind us in order to travel light for this last lap. But it wasn't to be our last lap.

We were awfully weak by now and made slow progress through the heavy going, and about two hours after we'd started a full bright moon rose which made us feel frightfully conspicuous. Moreover, we began to doubt our actual position, for a road we'd expected to find wasn't there. However, we tramped on by compass and reached a village which we hoped was a place named Riedheim, within half a mile of the frontier. But here we suddenly came on a single line railway which wasn't on our map. We were aghast – we were lost – and Buckley was fearfully exhausted for want of food, so we decided to lie up for another night in a thick wood on a hill. The meat lozenges I'd saved now came in very handy and we also managed to find water and some more raw potatoes. Then we slept, and when daylight came studied our small scale map and tried to make head or tail of our situation.

We had a good view of the countryside from our position, but could make nothing of it. Perhaps we were already in Switzerland? It was essential to know and it was no good looking for signposts since they'd all been removed within a radius often miles of the frontier. I think we were both slightly insane by now from hunger and fatigue; anyhow I decided to take a great risk. I took off my tunic and walking down into the fields asked a girl who was making hay what the name of the village was. It was Riedheim – as I'd originally thought. The railway of course had been made after the map was printed. I don't know what the girl thought of my question and appearance; she gave me a sly look, but went on with her work. I returned to Buckley, and when it was quite dark we left our hiding place. We had threequarters of an hour to cross the frontier before the moon rose – and we had to go with the greatest care. For a time we walked bent double, and then we went down on our hands and knees, pushing our way through the thick long grass of water meadows. The night was so still – surely the swishing of the grass as we moved through it must be audible for hundreds of yards. On and on we went – endlessly it seemed – making for a stream which we had seen from our hill and now knew must be the boundary line. Then the edge of the moon peered at us over the hills. We crawled at top speed now until Buckley's hand on my heel suddenly brought me to a halt. About fifteen yards ahead was a sentry. He was walking along a footpath on the bank of a stream. *The* stream. He had no rifle, and had probably just been relieved. He passed without seeing us. One last spurt and we were in the stream and up the other bank. "Crawl," said Buckley "Run," said I, and we ran. It was just after midnight when we crossed into Switzerland and freedom on our eighteenth night out.

CHAPTER FIVE

INVETERATE ESCAPERS

By Duncan Grinnell-Milne

The period of my adventures as a prisoner of war lies between 1 December, 1915, and the end of April, 1918 – nearly two and a half years. During the whole of that period the thought of escape was uppermost in my mind, and therefore I cannot hope to tell you in detail of all the attempts made or of all my adventures. The best I can do is to recount briefly some of my many failures and my final success.

I was only nineteen when I was captured, flying; and it seemed tragic enough then to be condemned to that most awful state of things for a young man in war time – inaction. Quite naturally my thoughts turned to escape.

My first camp was Mainz; and the first incident to stimulate my imagination occurred on Xmas Eve, 1915. Two officers – one British, one French – escaped. They weren't at liberty very long, but the details which slowly trickled through were somehow wildly exciting. They had obtained civilian clothing, German money, maps, a compass – how, I didn't know, but it made me want to find out!

I determined to escape too. I thought about it; I talked about it to one or two kindred spirits. I didn't know a thing of how to get going, but I set out to learn. I had one asset: I could speak German – not really such an asset as it seemed – and without wasting much time I started to dig a tunnel.

It was a very small tunnel and it had a very long way to go – at least eighty yards. It would have taken many weary months to complete – in fact I was secretly rather glad when the Germans became suspicious, and suddenly bundled a few of us who had been connected with it off to another camp.

Weilburg was the name of the new camp; not a bad place, where, under other circumstances, one might have been content to stay for the remainder of the War. But the itch to escape had obtained a firm hold on one or two of us. We were delighted, not with the camp, but with the fact that a tunnel had already been started by some Russians in a disused cellar. Here I had my first experience of making keys and picking locks, for at night the doors leading to the cellar were locked and the Russians had skilfully moulded pass-keys out of soft white-metal spoons. I learnt some valuable lessons from them. But it was far more than a tunnel; it was a conspiracy! After dark, through the passages of the building, flitted Russians in long black cloaks, caps pulled down over their eyes, mysterious bundles beneath their arms. In the cellar itself, stumps of candle threw long, distorted shadows, muffled figures – those of Guy Fawkes and his friends – moved as silently as ghosts. At least they tried to be as silent as ghosts, but every now and then someone would trip over a brick or an empty box or else clumsily drop one of the table-knives used for digging. There would be a crash, a loud clatter, immediately followed by a chorus of hissing and "shooshing" and hushing, as though one had aroused a nest of angry snakes. The candles would be blown out and we would wait, listening with bated breath, whilst overhead we could hear a sentry passing, coughing and stamping his feet in the cold. At length reassured, we would light up again and cautiously resume work.

Gradually we obtained a bigger proportion of British workers and fewer Russian conspirators; work went on more quickly if less romantically – but even so we were doomed to failure. The tunnel was too near the surface; it collapsed beneath a mass of melting snow just before it was finished, and we were temporarily heartbroken. But we soon found courage to start again; other schemes were afoot. We were beginning to know the rudiments of the game, of how to make odds and ends of material into rough suits of civilian clothing, of how to get compasses smuggled out from England, or of how to buy very bad maps from a corrupt German guard. A visiting clergyman, who imprudently left his bag unwatched during a church service, gave us the chance to see what an official travelling pass looked like, and we banged out many copies on a borrowed typewriter. A little later two of us very nearly escaped in the washing baskets which were carried out of the camp each week. So sure was I of the success of this scheme that on the night when we were to be shut into the baskets I applied a bottle of black hair dye to my red hair. But the baskets were too small, and when at dawn we gave up hope I was thankful to think that the hair dye hadn't worked. I should have touched wood – by noon my hair had turned a bright purple, and the Germans had a good laugh at my expense.

Scheme after scheme went wrong and all I got out of Weilburg was some valuable experience and a few weeks in gaol for helping two other fellows to escape.

The next camp I went to was Friedberg. There, for some three months I worked hard at a number of different plans, and at length after many failures three of us tried a new scheme. We were to walk out of the camp in broad daylight, two of us dressed as German officers, the third as a civilian. The supposed civilian, by the way, was my brother, who had recently been captured, also while flying. I cannot go into lengthy details of the slow manufacture of German uniforms – many other prisoners had a hand in it – but I can at least explain that the pre-war Russian overcoat was of much the same colour and cut as the German garment. Of course a good many important alterations were needed; and the remainder of the equipment of caps, badges, shoulder-straps, sword-scabbard, etc., required a vast amount of patient work.

However, the main business was wearing the uniform and somehow making it get us past the sentries on the gate. There was a lot of difficulty about this, but providing you had sufficient effrontery it was not impossible, for a large number of commissions – from the German War Office, from the Red Cross, from neutrals – had recently inspected the camp. *We* styled ourselves the Drainage Commission, and a very smart trio we were, smart enough to fool the authorities. But no one need ever attempt to explain to me the meaning of "stage fright". No actor ever felt as badly as I did on the morning when I led my two drainage friends past the sentries to the gates of Friedberg. After all, in England, nowadays, an actor rarely gets shot or put in prison if he fails to give satisfaction; whereas in our case there was a distinct likelihood of getting shot, and a certainty of being gaoled if we were found out. But the great bluff succeeded splendidly. The sentries clicked their heels and saluted as we marched triumphantly out of the camp without any opposition whatsoever; and the only sad thing I have to record is that within five days we had all three been recaptured after long and rather difficult cross-country marches.

Naturally we lost all our valuable escaping kit on being recaptured, a very discouraging state of affairs, but something over a month's solitary confinement in the civil prison in the town of Friedberg gave me plenty of time to ponder past adventures and also to plan future attempts. And when at length I was sent off to Fort Zorndorf, near the town of Cüstrin, some seventy miles east of Berlin, I was impatient to start again.

Life in a fortress isn't too much fun at the best; but the two principal objections to Zorndorf were that it was extremely difficult to get out of, and that it lay a very considerable distance from any neutral frontier. In fact the Russian front was as near as anything, and whenever Russians escaped or laid plans to escape, they generally made straight for home. Just before I arrived one Russian officer went so far as to make himself a saddle and bridle, intending, so he said, to catch a horse and ride back to Moscow. He actually got out of the fort dressed as a German officer, but he never caught his horse. It was he that was caught, practically at once – the sight of a German officer carrying a set of home-made harness was a trifle *too* odd!

Zorndorf, like so many old forts, was a sort of five-sided affair, mostly underground, with a few trenches and earthworks on top and a big ditch all round. On the far side of the ditch a thirty-foot wall rose to the level of the surrounding country. There was only one official exit, closely guarded – as, in fact, was the whole camp. When I arrived the few good schemes had already been used up. But the majority of us being there for attempted escapes, we went on trying. We talked of, we imagined, we worked at every conceivable scheme – from digging about in the very foundations of the fort for a possible secret passage, to calculating the chances of a man-lifting kite or of a hot-air balloon: and as far as that goes, we must have *talked* enough hot air to lift a regiment out of the place.

I first met Captain Hardy (who also describes his experiences in this book) at Zorndorf; he and I racked our brains over many a plot. The first thing we actually tried was a wild dash for freedom from the house of the German Commandant. He used to have us brought out of the fort to his house if we had anything to ask him or to complain about. The house was on the edge of a forest, and although close to and in full view of a number of sentries we thought it unlikely that they would fire for fear of hitting the Commandant. On the great day itself the sentries seemed very watchful but only one guard accompanied us, and while he was inside the house announcing our arrival we strolled off round the corner, jumped a fence and then sprinted away at full speed into the forest. There were three of us at the start, but the third fellow couldn't run fast enough. He was soon recaptured, unharmed we heard later, but at the time the sounds of shooting and much shouting made us redouble our efforts. Hardy and I ran on, got separated, lost ourselves in the forest, and hours afterwards, by an extraordinary chance, found each other in the night miles from anywhere. It was an unpleasant escapade, not even very funny. But then if you want to be really uncomfortable wait for a spell of bad weather in January, and, having made yourself thoroughly unfit by a few months indoors preferably in a gaol, put on your thinnest clothing and try an all-night cross country walk. We met with swamps, dense forest, streams in flood, villages and farms that had to be avoided – and the River Oder, which we vainly attempted to cross in a leaky boat. However, allowing for detours we covered over forty five miles in fifteen hours!

And in the morning we boarded a train for Berlin! It began to look as though we were on the high road to success – but, no, misfortune barred the way. Back at Zorndorf someone had forgotten to tear up a map on which was marked our proposed route. The Germans found it, sent a man ahead of us by rail; we were arrested on the train; and brought back to Cüstrin for a little solitary confinement. And when this was over, and we were back in the fort, we had to start all over again collecting escaping kit, manufacturing funny looking civilian clothing, hunting for ever scarce maps, designing new false police passes – in fact all the lengthy and serious preparation for escape.

As soon as we were ready, Hardy and I with a Belgian officer named Bastin tried a much more ambitious scheme. It had been worked out by some French officers who had left for another camp. They were responsible for all its brilliant ideas – and also, I'm afraid, for its failure. For it depended, at the end, upon a home-made ladder to scale the thirty-foot wall above the ditch; and the ladder was a foot too short! However, we didn't know that when we started. By an ingenious plan, also worked out by the French and involving being locked up in the camp chapel all night, we got out on top of the fort before daybreak, and carrying our kit, and the ladder in sections, we crept around the trenches under the very noses of the sentries, eventually sliding down a long slope into the ditch. There, behind a wall, we built up the ladder and waited for dawn. We had really succeeded wonderfully well till then; there had been a flock of sentries about, but we had dodged them all, greatly assisted by deep snow and the fact that we were wearing white clothing. The white clothing, covering us literally from head to foot, was made up of various odds and ends, but I remember that it consisted in part of female nightgowns, purchased for us by a German guard – heaven knows what he thought we were going to do with them! Yes, it was a splendid scheme – but the ladder was too short! And the wall was covered with ice so that one couldn't get a grip to pull oneself up from the top of the ladder… We were caught in the ditch.

Three months' solitary confinement this time, in Cüstrin Citadel, then back to Zorndorf for further vain attempts and more hard work collecting kit. I won't say that we ever gave up hope; but the outlook was becoming pretty desperate, when suddenly after a total of ten months in the fort, I was packed off to Ströhen Moor, a place west of Hanover and only about one hundred miles from the Dutch frontier.

Ströhen was quite the funniest camp I was ever in. To begin with, it was all-British – no Allies. Secondly it was notoriously unhealthy, which made everyone much more irresponsible, discontented and ready to annoy the guards in any way possible. Also it was, at the start, a very easy camp to escape from; people walked out of it with but little trouble. Several who escaped reached the frontier, one or two successfully crossed it. But all the easiest schemes were soon exploited; the Germans became thoroughly alarmed, and the mesh of the wire surrounding the camp seemed to grow finer each day. When I arrived it was time to think of something serious.

Yet only a day after my arrival I was taken into a scheme which, for simplicity, craziness and, also, likelihood of success, was hard to beat. It was proposed to charge one of the small side gates of the camp with a "battering-ram" at dusk. The lock was believed to be quite weak, and the momentum of charge would, it was thought, break the lock and carry us on into outer darkness; while the yells of a gang of accomplices in the camp would distract the attention of the sentries. The "battering-ram" was an iron bar – part of a gymnastic bar erected in the camp by the Germans – and about six men to carry it during the charge... I applied for a position at the tail-end! But I had come into the scheme rather late and there were already quite a number of applicants for the post of honour. Another job was found for me – a nastier one.

There were two rows of wire at Ströhen: one row, close-meshed, surmounted by barbed wire; the other, the row, a fence some three or four feet high, designed to keep us away from the outer row. The space between was called "*neutral* zone" – anyone found inside it got shot! Wherever there was a gate in the outer wire fence, there was naturally a smaller gate in the inner one; and it was my job to open the small gate, at the crucial moment, so as to let the "battering-ram" party go through at speed. I also had to watch the sentries, lest they should smell a rat – meaning me!

On the evening of the appointed day, the gallants assembled behind a nearby hut – iron bar, rucksacks, kit and all, in readiness. As it grew dark I commenced up and down near the wire, trying to look happy, with an eye on the sentry. Presently, when no Germans were looking, I gave the signal to "stand by." Then I strolled up to the gate, unlatched it and pulled it open. It squeaked but I couldn't let go or it would have swung to – and I had already waved and whistled for the charging-party to start. I couldn't see much in the dark, but I heard a scuffling sound as they got under way; and a second later they came thundering past. I have a recollection of feeling at that moment exactly like an old man at a level-crossing holding open the gates for an express to go by; and the next moment the express was derailed and I was left looking stupidly at the accident.

There was a tremendous crash as the front man of the party hit the gate. In the darkness he had missed the lock with the end of the ram and it was his face that charged the framework. But in spite of the five strong men behind him, his face wasn't hard enough to push down the obstruction, and he let forth a yell that must have curdled the blood of all the sentries round the camp. The iron bar was immediately dropped with a loud clang, and the party having picked itself up made off at top speed in the direction of the huts. I fancy I was rather dazed at the rapidity of these happenings, for I stood for a moment, still holding the little gate open, gaping at the "battering-ram" on the ground, until a loud report close behind brought me suddenly to my senses and I just managed to dodge into a hut before the infuriated guards came streaming into the camp, ready to start the inevitable search.

And not long afterwards, when numerous attempts had driven the Commandant to the verge of insanity, a properly organized search for escaping kit was made with the help of detectives from Berlin. We all felt very sorry for those poor detectives! From the time they entered the camp to the time they left, the unfortunate men were given no peace. Impeded at every turn, they were harried from one room to another; contraband captured in one hut was recaptured by the prisoners in the next. On leaving, surrounded by a band of cheering British officers, several of them complained that their pockets had been picked, their identity cards and police papers stolen. And one wretched man walked out with a notice pinned to his coat-tail: "You know my methods, Watson!"

Next day more prisoners escaped.

My brother turned up at Ströhen, fresh from gaol after an escape which had brought him close to the Dutch frontier. Together we started to work out a new and fairly scheme. We couldn't get material for German uniforms (and in any case very few officers came into the camp) so we decided to dress *me* up as a German soldier, and let me escort a couple of prisoners, my brother and another man, out of one of the main gates. The manufacture of the German uniform out of spare bits and scraps of clothing wasn't too difficult, but the rifle took weeks to make. We hunted for many days, in and around and under the huts, before finding a suitable piece of wood out of which to carve the stock – a bar wrenched from a cooking range formed the barrel – tin cans were cut up to make the breech mechanism. It was a masterpiece when it was finished – I believe it was put in a German war-museum later – at any rate the odd pieces of scrap-iron, wood and tin were faked up so that it would stand a really close inspection.

The party was eventually increased to five prisoners under my supposed command. They were disguised as British orderlies, of whom there were a large number at Ströhen, and who were frequently employed in bringing food and parcels from the station. In our case, we put all our kit into a big sack, labelled it for another camp as though it were being sent after a departed officer, and loaded it on to a wheelbarrow. The scheme for getting out of the camp, first unlocking and passing through an inner gate in full view of the Germans, was pretty complicated and required a great deal of preparation. In addition to the German uniform and rifle we had to make forged passes, false keys, etc. In fact there was so much to think of that we felt sure of forgetting some small but vital detail. But everything worked out remarkably well. I admit that I felt like the world's biggest fool when I collected my orderlies, yelled commands at them in German, herded them past the sentry and marched out of the gate, wheelbarrow and all. I felt that everyone in and about the camp, Germans included, was looking and laughing at me! But we got out all right, the whole lot of us... And then it went wrong! My brother was recognized. It wasn't his fault – he'd been in gaol so long that all the guards knew him well by sight. And once we were stopped, we knew it was all up.

I did about nine weeks solitary that time, followed by a couple of weeks in hospital, an attempt to cut the wire, some more gaol; and then off to Neunkirchen, in the Saar district – a nasty little camp in the middle of the town. We lived in a small theatre, over eighty of us in one room – which made escape practically essential. Exercise was what we chiefly needed, and we got all we wanted in the digging of a superb tunnel beneath the stage. This time we had almost every advantage, and if that tunnel had ever been completed a very large number would have left the camp. We spent all our spare time manufacturing compasses, copying maps, printing false papers, and making a sort of escapers' phrase-book in German – all so as to enable between forty and fifty prisoners to escape. The tunnel itself was fitted with electric light – rigged up with the help of electric torches bought from the Germans – and an electric buzzer to warn the workers of the approach of danger. A great pity it didn't work! Rain spoilt it, and bad drainage. For more than a month we fought the rising flood, until everything in the camp was wet and muddy, and the water began to overflow into our dormitory. Then, rather naturally, the Germans suspected something...

Weeks passed in the planning of fresh attempts, and after one or two short stretches in gaol I was beginning to plan something desperate, so as at least to be sent away from Neunkirchem, when I had a stroke of good luck.

An exchange of prisoners had been taking place for some time between England and Germany. Officers and men of both nations who had been captured early in the war were being sent to Holland, where they were given complete liberty but forbidden to return to their respective countries. This plan, essential for the health of the prisoners, of course meant abandoning all idea of taking any further part in the war. A few of us who still thought we would eventually escape refused the exchange, and when my turn came, I told the authorities of my intention to stay in Germany – though not, of course, of my reasons. Then came the good luck. I was sent with the other prisoners to a camp at Aachen. There my refusal was to be officially accepted, and I was to be sent back to a camp in the interior – one of the authorities hinted darkly at Fort Zorndorf!

Now the north-western side of the town of Aachen is under five miles from the nearest point of the Dutch frontier, so that at a glance an escape looks remarkably easy. But there were several things that made it difficult. We found that the camp was in the south-eastern part of the town, and the thickly populated outskirts would have to be cleared before one could turn west towards the frontier. There were three of us intending to escape, and from our rather sketchy maps it was plain that we would have to march fifteen to twenty miles in all, and at top speed. That was the real difficulty – time. We found out that after one day and one night the formalities would be completed; then we should be sent to another camp.

On the morning of our arrival we started desperately searching for an exit. Never before had it been necessary – or possible for that matter – to get out of a camp within twenty-four hours of arrival. Never had it been possible or so absolutely essential to reach the frontier and cross it in one short night. For with Holland so close it would be simple for the Germans, once warned of our escape, to guard every inch of the small sector at which we were bound to aim. A daylight attempt was impossible; we had to leave after dark and be in Holland before dawn. It seemed utterly hopeless. The camp was small, closely guarded;

we knew nothing of its routine or even of its topography; we had practically no kit. After roll-call that morning, we had a total of eighteen hours daylight and darkness, in which to escape *and* make good.

Round that small camp we marched innumerable times; searched the building in which we were housed, searched the yard, searched the palisade and the main gate for weak spots; searched everything with a horrible feeling that we were attempting the impossible.

And yet by 9.30 that night two of us were out of the camp. The third man, observed by a watchful sentry, had been unable to follow. But the two of us had left unobserved – neatly, efficiently, but unromantically enough, through a small, almost invisible, ventilating shaft in the camp lavatory; thence through another lavatory (used by the Germans) to a wire fence. Hurriedly, but as silently as possible, we tore our way under the wire, crawled past a couple of sentries; and crept out into an open field. Then under cover of a hedge we made our way cautiously to a road leading through the suburbs to the country east of Aachen.

The first great difficulty was surmounted: we had cleared out of the camp within the specified time. Now the second great obstacle faced us: to reach *and cross* the frontier before dawn.

The suburbs were difficult enough to clear; we never seemed to reach open country. There were villages, factories, coal mines to be avoided all along our route; in the intervals, densely wooded hills where we wandered about, our maps useless, and only a rough compass course to guide us. I had a feeling that we were still alarmingly close to the camp, that we were being followed, that we should never reach the frontier before dawn. It was generally agreed among escapers that the only safe thing to do was to spend a night or two approaching the frontier, and practically crawl the last few miles to the border. But here we were, marching along at our best pace, with no more than the faintest idea of our position. As we gradually turned from east to north and north-west, the country did open up a little but our maps became even vaguer.

The hours passed. There were fewer houses, but nevertheless we kept on blundering into obstacles: well-fenced farms, the outskirts of villages. And then as we hurried on beneath a dark and raining sky, tired, muddy, wet through from wading streams, our clothing torn to rags, we began to encounter obstacles of a different sort. All the woods were crossed by barbed wire fences; farmhouses contained wakeful men; we heard the click of rifle-bolts; shadowy silhouettes showed faintly on the skyline. We were close! But our maps were nearly useless; only memory of the Dutch frontier studied during over two years helped us – that and a compass course. The obstacles and unknown features of the country delayed us terribly. We had to make wide detours; once we had to retrace our steps after nearly bumping into a sentry... Dawn came suddenly out of a grey, hopeless sky. We had reached the end of the time limit set in the camp on the previous day.

In the first light we hurried on, crawled through hedges, skirted open fields, and in desperation finally *ran* a hundred yards to find cover in a bramble bush. There we rested, stared at our maps, studied the features of the country, and at length ascertained our exact position. We had succeeded! We had won the race. We stood up on the Dutch frontier – free!

CHAPTER SIX

A WINTER'S TALE

By J. L. Hardy

In the winter of 1915 we still knew very little of the science of escape. We had
no secret communications with home and hadn't yet learned to make ourselves
false passports; we were lucky if we possessed the copy of a map out of a railway
time-table, and my German at that time was also far from good.

Halle was a hard place. I believe I am, with one exception, the only prisoner
that ever broke out of it. It was a shockingly bad camp and yet there were
practically no attempts made there, because one simply could not see where to
make a start. It was an old machine factory – just a large courtyard, surrounded
by workshops in which we lived, and it was situated well in the middle of the
town. It was bare and ugly and dirty. There were plenty of sentries inside the
camp and sentries in the streets around it and more sentries in the munition
factory that adjoined it. At nights the whole place was a blaze of light, and
sufficient lights were kept burning even in our sleeping quarters to prevent
any nocturnal schemes. For months I looked in vain for an opportunity and
then I found that in my interminable march round that courtyard my eyes
were drawn more and more to the roof of a building in the German section
of the camp. The camp was shut in by buildings on three sides. Those on two
sides were occupied by prisoners; the third was a long, two-storied building,
which contained the guard room and the parcel room on its ground floor and
the German quartermaster's stores and censor's office upstairs. Prisoners
were only allowed here one or two at a time for the handing out of parcels,
and to prevent any unauthorised person being there a high barbed-wire fence
had been put up with a gate in the centre, at which a sentry was stationed.
When you went for a parcel the sentry allowed you through the gate and you

walked down a short passage into the parcel room from which there was no other exit. Half-way down the short passage was the staircase which led up to the next floor. Here, on a landing, were the two doors of the other rooms I've mentioned, the censor's office and the quarter-master's stores. The door of the quartermaster's stores was kept locked.

On the further side of this building, between it and the street, was a small narrow garden, lit at night by a bright arc lamp and fenced with high railings. There was practically nothing growing in this small garden – just a sentry.

Now if, I thought, I could get on to the roof of this building, let myself down into the little garden and then scale the railings (while the sentry obligingly turned his back or slept) I should find myself in the open street, and free. IF, yes – it certainly was an if – but, as I've already said, no one, so far, had managed to escape from Halle. There was a way on to the roof, I knew, through a skylight in the quartermaster's stores, but the roof looked very exposed; could one show oneself on it? Was it possible to cross that garden, so brightly lit and so open, under the nose of its sentry? And to scale the railings too? Besides, I had only seen the garden side of the building once, as I was brought into the camp, and wasn't familiar with its layout.

Well – there was one way of knowing whether these things were possible, and that was by trying; but I confess to a sinking sensation whenever I looked at that bit of roof.

First of all I had to devise a means of getting into the quarter-master's stores, where the skylight was. I might manage that by pretending to be on a visit to the censor, who, as I've said, lived on the same floor. Prisoners were allowed to visit him during working hours and I should therefore have to hide myself in the store room from the time he knocked off until it became dark enough for me to make my attempt. The stores were locked, so I should have to pick the lock and I should have to do it quickly and quietly, as someone might easily come out of the censor's office opposite at any moment. Harrison told us he had a weakness for sardine openers when picking. I liked the thin strong wire that is used for stiffening an officer's cap. I got myself a couple of bits and started practising on every available lock in the camp, and in time I got so good at the job that I felt the particular lock in question would have no terrors for me.

J. R. Ackerley.

Harry Beaumont.

H. A. Cartwright.

Hugh Durnford.

A. J. Evans.

D. Grinnell-Milne.

J. L. Hardy.

M. C. C. Harrison.

E. H. Jones.

Heinz H. E. Justus.

E. H. Keeling.

Ernest Pearce.

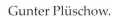
Gunter Plüschow.

Hermann Tholens.

Lawrence A. Wingfield.

This was my second attempt to escape from Germany and I decided that this time I would put my German to the test, and travel by train. I had, as a matter of fact, no other choice, the weather bitterly cold and a distance of 300 miles to the frontier. We had heard that it was very dangerous to travel within forty miles of the frontiers, so I chose Bremen as my destination and planned to go on foot from there westwards and try to cross into Holland through the marshes near the coast.

I don't remember fixing a particular day beforehand, but I must have done so. Only one friend – Captain Cutbill of the Suffolk Regiment – knew of my plans and I proposed to do the stunt alone. I used to lie awake at nights and worry over it. I used to picture myself cornered in that garden like a rat, dodging about while a frightened and furious sentry blazed away at me. I know I was more frightened of this particular attempt to escape than of any other I've taken part in, but the chance was there, and I was determined to take it. The day arrived. I dressed myself in my room, my uniform over civilian clothes. I owned a compass and a small map of the country between Bremen and Holland and was taking what food I could conveniently carry in my pocket. I had a civilian shirt and cap, dungaree trousers and a Norfolk jacket. At about three o'clock in the afternoon Cutbill and myself presented ourselves before the gate and showed the sentry two letters which we said we wished to hand to the censor. He let us through, and as soon as we were in the building we crept quietly up the stairs, passed the censor's office on tip-toe and reached the store-room door. I produced the two small wires and shoved one into the lock. My friend held it and braced while I pushed in the second and felt for the bolt. I was in a frantic hurry, expecting every moment that the door behind us would open and some spotty little clerk would see us and give the alarm. At last I felt the bolt slip further and further, and suddenly the door opened under my hand. I said good-bye to Cutbill, went in and closed the door and picked the lock too from the other side. The stores, I found, were divided into two rooms, so I had yet another locked door to tackle. This went as easily as the other, and I was now in the little room from which my adventure was to start. I looked round first for something with which to let myself down from the roof when the time came. It was too high to jump. I found some old leather straps

which I plaited together into a rope and then sat down to wait for darkness. I had a sleep, read some ancient German newspapers and was feeling quite all right when suddenly I heard a key in the outer door. Oh! Lord. I was caught. The sentry must have reported that whereas two officers had gone up only one had come down. I knelt down and looked through the keyhole. To my immense relief, instead of several sentries I saw one German N.C.O. and a number of orderlies, who were carrying bedsteads out of the room. I felt very thankful for the locked door between me and them.

At last the fatigue party cleared off, locking the door behind them and left me to myself again. At about six o'clock it began to get dark and started to rain. All the lights outside had been switched on. I judged the moment had come. The old hands shook a bit as I pulled a couple of packing cases into the middle of the room, climbed on to them and pushed open the skylight. Then I scrambled on to the roof. In a moment I was back again and closed the skylight behind me.

The thing was impossible. Never had I realised how impossible it was. The fact that prisoners weren't able to go too near the sentries' beat had prevented my realising that at least three of them had a direct view of my roof and there was an arc lamp immediately over the skylight. It was as bright as day there and the sentries had probably seen me already as clearly as I'd seen them. I stood there quite dumbfounded and feeling absolutely desperate. I'd burned my boats behind me with a vengeance, for no one was allowed in this building after 4 p.m. If I tried to get back I should be arrested and everything discovered, including the fact that the senior British officer had reported me present at roll call. The others would think I'd funked it. I *did* funk it. What on earth was I to do. Then suddenly I saw a chance. The rain outside had now turned into a downpour. The sentries would probably be sheltering in their boxes. It was a risk – but worth taking.

I jumped for it. My hands gripped the edge of the trap door – one heave and I was up, standing in the deluge on the roof. My surmise was correct. Not a soul was to be seen in the courtyard of the camp. I made fast my rope – took a pull on it, threw myself clear of the gutter and slid down. The rope broke and I landed in a sitting position in the garden about four yards from the sentry,

who stood in his box. Next moment I was on my legs again and bolting for the railings. I expected every moment to hear a shout behind me, but my man had bowed his head to the beating rain and saw nothing. The railings must have been easy. I don't remember them. I was in the street. There was no one about, and turning to the left I ran with my head in a whirl. I was already soaked to the skin, but in a state of absolute elation.

Now it had been my intention to break out without leaving any trace, and I'd meant to tie something on to the end of my rope and throw it back on to the roof. But the breaking of the rope had made this impossible and I felt certain that as soon as the rain stopped and the sentry came out of his box, he would see the end of the rope hanging there and give the alarm. The rain had already stopped, so I must therefore take it that my escape was now known. There were several people about in the streets again and I realised that whatever I did, I must get out of Halle quickly.

I felt I must look a very suspicious figure, dripping wet as I was and, for one moment, I hesitated at the station entrance, but it was the only hope, so I hurried to the booking office and asked for a fourth-class ticket to Berlin. The clerk looked me up and down, drummed his fingers on the ledge and asked what I was going to Berlin for. I thought of saying I was going there to work. Probably he thought so too and was merely going to offer me a cheap workman's ticket. But escapers see a hundred subtle traps where none exist. I said: "My father has died, and I'm going to his funeral."

He gave me my ticket at once, with a sorrowful look, and I went up on to the platform. I looked pretty young at that time and I used to put on a very bad limp, half close one eye and open the other in a glassy stare. This gave me the appearance of an imbecile, but was held by my friends to be a great improvement on my natural expression.

I hadn't long to wait before a train came in and I hopped straight into a fourth-class carriage. I had no idea in which direction it was going. All I knew was that I had got to get clear before the camp telephoned my description to the station police. Off we went, but after about two hours the train stopped in a place called Kothen, where an inspector got in and examined my ticket. He made the usual sort of bawling row when he found I was in the wrong train, called me an idiot and made me buy a ticket back to Halle. I dared not argue with him. He seemed surprised that I had the money for the ticket. He pushed me into a carriage full of soldiers and there I sat staring at the notice opposite me.

Vorsicht Beim Gesprach. Spionen Gefahr!
Watch your words.   Danger of spies!

How nice for me. I felt very small among those troops. When we got to Halle I sat well back and pretended to be asleep, and let the train take me on to the end of its journey – Leipzig. Here a new difficulty arose. I couldn't leave the platform without passing the barrier, and I dared not show my wrong tickets, which were bound to lead to an awkward discussion. One ticket from Halle to Berlin, one from Kothen to Halle, and here was I at midnight in Leipzig.

The station was emptying and I began to feel rather conspicuous. I badly wanted a smoke but I had no matches, so I tried to get a light off the tail lamp of a train. Apparently this was *verboten* because I was hauled up by an official and a little crowd formed. Up came a policeman, who asked for my papers, and I produced my two tickets. In the following confusion and whirl of conversation, in which everybody joined but myself, he forgot about the papers. I looked anxiously from face to face. I stood all crooked. The large eye glared, the little eye blinked. In broken sentences, in muttered phrases, I killed my father again in Bremen and set out to his funeral.

They were sorry for me – even the policeman was sorry. We all trooped off to the barrier, where my tickets were taken from me, and I was told that there was a train leaving for Bremen at five o'clock next morning. I went and sat in a large general waiting room, which was warmer than the platform. After about half an hour a policeman came in and asked someone for his papers. This was awful. I couldn't get up and walk out of the place. I thought of referring him to the inspector, but before he came round to me, he started having trouble with a German working man with a certain amount of drink on board. There was a terrific shouting match which ended in a battle, and the policeman rushed off with his prize. After this I kept on the move till my train was in and then got settled in a corner and pretended to fall asleep. We pulled up in due course at a large station and I put my head out of the window. Was this a nightmare? It was Halle again. But all went well. During the whole of that journey no passports were asked for, and at six o'clock in the evening we ran into Bremen.

I think I lost my wits completely in Bremen. I walked and walked – I had to keep going, because it was infernally cold, but I must have gone in circles because I couldn't get out of the town. There were nothing but bridges – all bridges were guarded, that was the sort of thing that prisoners believed in those days. By about nine o'clock that night I began to feel pretty done. I had no great-coat and there was a biting east wind blowing and snow began to fall lightly, and lie unmelted on the ground. I went back to the station and decided to go by train a few miles further westward, risky though it might be. I took a ticket to Delmenhorst. It would at least be warmer in the train, and I thought I might find a haystack or barn out in the country where I could rest for the night. I discovered a radiator, which I froze on to until my train came in.

We reached Delmenhorst at midnight. It was pitch dark outside. I walked briskly out of the station as though I had some definite destination, and I set off in a westerly direction. I did about four miles in what I believed to be the right direction, but there was such a fierce wind that I couldn't keep matches burning long enough to read my compass. However fast I walked, I could not keep warm, and I was dropping with sleep, and generally feeling awful. At last I came to a cottage with some sheds behind it, but I was routed out of that by a dog, and his barking brought lights into the windows. I bolted down the road.

I kept leaving the road then and crossing fields, because I thought I saw straw stacks, but when I got there I would find dumps of pine trees, through which the wind whistled. I would have given *anything* for a great-coat. I turned back for Delmenhorst. Trains – trains were good. You couldn't freeze to death in a train. But the station was closed for the night. I went and sat in a graveyard with my back against a tombstone. Too cold. The whole place was frozen. I wandered about like a lost dog and found myself on the railway line, followed it up and reached the station that way. I climbed up on to the platform and looked to see if there were any fires in the waiting rooms. There weren't. But there was a lovely stove burning brightly in the telegraph office. The door stood open.

The room was empty. I hesitated. It was a *lovely* fire! I would go in and stop there just long enough to get the frost out of my hands.

But it was surrender really – and in my heart of hearts I knew it. I threw my chances away because I hadn't the guts to stand the cold that soldiers on every front were putting up with – and because I was alone.

I hadn't been there long when an official came into the room. He stopped with a jerk at the door, and looked me up and down in astonishment.

"*Um Gottes: Willen, woher dann?*" said he. I stood there like a fool. The lovely warmth of that fire – I could hardly keep my eyes open. I thought "*Woher?*" – does that mean "Where are you from?" or "Where are you going to?"

I said: "Give me a minute to get warm, and I'll tell you who I am."

"All right," he said, "rest here a bit;" and he went out and locked me in. There were windows. I could still have made a bolt. But I shouted: "I'm an escaped British officer," and I lay down on the floor and went to sleep.

CHAPTER SEVEN

FUGITIVES IN GERMANY

By J. L. Hardy

In the spring of 1916 I found myself in Magdeburg camp. I had just finished a term of imprisonment for my unsuccessful attempt at escape from Halle and Baschwitz, whom I knew slightly, approached me almost at once because he knew I hadn't given up hope. Baschwitz was a Belgian officer, about thirty years old, very short and thick set, with extraordinarily small feet, and he was extremely muscular. He had very large wide open blue eyes and a turned up fair moustache. He spoke perfect German and very good English. At nights he wore a Schnurr Bard Binder, which is a sort of strap for keeping your moustache in position. It sounds as if he were foppish, and from our point of view he was; but he was also perfectly brave, and when, in the course of my story, I say "we planned" I generally mean "Baschwitz planned," and when I say "we were determined" I mean "he was determined". We met every day and we walked together every day – we walked in fact all day round and round that wretched camp looking for *some* weak spot in the defences. I think any ex-prisoner will agree with me when I say that Magdeburg was an extremely strong camp. There was a great deal of barbed wire, wide neutral zones, something like thirty sentry posts, and the whole place at night was ablaze with arc lamps. The spot that drew *us* was a little triangular courtyard behind the Wagenhaus – the building in which we slept. We could look down into it from one of the windows. One of the three sides of this little yard was formed by the back of our building, the second side was the usual double-barbed-wire fence, and the third consisted of a ten-foot wooden paling along the top of which had been fixed the usual iron stanchions carrying barbed wire. Access to the yard was gained only by a door in our building, and against the wooden paling had been built a latrine for the use of German soldiers of the guard. This latrine had no roof. The camp orderlies, who were of course prisoners of war, were allowed to use this yard as a drying ground for washing, but no officer prisoner was allowed there, and a sentry was posted there day and night to see that this rule was obeyed.

Now, there wasn't a chance of scaling the double wire entanglement. It was pretty high, and moreover, a rat could not have run across that yard without the sentry seeing it. On the other hand if one could get into the latrine unspotted, it might be possible to cut a hole in the paling large enough to crawl through. Parallel to, and outside the paling, ran a low railway embankment along which sentries were posted. One of them unfortunately, was placed exactly opposite the point where one would emerge. It was, I must say, hard to imagine any possible combination of circumstances that would make this enterprise feasible. First, we must be disguised as orderlies in order to get into the latrine – well enough disguised to deceive the sentry. This was easy; but in the second place we must be absolutely safe from disturbance while cutting through the paling, and to make sure of this we must do it at night, when the yard was closed, and no one allowed to use the latrine. That meant that we would have to get into the latrine just before the yard was closed, and hide there till dark – which would necessitate faking the evening roll call.

That would not account however for the sentry on the embankment outside. The only hope of evading him would be to choose a night when the rain was so heavy as to drive him into his sentry box and keep him there. It was a point in our favour that his box stood sideways to the paling, so that when he was in it he would not be looking straight towards us.

Baschwitz had a lot of friends at Magdeburg, and the job of getting civilian clothes fell to him – for, of course, we should want civilian clothes for the journey to the frontier if we managed to get out of the camp. Some of the prisoners had dungaree trousers and one or two had civilian jackets, but it was hard to know who to approach, for we didn't want our intentions discussed or betrayed. However, we marked down certain garments and decided not to approach their owners till the last moment. Then suddenly we discovered that our whole plan was rotten, our castle built on sand. I was watching from the landing window one night and saw the rounds – a German officer and N.C.O., two sentries and a couple of police dogs, go into our courtyard and examine the latrine. Rounds went out every hour at Magdeburg, and every hour they visited our courtyard – and we had never realised it. It looked as if there was nothing doing and Baschwitz and I mooched miserably about the place, hoping to see some other loophole. There was none. In a half-hearted way we pushed on with some preparations – for instance, we got hold of a key-hole saw from an old Belgian colonel who was allowed to do carpentering. We got hold of five or six pounds in German money either won at cards or else bought at excessive rates from some other prisoner. We felt we *had* to be ready if any chance came. But the days dragged on and nothing happened. And we sat there and sat there.

We began to look into the matter of faking the roll call. We slept up to forty prisoners per room, and at night we were ordered to be in bed when the German officer came round with his escort. The German officer who was responsible for Baschwitz's room was not very thorough in his methods. He just made sure that every bed had its occupant, but he didn't wake prisoners who were already asleep, and Baschwitz felt certain that a life-like dummy would fool him all right. But the officer who took the roll in my room had got dummies on the brain. If you lay still, he used to make one of the sentries prod you till you sat up. What he did not do, was to count the beds, and all I had to do to fool him, was to dismantle my bed, hide the sections, and move the other beds up to hide the gap. As for morning roll call that could be worked by getting the senior officer to report "two officers sick in bed". Two prisoners who had just attended roll-call would then rush straight back to their beds – there to be counted again. So Baschwitz made a start on his dummy. He got some plaster of Paris from a prisoner who was a sculptor by profession, and he got hair from the barber's shop, and in the end, I can tell you, he made a wonderful job of it – a dummy with a nice pink complexion and an aquiline nose.

About this time I was sent for by the Commandant and interrogated as to why I was so much in Baschwitz's company. The Germans were getting extremely suspicious. They knew we had a plan, but they couldn't make out what it was. Eventually the Commandant, having made a tour of the camp with his officers was struck by the very same thing as had struck us. The weak spot, he saw, was the little courtyard, and the weakest spot of all, the latrine in the courtyard.

He ordered that it was not to be used any more, and that the door was to be nailed up. In giving this order he played entirely into our hands, because once hidden in there we were certain not to be disturbed, and we therefore decided that there was no reason why we should not make our attempt by day.

Well, at last we had everything ready. Civilian clothes – about 120 marks in German money, a compass and the small map out of a railway time-table. All we had to do now was to wait for stormy weather, to keep the outside sentry in his box. We had decided to make for the Baltic coast, get across to Rügen Island, and try to smuggle on board a ship at a port on Rügen called Sassnitz. The weather at this time was set fine and we had a job to pass the time away. It was rather hard on your nerves, because you went to bed every night with the possibility in your mind of waking up in the morning to find that the weather had broken at last and that the job had to be done quick. Also there were constant rumours of attempts about to be made by other prisoners, generally Russians. Thank heavens, the stock of wine in the canteen usually gave out before they got anything started. Weeks passed, and then, one morning I got up to find it pouring out of a grey sky. The day had come. Somehow it was a bit of a shock. Every German sentry in that camp had instructions to fire without warning on an escaper. The prospect made me feel slightly sick.

I looked into Baschwitz's room, and gave him a meaning wink. He whispered: "After the breakfast, we go." "You bet," says I.

I went back to my room and started to get things ready. I wrapped our two civilian jackets into a small bundle and gave them to a British orderly who was going to help us by dropping them over into the latrine, which, as I've said, was roofless. I watched him do it from the window. He crossed the yard, concealing the bundles from the sentry as he went, and choosing his moment threw them over. But the sentry seemed to have noticed something for I saw him go to the latrine and try to look over. Luckily it was too high for him – but we didn't like this suspicious move and decided to wait till he was relieved.

Breakfast was a ghastly meal for me. Then I took my bed to pieces and hid it, moving up the other beds as I have said. I got a bit of raw bacon to grease the saw with, buttoned up my uniform great-coat and followed Baschwitz downstairs. Oh Lord! If there's any escaper reading this now, he knows how I felt. When we got to the door leading into the courtyard we slipped off our great-coats, threw them to an accomplice and walked out dressed as orderlies with our civilian clothes underneath. There were several orderlies in the yard, and the sentry ignored us. We reached the latrine, and the Tommies stared at us as we hurriedly scrambled over the wall when the sentry's back was turned and dropped inside. So far, all well. And now for the job!

We knelt down and examined the planks we had to cut through. They were thick, and we had first to cut a hole with a penknife before we could use the saw. This took about twenty minutes, and then I got the saw through and started to use it. Holy smoke! The row it made! The whole paling seemed to vibrate. I thought: "This is impossible. The sentry is bound to hear it", for you must remember that neither the sentry in the yard or the man outside the fence was more than ten yards away. More bacon grease – no use, just as much noise. Then we looked up and found we were in full view of the German censor's office, which was at the top of the building. Someone would come to the window and spot us before long. Moreover the rain had stopped, and the sentry outside was walking his beat, it made us desperate. We took the saw in turns. We were bound to be collared at any minute now. We took off our orderlies' clothes and sawed away furiously, and still no alarm was sounded, and at last had cut through two boards, but the wood was wet and swollen and we had difficulty in pulling them out. First we screwed a piece of wood across them to keep them together, and then at last we managed to open the hole. I was to go first. I wriggled through and found myself in a shallow ditch overgrown with weeds. The sentry was standing outside his box, but with his back to us, watching something on the other side of the embankment. I turned left, away from him, and looking round saw Baschwitz had got through and was refixing the boards in place. He smeared earth over the cut, brushed away the sawdust and crawled towards me. A few yards ahead of me the bottom of the ditch rose to a level with the railway line, so that beyond this point we couldn't conceal ourselves any more. We had got to come out into the open.

It was a nasty moment when I finally reached this point and stood up. A nasty moment when I found myself face to face and within two yards of another sentry in charge of French prisoners working on the line. He had nothing to do with our camp, but he stared at me as startled as I was. I nearly ducked; but Baschwitz from behind said in German: "Where can that damn dog have got to. If we've lost him there will be trouble." We both started to whistle and call "Wa, komm, komm," and peer about the place. Still doing this we walked slowly across the line and slid down the other side of the embankment. Out of the corner of my eye I saw both sentries staring at us. Where had we come from? Each probably thought that the other had passed us. They did nothing. Just stood and stared. We walked down to the edge of the river in a dream, and entered the town. Says Baschwitz, who had never broken out of a camp before, "Ich kann is nicht glauben" ("I can't believe it").

Baschwitz bought two single tickets to Berlin, and we travelled there in separate compartments. All went smoothly. No papers asked for – no awkward questions – no conversations. In Berlin we joined up again and walked to the Stettiner Bahnhof, loitering on the way so that we did not arrive there till about four in the afternoon. We bought our tickets for Stralsund – they would be something to show if we were questioned – and then had to hang about for another hour before our train left. Again we travelled separately – myself shamming sleep most of the time, and Baschwitz airing his perfect German with anyone who cared to talk to him. We ran into Stralsund at midnight and walked through the steep cobbled streets of the beautiful old town, passing an occasional Schutzman on his beat. I knew the place, and we were soon lying in a field about two miles out on the Greifswald Road. Our legs ached frightfully; I can't imagine why. Prisoners seem to be bundles of nerves. Our legs ached so that we had to lie on our backs and hold them in the air.

There we lay under the stars and ate a little of our food and smoked cigarettes and talked till dawn. About six o'clock, feeling very dirty and unkempt, we started back to the town, and reached the harbour about half-past six. There was hardly a ship in the port – not a very bright outlook for our enterprise, and we could only hope things would look more lively at Sassnitz. To cross to Rügen, you buy a ticket at a small station on the quay; the train runs on board the steamer and runs ashore on the other side, and so across the island. Again no papers were asked for. When we reached Rügen the train filled up a bit, and I remember Baschwitz whispering to me that the people were speaking a dialect which he couldn't understand in the least. When we got to Sassnitz we found it a town of white houses and red roofs, of precipitous cobbled streets and quaint little shops, the whole built practically up and down the face of a cliff. Below us lay the harbour with its long mole, the blue sea, and far away on the horizon, seen faintly as a dim cloud, lay the coast of Sweden. Imagine our consternation when I tell you that there was not a single ship in port, and not a single civilian to be seen about the harbour. The quay was deserted except for sentries, and obviously there would not be a chance of getting near the place when a ship *did* come in. However, we had heard that Ancona, a village about fifteen miles up the coast, was still a busy fishing port, and we decided to push on to this point and try to bribe a fisherman to take us over. Failing this we should have to get off Rügen and make for the Dutch frontier. We had a sleep and then started off for Ancona. We followed a track which led for mile after mile through woods on the edge of the cliffs. Where the cliffs rose to a great height we would occasionally spot a sentry gazing out to sea. Once or twice we passed them close to, and though they looked us up and down we were not challenged. About eight o'clock in the evening as we passed through a small village we found ourselves being followed by a group of men. Baschwitz turned round on them and asked boldly if we could get lodgings there for the night. Someone said we could get a room with the widow Schröder, who kept an inn on the outskirts of the next village. We walked on, not certain as to whether we were still followed, and reaching the inn thought it would be best at least to apply for a room there. In the little bar parlour there appeared to be no one but a little old woman behind the bar. Could we have a room? No, in her shrill, angry German. No room. No room for people she didn't know. She didn't like the look of us and the Herr Unter-Offizier would like to see our papers.

What under-officer? We started to bluster, but the old wretch had done the mischief; for a man came forward out of a dark corner – an N.C.O. of Landsturm, with a red beard.

"Yes," says he, "let's have a look at your papers." He opened a door and called two of his men. We were trapped! The inn was a guard room full of soldiers. The game was up.

And then old Baschwitz started in coolly and quietly to lie and lie and lie. We were cousins, he and I. He had been invalided out of the army before the war for malaria. I was blind in one eye – I should have said that I always assumed a limp and a squint on these stunts. We were working in a factory in Stettin. We had permits allowing us to cross to Sweden for a purpose – (Ach! geheim, secret). Our papers had been taken from us at Stralsand for verification. Some of the soldiers seemed to believe our story, but the terrible old woman and her ghastly daughter egged the under-officer on. He said: "You are under arrest. I shall now go and telephone to see if your story is true." He marched us into the guard-room and told his men to watch us, and then went out to the post-office. We were in a low-ceilinged kitchen with a tiled floor. Soldiers were playing cards and lolling about. Half-a-dozen rifles in a rack – equipment – old newspapers; some loaves of war bread – the usual paraphernalia of a guard-room. I said to Baschwitz – I whispered: "We shall get out of this." He shook his head miserably.

Soon the under-officer returned and said he could not get through to Sassnitz and we must spend the night in the guard-room. He had got far more suspicious of us now. I would like to give you a more vivid impression of him – this elderly man – but my own recollection is vague. Was he thin or stout? I don't know. He was brave and conscientious, and he had only a few hours now to live.

He made us lie down on a mattress in the corner of the room, having first made us take off our boots. He brought a small table forward and placed the lamp on it so that the light shone on us. Then he ordered two sentries to sit in chairs with loaded rifles – to hem us in, and he then armed himself and sat in a chair near us.

We fell asleep. I don't know how we could. The bottom had fallen out of our world, but we fell asleep. We slept seven hours and woke to an amazing sight. It was five minutes to five by the guard-room clock. The relief had gone out, and the relieved sentries were not yet in. There was no one in the room but our two sentries and the under-officer. And – all three were asleep.

The under-officer was stretched on a sofa with a handkerchief over his face, the others drooping over their rifles. I woke Baschwitz and he stared and grabbed for his boots. Even the door was unlocked and we tip-toed across the room, and, once outside, ran pelting down the road and then into the fields. We had no plan at that moment. We just ran and ran until we were exhausted.

I can tell you now what happened in the guard-room after our departure. The incoming sentries woke the under-officer. He wasted no time. He guessed, no doubt, that we were prisoners of war, and he, a German, had failed in his duty. He pulled off a boot, put the muzzle of his rifle in his mouth, a toe on the trigger, and blew his brains out.

The rumour went, I don't know how, that we had murdered him. Of course we didn't know this till later. At any rate half the population turned out after us. We hoped to hide till nightfall and then steal a boat and get back to mainland, but we were spotted hiding in a little copse and our pursuers came up from all directions – sentries with rifles – civilians with shot guns – people on push bikes. It was pretty ghastly, and we lit cigarettes to try and appear unconcerned and walked out into the open. We were covered from all directions, but not a shot was fired. We were cursed a good deal and marched to a little lock-up, where we spent the next twenty-four hours eaten alive by fleas and bugs, and without any food. A strong escort fetched us next morning and we were taken to Stralsund prison with the populace howling "Murderers!" after us. It was then that we learnt what had happened in the guard-room, and we should have been in a pretty fix if the sentries who had been with the under-officer hadn't told the truth about his death. If they had chosen to conceal the fact of his suicide and the reason for it and blame us, I shouldn't be telling you this story tonight.

After a week in Stralsund prison – a week without a smoke – awful – we were sent back to Magdeburg. Here we spent months in cells – cells measuring four foot by twelve foot. We had an hour's exercise a day and the prison staff were civil and decent but very strict. From there to Burg and here they parted us again, and I was sent to Fort Zorndorf. It was an awful blow. These adventures had made a tremendous tie between us. Finally Baschwitz did escape – alone. Later I had the luck to get away too. We met in London. It was early in March 1918. I was going back to France and he was going on an adventure very much more dangerous than that. It was wonderful. It was priceless. There was an enemy whose tail was still up, who thank God, was still in his strength. It was like a dream – it *was* a dream – that had come true.

CHAPTER EIGHT

WHAT A SKELETON KEY WILL DO

By M. C. C. Harrison

I must make it clear from the beginning that the escape I am going to describe here took place from the *civil* prison at Magdeburg and not from the prisoners of war camp, which was some little distance outside the town.

I was sent to this civil prison at Magdeburg with a few other officers – Russian and English – in December 1916, after my third unsuccessful attempt to escape from Germany, and I want you to have a picture of the inside of that prison in your mind. The entrance was a large doorway in one of the main streets of Magdeburg. We passed through this doorway into the police buildings, then along a stone passage, and up three flights of stairs to an iron door, against which our escort knocked violently. I shall refer to this iron door a good deal, and shall call it door X. An armed sentry on the other side opened this door and locked it again directly we were through. We now found ourselves at one end of a straight corridor in the civil prison. The corridor was about a yard and a half wide and we could see fifteen cell doors on the right hand side and, at the far end, facing us, the door of the guard-room. I hope that is clear. A straight narrow corridor. Door X, through which we had just come, at one end; the guard-room, facing it, at the other. Fifteen cell doors, including the lavatory, on the right-hand side.

From about the middle of the left-hand side another very short blind corridor led off at right angles. This small corridor – or recess – contained the office and three cells. Otherwise the left-hand side of the main corridor was blank. The commotion we made as we were herded through door X caused a familiar voice from inside one of the cells on the right to shout out, "Is that you, Harrison?" It was Templer, with whom I'd already made one attempt to escape and with whom I eventually succeeded in reaching England. I will tell you about that escape in the next chapter. I did not get a chance of seeing him there. He was released a day or two after my arrival and sent to Magdeburg camp, where he did me a very great service.

We were now being ushered along the passage to the office in the recess on the left. There we were searched in the presence of the Prison Commandant and the jailer, and we were then locked up in separate cells. Mine was one of the small ones, only 3ft. 4ins. wide. I at once started thinking about the same old problem, "How the devil was I going to get out of the place?"

There were occupied cells on either side of me, above and below, so it was out of the question to go through the floor, walls or ceiling. The window was only a foot square and heavily barred, and it overlooked a courtyard entirely surrounded by buildings.

I did not fancy the idea of trying to go that way. There only remained the door. Personally I always preferred escaping from prisons *via* the doors. I maintain that one of the easiest obstacles the escaping prisoner can have to compete with is a *locked door with a somewhat bored sentry guarding it*. The mere fact that the door is locked eventually makes the sentry careless and it is only a matter of time before a diversion can be arranged to distract his attention for a few moments at any rate. He may be a decent sort of fellow and willing to discuss war news or food, or he may be of an excitable nature and take an interest in some other form of diversion.

On this occasion there were, however, two locked doors to be negotiated – that is my own cell door and door X at the end of the passage. There was the sentry between these doors; there was also the rest of the guard in the guard-room with the under-officer sitting at the open door looking down the passage.

The art of picking locks is a trade rapidly acquired by prisoners. Two bits of stiff wire, each bent into the shape of an L, is all that is required. With one you lift the spring of the lock and with the other you feel for the notch in the bolt and slide it along. I generally used two sardine tin openers. I never experienced much difficulty, but the locks in the doors in Magdeburg prison were of modern design and I found it a slow job. Two complete turns of the real

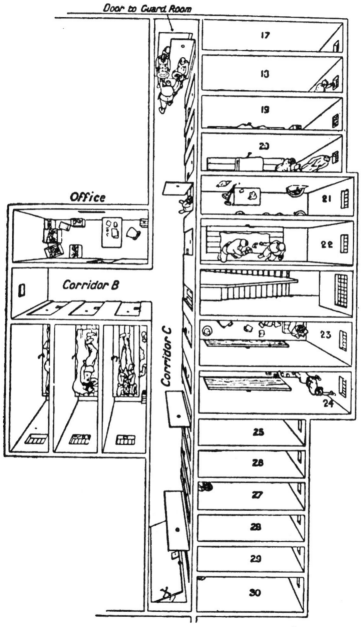

MAGDEBURG PRISON—'KRIEGSGARNISONARRESTANSTALT'

key were necessary to lock or unlock these doors and the extra time needed for picking them might well have proved disastrous, with so many Germans on duty in the passage, guard-room and office.

The obvious solution was to make a key. I noticed that the same key was used for *all* the doors in the prison; for door X, the cell doors and the door of the office where our parcels were kept.

The prisoners met at exercise for half-an-hour every morning and half-an-hour every afternoon. When we were returning from exercise one day an Englishman and a Russian started bickering and almost came to blows in our corridor. This was according to a prearranged plan. I shoved them into the nearest cell – as if for a joke – slammed the door and shouted to the sentry for the key. He thoroughly entered into the spirit of my joke and promptly handed it to me. I hastily took an impression of it on a wad of Oxo cubes which I held in my left hand, locked the door and went on to my cell, and left the sentry to release the brawlers.

I did not fancy the idea of making the key myself in my cell. It would make too much noise. So I had to think out another way. I knew that officers in the prison who required dental treatment were marched under escort to a dentist in the camp. I have already told you that my old friend Templer who was in the prison when I arrived was now in that camp. So I made a drawing of the key and wrote a note to Templer asking him to make me a skeleton key. That evening I developed violent toothache, and so appalling was my agony that I was promised a visit to the camp dentist the very next day.

As I expected, Templer was one of the first to greet me in the camp. In a language which my escort could not understand I managed to say to him: "I have a note for you, follow me," before I was told to keep my mouth shut. While I was being marched up the stairs to the dentist's room, I dropped the note containing the drawing of the key, and had the satisfaction of seeing Templer place his foot on it.

About twenty minutes later, when the dentist was grinding away at a perfectly good tooth, I heard a loud and heated discussion break out in the next room, and amongst many voices easily recognised that of Templer. He played his part so well that I doubt if even the other English realised that he was conveying to me the fact that the key would be ready the following Wednesday and exactly where I could find it and grab it as I passed.

I was determined to waste no time, so I had toothache again on the following Tuesday, and was warned for the dentist on the Wednesday. Everything seemed to be going splendidly. But imagine my dismay when Wednesday came and I was marched, not to the camp, but to a dentist in the town. The camp dentist had been sent to the front. How was I to get my key from the camp? I hoped that a new dentist would eventually be appointed to work in the camp, so I went on agitating for visits to the dentist as often as possible. But although I must have had a hole bored in every tooth in my head, I never saw the camp again.

Meanwhile friends of Templer's in the camp, all of them unknown to me, had made a key out of a part of an iron bed-stead. Templer himself had been moved elsewhere shortly after my visit to the camp, and when the others, who were all foreigners, realised that I could not get to the camp, they decided they would have to send the key to me.

So one of them put the key inside his boot, went to the Commandant's office with some utterly frivolous complaint and refused to leave. He was, therefore, marched straight off to the prison, where he handed the key over to me that same evening.

The key was a complete success and I soon found that with careful manipulation all doors could be opened and relocked reasonably quickly.

I hid the key in a ventilator in the passage as civilian detectives often came into the prison to search our cells and our persons. As long as they found some contraband in our cells they were quite satisfied – so we never disappointed them. What we did not want them to find, we hid in the office, which of course was never searched. By making suitable diversions for the sentry, jailer or parcels censor, we found ample opportunities to do this. You will remember that our key also fitted that door.

I have not space to say much about our first attempt to escape – and in any case it was a short-lived affair. This is what happened. In order to ventilate these tiny cells, the doors were left open for an hour every evening between 8 and 9 p.m.

The prisoners were not allowed out of their cells and the under-officer as well as the sentry remained on duty in the corridor during this hour. Campbell, A. and S. H., Graham Toler, Middlesex Regiment, and myself decided to try and slip through door X one night during this hour, while other prisoners arranged a diversion in the recess by the office.

Towards the end of February, a day or two before we were ready to go, Cartwright of the Middlesex Regiment was brought into the prison. I had previously tried to escape with him and as a result the Germans had decided to separate us.

It was a mere coincidence that we should now meet in the same prison as a result of further unsuccessful escapes.

Of course Cartwright had to come with me. On 5 March, about 8.30, we decided to make our effort. The demonstration was so successful that the whole guard turned into the office recess to see what was happening.

Meanwhile, five of us passed through door X and down the stairs of the police building, but we found the door leading to the street locked. Before we had time to pick the lock, an eruption of bellowing from above told us that we had been missed. We hastily sought what cover we could in the basement, but although we survived the first hasty search we were caught two hours later and were nearly shot on our return to the prison by our infuriated jailer, whose Sunday evening had been ruined. Campbell saved the situation by holding the muzzle of the rifle over our heads as the jailer tried to fire at two yards range.

We subsequently heard that on any other night but a Sunday the door that had blocked us would have been open till 9 p.m. What a mess we seemed to have made of a glorious opportunity.

Our clothes were stripped off us in the office before we were put back in our cells, and in the subsequent search we lost nearly all essentials for an escape that had taken months to collect.

Mercifully our key was safely hidden in the passage and survived all other searches.

The authorities never discovered how we had gone, and they came to the conclusion that we must have had outside assistance.

They put a large slab of metal over the keyhole on the outside of door X and posted two policemen on special duty on the stairs every night.

We discovered that these policemen did not go on duty till 6 p.m., so from our point of view it was obvious we must now get to work and stage an escape by day.

The first essential for a successful escape by day is good civilian clothes, so during the next few weeks we concentrated on gradually converting our uniform.

Cartwright had an old-fashioned single-breasted black military overcoat. With a little amateur tailoring this would do. He exchanged a pair of his khaki breeches with a Belgian for blue trousers with a red stripe, and got a civilian hat smuggled down from the camp by a Belgian orderly between two plates when he was bringing us our midday meal.

My own kit was rather more difficult. I knew I could dye my khaki trousers with ink or blacking, for I'd used both of them on previous occasions, and Cartwright was able to spare me some cloth from the seat of his breeches, with which I made a cap. Most Germans seemed to wear Homburg hats but this was the best I could do. I was, however, in invisible ink communication with home and I was glad to receive from my mother before we left a soft felt hat wrapped up in oil silk and sent out in a pot of jam. The felt was very thin and soft but by rubbing soap into it, I was able to harden it and make it keep the same shape as a Homburg hat. But my coat was nothing like as suitable as Cartwright's. It was a Grenadier Guards officer's overcoat, which I had had sent out to me some time before when I was planning to escape as a German officer. It had already undergone alterations both by German tailors and myself, but it was still a long double-breasted garment with a high stiff collar. I decided to take about eight inches off the length and make a roll collar out of the strip. So long as I left the badges of rank and brass buttons on it the authorities would be satisfied it was still a uniform coat. But the sentries seemed exceptionally inquisitive and were always peeping through the spy hole in the door of my cell and there was I inside tailoring away at my coat. This was very disconcerting.

The spy hole was a circular bit of glass about the size of a penny with a sliding shutter on the outside. It would not have been wise to have stuck a bit of paper over the glass to block the sentry's vision, as this would only have been removed at once – and would also have aroused suspicion. I reported my difficulties to Cartwright and he painted me a suitable picture to place in my spy hole. By suitable I mean a picture calculated to appeal to the minds of peeping Toms. It was the back view of a lady undressing with just one more garment to remove. This picture achieved its purpose. The sentries nudged each other to come and have a look at it. They thought it a huge joke and left me to work in peace inside.

I was afraid, however, that the picture might be confiscated, so I melted some lead paper and stuck it on the back. I then attached it, with a piece of cotton, to the hot water pipe in the corner of the cell. The result was that as soon as the door opened – it opened outwards – the thread became taut and the picture was pulled out of the spy hole and automatically hid itself behind the radiator. One morning a German General inspected the prison. His idea of doing so was to tiptoe along the passage and peep through every spy hole in turn. When he came to my cell door and saw the picture in position, to say he was furious would be putting it mildly.

He had the door opened and stood there shouting at me. As soon as I could get a word in I asked him politely to what picture he was referring. "Why, this, of course," he said turning round – but there was nothing there. I suggested that it must have been a hallucination – but he was clearly dissatisfied. I expected he would visit me again the next morning and he did. This time, I had spread a round patch of toothpaste on the floor near the entrance to look like the back of my picture. He had opened the door even quicker this time, and pounced on the toothpaste, which came off all over his fingers. I burst out laughing. There was nothing he could do, as I was already in about the worst cell in Germany.

Obviously I had to keep up the belief that the picture was there merely as a practical joke. The jailer was instructed to get my picture at all costs, and one day he thought he had it. He opened the door like lightning and seized an envelope I had stuck there for his benefit. Triumphantly he wrenched out the pink paper lining, whereupon pepper flew up into his face. The picture had, of course, already concealed itself behind the radiator. Detectives were called in, but the picture still survived.

Meanwhile work on my coat proceeded satisfactorily, and by the end of April it had become quite a good shape with a perfect roll collar. The next thing was to dye it a suitable colour. I conducted various experiments in my cell and discovered that a strong solution of permanganate of potash would turn it quite an attractive chocolate shade. I decided to do the job in my bath, so as to ensure the coat coming out an even colour all over. I was allowed to order plenty of permanganate crystals on the pretext that they formed an excellent disinfectant for bed bugs, which were very plentiful in my cell.

Once a week we were locked into a cell which was fitted with a long bath. This cell was on the floor below and we were taken there and back by the jailer, but he generally left us there for twenty minutes undisturbed.

In my anxiety to ensure the coat taking an even colour all over, I put far too many crystals into the bath, and I found to my horror when I let the water out that I had dyed the whole of the bottom of the bath as well as the coat. However, I kept up the bed bug story; my coat – which was now a lovely colour – was not discovered – and the only result was that I was ordered to pay for a new bath.

We did not want the detectives to find our escaping kit in our cells so we put the stuff, hats, caps, etc., in the safe keeping of the Germans without their knowing it of course. This is how we did it.

When we went to the office to collect the contents of our parcels the Germans concentrated their attention on watching what we took out of the room. We hid forbidden articles there from time to time during these visits and counted on finding an opportunity to get in there with our false key to retrieve them when required.

We both now had all the necessary clothes with little fear of losing anything in the event of a detective search. Our coats still had their badges of rank and brass buttons, Cartwright's hat and my cap were both hidden in the office, which was never searched.

Magdeburg was about 400 kilometres to the Dutch frontier as the prisoner walks, and we had ample provisions collected for the journey. Germans of the class to which we aspired to belong seldom carried more than a small brown paper parcel. Additional food we decided to stitch to various parts of our anatomy in such places as would give us typical Prussian figures.

It was now early in May 1917 and all that remained to be done was to perfect our plan for getting out of the prison. At this time I was in cell No. 20, which was unpleasantly close to the guardroom. Cell No. 28, which was at the other end of the corridor, near door X, was the only vacant one. I knew it was no use asking to change, so I had to devise some means of getting the Germans to order the move. For two consecutive nights, therefore, I kept the guard on the alert all night, by scraping away at intervals with a broken bottle against the wall. This imitated the noise of a metal file at work. Every time they burst into my cell to see what was happening I was fast asleep. Directly the incident was reported to the Commandant he rushed off with his entire staff to examine the bars of my cell, to see if they could detect what I had been working at. Meanwhile I was moved to cell No. 28 at the point of the bayonet and incidentally nearly shot through the sentry pulling the trigger of his rifle by mistake.

I was now only two cells from Cartwright and we were both near door X. One of the larger cells in the centre of our row was fitted out as a lavatory and this we used for informal meetings to discuss details not only between ourselves but with our Russian and English accomplices. The guard had orders never to allow more than three of our cell doors to be open at the same time.

The scheme which we now contemplated hinged on the possibility of getting three suitable cell doors unlocked legitimately by the sentry and left wide open across the passage, thereby partially blocking the view the guard commander would get from his position by the open door of the guard-room. If this were done the guard commander would not be able to see much more than the hinges of door X, and further the doors of some of the cells would be completely hidden from his view. If the sentry at this moment could be enticed up to the guard-room end of the corridor, he, too, would not be able to see what was happening near door X.

The problem we now had to face was – could the cell doors of Cartwright and myself both be opened with our key and re-locked after us, and could we then unlock and pass through door X while this temporary diversion was going on. You can easily appreciate that the most careful timing was necessary. One of our greatest difficulties was explaining to Russian officers in a language foreign to us both, exactly what we wanted them to do, and satisfying ourselves that they understood.

We elected to make the attempt soon after the midday meal had been cleared and before our own jailer had returned from his lunch; a lot of people are feeling rather sleepy just about then. Our plan was this: On the chosen day – 12 May – at 1.45 every officer was to be in his cell. Five minutes later the Russian in cell No. 29, next to mine, was to knock at his door, and directly it was opened tell the sentry he wanted to get a paper from Loder Symonds in cell 17, next the guard-room. The sentry would accompany him along the corridor towards cell 17, and as they passed Cartwright's cell the Russian next door (cell 25) would knock and say he wanted to wash up his dinner plates. As the sentry had already opened only one door there was no reason why he should not open this one as he was passing it. As soon as the sentry had reached Loder Symonds' cell next the guard-room, the Russian from No. 25 would rush back from the lavatory leaving the door wide open across the passage, and open Cartwright's cell with our key. Cartwright would come out and relock his own door. Then getting what cover he could from the open doors of cell 25 and the lavatory he would let me out, and relock my door. We would then tiptoe to door X and open it but first we would unlock the door of the cell next to it, which belonged to Campbell. As soon as door X was unlocked we would hand the key to Campbell, who would relock it after us. The Russian from cell 25 could then take the key, relock Campbell in his cell and hide the key. All this time the sentry would be engaged with Loder Symonds in cell 17 at the far end of the passage.

How long could Loder Symonds keep him engaged? How long would it take us to unlock and relock four doors with our amateur-made key? It was just a question of time. We reckoned that two minutes or thereabouts would have to do.

The day came. Our watches were carefully synchronised and on the stroke of time we heard the first Russian in cell 29 knocking.

This was a great relief to us as we stood fully dressed in our cells. The second Russian in cell 25 also knocked at precisely the right moment, and soon after had Cartwright's cell open. I then heard my own door being stealthily unlocked. I came out to stand close against the wall beside Cartwright, but noticed, to my horror, that the second Russian had not left the lavatory door open, so the view down the passage from the guard-room was only partially blocked by the smaller door of cell No. 25.

We now had to exercise even greater care. While Cartwright relocked and bolted my cell, I went and unbolted Campbell's. Cartwright then came and unlocked it, handed me the key to open door X and took up a position of observation through the spy hole of the open door of 29 – the first Russian's cell. He at once whispered that the sentry was walking back towards us. Apparently Loder Symonds had not been able to keep him in conversation.

Were we to be caught? No. Loder Symonds made a last determined effort, and managed to entice him back with an offer of food.

I unlocked door X, handed the key to Campbell and passed out followed by Cartwright. But just outside we found a charwoman cleaning the steps. I at once said "Malzeit", that is "good-day", in the same manner as was usually adopted by civilian tradesmen when the sentry let them out, and we walked on through the building, down the stairs and out into the street. It took us quite an hour to get clear of the town as we dared not leave it by any main exit. We chose a canal towpath and soon after reaching open country we thought we must be about to be recaptured when we saw a trooper galloping after us. However, he passed us, taking no notice of two perspiring civilians in overcoats on a boiling hot May afternoon

The scene in the prison after we had gone is worth recording. The charwoman whom I had frequently seen on my visits to the dentist recognised me, and after she had recovered from the first shock she fetched the police sergeant, who knocked at door X and told the sentry that two prisoners had escaped. The under-officer was at once sent for but he pointed proudly to his row of locked cell doors, and told him to go away and mind his own business. About twenty minutes after we had gone, the Commandant came to the prison to inform me that I was to pay some large sum of money for damage done to a cell at a previous prison. He went to the office and gave orders that I was to be fetched. I have not yet mentioned that our key was a shade smaller than the original, and unless carefully handled the lock could not be turned with the proper key afterwards. We had on one occasion previously witnessed the trouble they had opening the office door after we had been in there to get at our parcels. Now they could not unlock my cell door, my spy hole was bunged up, and it took them twenty minutes before a locksmith was procured and got the door opened. I would have given a good deal to have seen their faces as they gazed into the empty cell. For some reason or other they elected to think I must have got into Cartwright's cell. It took another ten minutes to get his door opened. Still they did not give chase. All cell doors were opened, prisoners were counted and recounted. We must have had quite an hour's start before they gave chase.

The mounted trooper that I mentioned a short time ago was one of the search party but he being a true German had to obey orders and go to the place where he was told to look for two escaping officers.

We struggled along for ten kilometres in our heavy overcoats with food stitched all over us, and then about 5 p.m. we managed to slip unobserved into a wood. There we repacked our kit for the customary night marches. The first twelve days passed without incident, by which time we had covered 300 out of the 400 kilometres to Holland. Here we passed close to a prisoners' camp from which two Russian officers had recently escaped, and we came in for the tail end of the hue and cry looking for them. It was generally just bad luck that caused the escaping prisoner to be recaptured, or so we always imagined. After a long walk we were always full of confidence that our next attempt would prove successful, and it was with this glorious feeling and not with depression that we were brought back to that delightful spot, the Magdeburg jail.

CHAPTER NINE

THROUGH THE BATHROOM FLOOR

By M. C. C. Harrison

I will now describe how I did eventually get away from Germany in August 1917.

Planning an escape was often far more difficult than its subsequent execution, and before making the actual attempt we had to consider three distinct phases; first, the actual break away from the camp, secondly the walk through Germany in order to get to a frontier, and thirdly the actual crossing of the frontier. I am going to deal with each of these separately, and then you can see which of the three problems gave us the most trouble.

My previous failures had led to prolonged terms of imprisonment, and after thirteen months in jail, I was, on 2 August, 1917, moved to the reprisal camp of Strohen, in the province of Hanover. The camp was a bleak spot situated on an immense bog, and was several miles from any other form of habitation. It consisted of about thirty wooden huts surrounded by two barbed wire fences four or five yards apart. Each was about ten feet high. Sentries were posted at intervals of sixty or seventy yards on either side of these fences, and there was a machine-gun turret at each of the four corners. The whole place was brilliantly lit up at night by arc lamps. Outside the camp and about twenty yards from the outer barbed wire fence there were two more huts. One was used as a guard-room and the other as a bath house. The bath hut was connected to the camp by a wired-in passage, but the gate at the camp end of this was kept locked except between eight and nine in the morning, when the prisoners were allowed to wash themselves in the presence of the entire guard.

The point to remember is that the bath hut was outside all the camp defences, that is, both wire fences, both lines of sentries, and all the arc lamps.

When I arrived in the camp for the first time on 2 August, 1917, I took a strong dislike to the place at sight. I never liked camps surrounded by nothing but barbed wire. The sentries on either side of the fence can see what you are doing as you approach the edge of the camp. Tunnelling from this camp was out of the question, as the Germans took the utmost pains to guard against it, and inspected the floors of all the huts at least twice a day. There were about 450 prisoners in the camp, and with the exception of fifteen or twenty Indian officers, they were all British. In the eyes of the Germans they were all of bad character, and most of them had made at least one attempt to escape. It was a great relief to feel that anyone in the camp could be trusted. When prisoners of different nationalities were mixed up in a camp the Germans used frequently to employ spies dressed up as Russian or Belgian orderlies. For this reason it was generally impossible to perfect any scheme unless it could be kept secret from everyone in the camp, and the way I now proposed to go had the obvious weak link that directly work was started, the whole camp would know exactly how I meant to go.

I now come to the first problem, that is, breaking out of the camp. The bathroom hut was divided into three rooms; one was used as a dressing room; the second contained six or eight showers, and the third was for heating appliances. The prisoners weren't allowed into this last room. The dressing room measured about twelve feet by ten feet. I have already said that the hut was connected to the camp by a wired-in passage, and at 8 a.m. the entrance gate at the camp end of this passage was opened and the entire guard not actually on sentry duty at the moment took up various positions inside the bath hut. About four or five actually came into the small portion partitioned off as a dressing room, while the remainder took up positions in the neighbouring compartments, from which they could keep the prisoners under observation through holes in the walls.

If 450 English are only allowed one hour in which to undress and wash in two small rooms the congestion can be imagined. The bathroom was absolutely crammed, at any rate, between 8.15 and 8.45. At 9 o'clock any prisoners still there were pushed back to the camp more or less at the point of the bayonet by the guard who came off duty then. It was obvious that if only you could remain in the bath hut after the guard had gone and stay concealed there till dark, the rest would be easy, as you would be outside both barbed wire fences and both lines of sentries.

The morning roll call was just before the bath hour, but there was also an evening roll at 6 p.m., quite four hours before it was dark. This could probably be faked somehow or other.

Anyway, now that I'd got the general scheme into my head the next thing to be done was to find a companion.

I soon picked out Templer, with whom I had made my first attempt in 1915, and who helped me in getting a duplicate prison key made at Magdeburg. He was one of the most gallant officers living. At the outbreak of War he was a cadet at Sandhurst – he was captured in 1914 and by August 1917 had made eleven attempts to escape. I am sorry to say he was killed fighting in France shortly before the end of the War.

He was glad to meet me again, but it turned out that he had already thrown in his lot with two others in another escape scheme, and it was doubtful if their plans would permit of a fourth. I was delighted when he told me a day or two later that his scheme had fallen through, and that he was prepared to come with me *via* the bathroom, provided he could bring both his pals too.

The floor of the bathroom hut was raised about six inches off the ground, and we decided that the best plan was to make a trap door in the corner of the dressing room and scoop away the earth from underneath until there was room for us all to hide below the floor.

I have already said that we only had access to this hut between eight and nine in the morning, and that there were four or five German sentries in the dressing room during this hour, but we believed that the congestion there between 8.15 and 8.45 would enable us to work unobserved. Only one of us could actually work at a time and the remaining three would take up positions by the nearest sentries and dry themselves with large towels or make suitable noises with their boots when the saw was in use.

For the past two years I had, in spite of many searches by detectives, managed to keep a metal saw concealed in my thermos flask between the vacuum and the outer case. This now came in extremely useful. On the morning of 6 August we started work by feeling between the boards with a bit of stiff wire in order to find a suitable place for our trap-door. We had to saw through two planks to complete the trap-door; this took four days – and in another two days we had pushed away to one side with our hands enough earth for one person to get underneath. All this was very precarious work, for it was done from above with four or five sentries in the same room. But from now on by 8.15 every morning one of us was able to get through the trap-door and under the floor, where he could work in comparative peace. We generally had to call him up at 8.45 when the numbers in the bathroom started decreasing. Whoever was underneath worked without any clothes on at all, and made straight for a shower bath directly he came up. Muddy clothes found in the possession of a prisoner always aroused suspicion.

The Germans examined the floors of all huts every day as a precaution against tunnelling. The bath hut was no exception to this and was examined daily after the prisoners left it, so we had to cover our tracks very carefully, and we found that a mixture of seccotine and dust almost completely hid all traces of our saw cuts.

After we'd been at it for ten days and had nearly completed our task we found that another pair had hit on the same idea, and were making a trap-door in another part of the dressing room. We interviewed them at once and found out that they'd come upon bricks underneath and were proposing to make yet another trap-door. We couldn't have the whole floor covered with trap-doors, so we decided it would be far safer to make additional room for the two of them in our compartment. This did not delay us as long as we expected for at the same time one of our own number fell out.

But a few days later we had another shock. On 16 August an officer named Lieut. Knight, Devon Regt. and R.F.C., made a successful and highly ingenious escape from the bathroom, and this might have cooked our own plans. However, he had covered his tracks well. He had gone into the bathroom with the crowd and stood in a recess in one wall about ten inches deep and one foot wide. He had brought in with him, under his coat, three long canvas frames whitewashed the colour of the wall and made to fit into each other and into the recess. These he built up in front of himself unobserved, and stood behind the camouflage for twelve hours. Although several Germans entered the bathroom during the day he remained concealed and escaped that night.

By 19 August we had made sufficient space for five people, and decided to go next day. We knew that as soon as we were missed from roll call, the guard would immediately be ordered to make a thorough search of the whole camp.

The disguise to our trap-door had proved good enough to pass the daily routine search, but it might well be detected in the intensive search that was bound to take place directly the authorities knew that five officers were missing, and since we should still be lying concealed under the floor waiting for darkness they would have a good four hours in which to find us. It was out of the question to bluff the 6 p.m. roll call for so many absentees. So we decided to try and make the Germans think we had escaped some other way, and the member of our party who had fallen out volunteered to cut the barbed wire fence on the other side of the camp.

The next problem to consider before we left the camp was how we were to get to the frontier. Templer and Insall, a Flying Corps V.C., were coming with me and we decided to walk by night keeping clear of roads and tracks as much as possible and lie up in woods by day. Ströhen is only eighty miles as the crow flies from Holland, but we agreed to get off the bog on the side furthest from Holland, then go north till we were clear of the marshy ground. This route would give us a walk of about 120 miles, but it seemed better than making straight for Holland since we would be missed quite four hours before we could hope to break away from the camp.

We attached so much importance to finding a hiding place before daylight that we agreed that we would always take the first cover we found after 3 a.m. From previous experience we had found it was an increased risk to march much after 3 a.m. on the off-chance of finding cover later on. The most popular hiding places were amongst low fir trees not more than six or seven feet high.

Among other things we took a supply of garlic to rub on our heels in case we were chased by dogs, and some pepper for the same purpose. Pepper would also be useful if we had a difference of opinion with anyone on the way. If you hurl a handful of pepper in anyone's face they don't see to shoot at you as you run away. As we were only going to walk at night, clothes weren't of great importance. As a matter of interest I actually wore my Grenadier Guards coat that I had used in 1915 for an escape as a German officer. I had worn the same coat eighteen months later, as I described in the previous chapter, for my daylight escape from Magdeburg prison when I was dressed as a smart civilian. I now cut a bit more off the length and used it as an ordinary workman's coat.

Now a word about our provisions. It is remarkably easy to keep going for quite a long time on biscuits, meat tabloids, and other concentrated food, but escaping prisoners cannot carry bulk, and the lack of this is bound to tell on the system in time. If you try to cross a frontier in a starving condition you will probably make mistakes and get caught, and we therefore decided that the main thing was to look after our health as much as possible. To save weight we carried no tinned food. In fact, beyond a little chocolate for munching at night we had practically no food other than porridge, bacon and billtong, which is dried meat, used largely in South Africa. We took with us, however, a Tommy's cooker, which is a miniature saucepan and a solid methylated spirit stove all in one. Our intention was to loot vegetables every night, and make a stew the following day. On this diet we hoped to reach the frontier in the best possible condition, for we knew the hardest problem of all lay in getting across it successfully.

We learnt from other prisoners in the camp who had been recaptured on the Dutch frontier that all bridges over the River Emms were guarded and also that there was a chain of sentries on the frontier itself, so we decided to enter Holland fairly far north where the frontier runs due north and south, and the Emms is parallel to it about six miles inside Germany. We didn't expect to find the frontier here clearly defined on the ground, but our map showed a dyke parallel to it and just inside Holland.

We decided that we must swim the Emms. If we made a reconnaissance of it one night we should be able to get across it early the next night, and thus have the maximum amount of darkness in which to cover the most difficult part of our journey. We didn't fancy the idea of having to lie up for the day between the Emms and the frontier.

Soon after 8 a.m. on 20 August, 1917, we entered the bathroom attired as usual. Friends helped us to carry our stores under their coats. As soon as the room was crowded we slipped through the trap-door one by one. I went down first and got to the end of the hut nearest the guard-room. The space between the two huts was less than ten yards across and was used as a parade ground for the guard. I could actually see into the guard-room through a small crack in the side of our hut.

When the five of us were underneath our kit was passed through and stored by Insall, who was the last in. By 8.30 the trap-door was sealed on top of us with a solution of our seccotine and dust, by a friend who proposed escaping by the same means at some later date. At 9 we heard the bathroom being cleared. About 10 o'clock we heard the Germans above making the routine examination of the floor. As our absence had not yet been detected there was no reason why our trap-door should be discovered now any more than on the previous day. Nothing of interest was likely to happen till we were missed at the evening roll call at 6 p.m. Several times Germans entered the bathroom above us, but probably only to look for soap, which was by now almost unobtainable in Germany.

The air underneath the floor was stifling. Several Germans had baths immediately above me and I wished they would not upset quite so much water. We had some loose provisions and thirst quenchers to munch to help to while away the time. The spiders were plentiful and we being very superstitious took great care not to kill any.

At last the bugle was sounded for the evening roll call. We were now going to be missed, and presently an eruption of bellowing from the camp told us that we *had* been missed. The whole guard was immediately turned out on to the parade ground about five yards from where I lay. The Commandant himself arrived on the scene and stampeded up and down in front of them, shouting out orders and despatching them to various parts of the camp. Some came into the bathroom, but as they entered fresh guttural explosions from the Commandant resulted in them doubling back to their parade ground beside me. Evidently the cut wire had been found, and from where we lay we could hear the Commandant order various patrols to go out into the country to look for us.

It is quite an unusual experience to be an eye-witness of the scene that takes place in the camp after your own escape has been discovered. Soon after dark we heard several shots fired, presumably indicating that some of these patrols had bumped into each other. The guard remained very active till after 2 a.m., and we had almost made up our minds that we would have to stay where we were for another twenty-four hours, but by 2.30 all seemed quiet. We then crawled back through the trap-door into the bathroom, carrying our boots. It was a great relief to get fresh air and freedom again after lying in a cramped position for over seventeen hours on the damp ground under the hut. We collected our kits and took up positions of observation at the various windows, from which we could see the nearest sentries.

I was given the job of picking the lock of a door on the side furthest from the camp. I had noticed that this door was locked during the day when we went to the bath, and as there was no traffic through it generally, I was very surprised to find it was not locked now. At first I suspected a trap, so I opened it with great care. But all was clear on my side.

With the camp arc lamps it was just like daylight outside, and as soon as the others had reported the nearest sentries in favourable positions we passed out, still carrying our boots. We took what cover we could from the shadow of the hut.

When we had gone about fifty yards we put on our boots and split up into our respective parties, Insall and Templer coming with me. I never heard what actually happened to the other two beyond the fact that they were subsequently recaptured.

It was already after three, and it was going to be daylight at five. We knew there were plenty of patrols out looking for us, so we hastily got as far away from the camp as we could on the side furthest from Holland. Shortly before 5 o'clock we found a little copse in which we hid for the next day. Of course we had not had time to collect water and could do no cooking. We were only about three or four miles from the camp. We almost got eaten alive with mosquitoes here, and we were very glad when it was dark enough to move. It was some time before we found any water. We were still intent on getting as much ground as we could between us and the camp. We didn't find particularly good cover at the end of our march, but we were far more comfortable than on the first day.

On the third night after considerable difficulties we finally got off the bog on the east side and started moving north to get round it. It was not till the next night that we were able to move in a westerly direction towards Holland. For the next three nights we had the most appalling weather, but in spite of this, thanks to the excellent food we were getting, our condition did not suffer. We would often spend a whole hour of valuable darkness looking for potatoes, cabbages, beetroots or mushrooms. After 3 a.m. we always took the first good cover we found, although it was sometimes nearly daylight before we found any; and once, when the approach of dawn forced us to hide in a small copse, we found to our horror when daylight came that there was a small cottage in it. We couldn't get more than twenty yards from this building, and dared not unpack our kit all day in case we might have to run for it at any moment. To make matters worse there was a dog. To keep him off, we had to keep rubbing ourselves with garlic all day. Thanks to the garlic he did not detect us till about an hour before dusk, when he started barking violently. We at once moved off, thankful that darkness would soon come to our rescue.

The general routine each day was much the same. Directly we found cover after 3 a.m. we lay down in it. The cold of dawn always awoke us if we were asleep. We would then have a look round and make certain our position was the best possible, then we would start digging sods with penknives, with which to cover ourselves in case anyone walked near us. This got us nice and warm again, and we then cooked our breakfast of porridge and cocoa. This was a longish job and as soon as it was finished we would prepare our lunch, which consisted of whatever vegetables we had found the previous night, mixed with our billtong or bacon. These meals were always delicious, and we never stinted ourselves over them. We had generally eaten as much as we could by midday when we slept in reliefs till the cold of dusk forced us to get active again.

A light supper in the form of more stew or cocoa and we were ready for the next night's march. One night we found a can of milk outside a farm. We drank as much as we could and filled a football bladder that we were carrying as a water-bottle. We had lived without fresh milk for three years, so it can be imagined how we enjoyed that drink! Of course, our porridge was tremendously improved the next day. We hoped to find some more on another night, but as we failed to do so, we decided to milk a cow. Unfortunately the cow we selected turned out to be a bull and resented the liberty we were taking. We lost bits of our garments getting out of his field in a hurry.

After eight night marches we lay up on high ground six or seven miles from the Emms. From our cover we were able to get a glimpse of the country between us and the river, and to decide on the best line of approach. As we were getting near the danger zone we were careful not to move off before 11 p.m. The approach to the river wasn't as difficult as it might have been. It was slow as we got into difficulties with a tributary and one or two small streams before we reached the Emms about 2 a.m. By 2.30 we had discovered a suitable place to swim across where the river was only about forty-five yards wide with cover on both banks for undressing and dressing again. It was very tempting to swim across there and then and rush for the frontier that night. However, we stuck to our good resolutions and retraced our steps back to the last good cover we had passed.

The next day we studied our maps almost incessantly until we knew by heart all prominent features between us and the frontier. Soon after eleven we sallied forth and reached the river a little before midnight. We undressed in our copse, packed our clothes tightly in rucksacks, put our watches and compasses in our hats, which we jammed on our heads, waited to let a patrol pass, and then swam across. We were dressed again on the other side very soon after midnight.

We now had only six miles to go with nearly five hours of darkness in which to do it, and we had already passed the first line of sentries. We were under the impression that the only other line was on the frontier itself, but we followed our original resolution to take no unnecessary risks and took all military precautions. One of us went slightly ahead of the remaining two and lay down every thirty yards to scan the horizon. After covering two miles, to my surprise I saw a sentry, and as we were trying to pass him, keeping as close to him as we could, so as not to run into another, the moon suddenly came out. It was now 1.45 and we knew the moon would not set till 2.30. We had to lie where we were beside a cabbage patch, and not twenty yards from the sentry with our hands hidden and our faces jammed to the ground. It was 2.45 before we felt it would be safe to move. During the two hours that we lay in this position three lots of patrols or reliefs of sentries passed within five yards of us.

When we eventually got a move on again it was quite dark. The next wire fence we climbed caused an alarm bell to ring in a neighbouring cottage. We all three hastily got over the fence and lay down just in time to see a soldier run along the track about five yards in front of us. As soon as he had passed, we moved on and lay down in the next field. Looking back we could see Germans with electric torches moving right along the fence.

Whatever the defences were here we had evidently passed them. We were now close to a village named Sustrum. I imagine that the regiments furnishing the frontier and river guards were billeted in this and the neighbouring villages.

We now had about two hours in which to do four miles. About ten drainage ditches full of water and with wire fences delayed us a little. In order to negotiate these quietly we had to cross them under water. Mercifully these ditches were only in the neighbourhood of the villages, and soon we found ourselves in admirable country for our purpose. A marsh obviously too heavy to be patrolled in the ordinary course of events, but not too heavy to impede us seriously. There was a slight head wind, a *tremendous* advantage, as sentries on the frontier would not be likely to hear us approaching.

The stars were out, so by keeping our right shoulder to the north star there wasn't much chance of losing direction, and we didn't have to rely on our compasses. How fast we went I can't say. We scanned the horizon every thirty yards as before. By now our vision at night was excellent. The probability was that sentries on the frontier weren't left on duty for more than two hours at a time, so we counted on being able to see them before they could see or hear us. As we had wasted so much time waiting for the moon to go down we moved as fast as we thought it safe. It is a well-known fact that on this business you do not cover the ground nearly as quickly as you imagine. As the frontier itself is not clearly defined on the ground I don't know exactly at what hour we crossed it.

When we were near it we came across some more of these humble ditches with water in them which required great care to negotiate without making a noise. Once I imagined I saw two sentry huts, so we steered midway between them, anxiously hoping to come across the dyke which showed from our map to be in Holland.

Then we crossed a larger ditch with a bit of a bank, and of course we thought this was the dyke. In order to avoid the danger of giving ourselves up before we really had crossed the frontier, as had frequently been done, we were determined to go on walking due west even after we knew we were in Holland.

About 4.45, just before it was light, I was pretty tired and I saw a weird sight. A long straight cloud, through which I could detect a V cut in it. I soon realised it was not a cloud. What was it? For a moment it reminded me of the view you get of Fair Head on a clear night from Bellycastle, where my people were spending the summer.

Was I going to wake up in a moment and find I was dreaming? No. I pulled myself together and realised it was a bank about 30ft. high, with a gap in it. The dyke, beyond a shadow of doubt. The finest sight I have ever seen. We kept clear of the gap where we guessed there would be a Dutch guard, possibly pro-German. We climbed the bank about 200 yards south of it, swam the canal on the further side at 5 a.m. and walked with a light foot due west on into Holland. We were unlucky and got mixed up with a quantity of German deserters in a quarantine camp for eleven days before getting a boat from Rotterdam.

A day or two later we reached England. Later on we were summoned to Buckingham Palace, where His Majesty honoured us each with a private interview.

CHAPTER TEN

A GAME OF BLUFF

By E. H. Jonas

My story begins at Yozgad, in Asia Minor. Yozgad lies in the heart of the rugged mountains of Anatolia, almost due east from Angora. It is over 4,000 feet above sea level, and was probably as inaccessible as any prison camp in the world outside Russia. The nearest railhead (Angora) was 120 miles away. The nearest seaport (Samsun, on the Black Sea) was a little further – about 130 miles. Three hundred miles as the crow flies would have taken us to friendly territory – either to the Crimea or to the Russians at Erzinjan or to Cyprus. But we were not crows.

So far were we from being crows that until August 1918 not a single attempt at a conventional escape was made from Yozgad. For over two years one hundred British officers and some thirty or forty British rank and file waited patiently for the Armistice. Nobody attempted to run for it. It sounds incredible, but we just endured and waited. Why?

It was not the difficulty of getting out of the camp. We at Yozgad had no barbed wire, unclimbable fences, electric lights, sentries every few yards, moats, and all the rest of the obstacles which escapers from German camps had to face. Except for a few middle aged sentries, armed with old muskets, who dozed in their sentry boxes all day and all night, we had no obstacles to getting away. Breaking camp was comparatively easy, indeed it was done occasionally for a lark. On one of these occasions two officers, on mischief bent, were seen outside the camp at night. The alarm was raised. The guard was out. Extra sentries were posted. But by dawn both had broken back *into* the camp, and escaped detection. Turkey is a topsy-turvy country. Where else in the world have prisoners of war broken back into prison?

The real sentry at Yozgad was not the old gentleman with the blunderbuss. The sentry was the desert, the distance, the mountains, the brigands outside. Every single officer and man in that camp knew he could break out if he wished. But every one of them knew that once he got outside, the chances of final escape were about the same as those of a snowball surviving in the South Sea Islands.

Even so, many would have tried it. The fear of personal punishment would not have stopped them. What really scared them was an official warning by the Turks that if anyone escaped the rest of the camp would be "strafed".

Most of us had been captured at Kut and we knew what the Turk could do in the way of "strafing". I need not enter into details. A single statement will suffice. At Kut 2,860 British officers and men surrendered to the Turks. Two and a half years later, at the Armistice, 935 returned from captivity. Two out of every three had disappeared. We in Yozgad knew how and where and when and why many of these men disappeared. Can you blame the prisoners in Yozgad because they weighed in the balance a very slender chance of personal freedom against the safety of their comrades, and found it wanting? I believed at the time, and I believe now, that it would have been better to try to escape, to keep on trying, and to help other prisoners to get away. It might have made us worse off in body but we should have been happier in mind.

But as things were, the camp would not tolerate escape. Many of us, probably, thought of trying it. But during the two years I was at Yozgad only one officer, as far as I know, got as far as getting his escaping kit ready. This was Lieut. C. W. Hill – the man who recently raced Capt. Kingsford Smith by air to Australia. His intention was discovered by his fellow prisoners, and the senior British officer in the camp put him on parole. The alternative to giving his parole was that the Turks would be informed, for the camp must not be endangered.

I racked my brains for some way of getting out without involving the camp in a "strafe". Very early on I thought of simulating insanity with a view to exchange. But the idea was too dangerous and too difficult. So I discarded it – for the time being.

My chance came in a most unexpected way. It came through spiritualism. A group of us began studying spiritualism early in the spring of 1917, and we took it up for the same reason as we took up philosophy, mathematics, French, Spanish, and a score of other pursuits – to pass the time and to break the hopeless monotony of our days. We commenced very seriously; we made a "Ouija Board", which is a polished board encircled by the letters of the alphabet – a sort of planchette – and night after night we experimented. Two at a time, we would close our eyes, place our forefingers lightly on an inverted tumbler in the centre of the board, ask a question, and wait for the tumbler to move to the letters and spell out the answer. We found the tumbler would move without our consciously pushing it; it even touched letters. But the letters it touched never spelt anything – they were meaningless nonsense.

This went on for a fortnight. We could get no sense. We got disheartened. The group of investigators dwindled till there were only four of us left. We decided to have one more seance and if we got no replies we would give it up.

Then I began to cheat. With my eyes closed, I pushed the glass to the right letters. I invented answers to the questions put, and spelled them out on the board.

I have no excuse to offer for cheating. It was just mischief. I have always been fond of a leg pull and I fully intended to confess when the seance was over. But the excitement which the answers aroused in my friends amused me too much. Everybody had enjoyed the chat with the spook. So I postponed the confession and carried on for a few evenings, before an ever-increasing audience of prisoners, extracting answers from the Ouija, and inventing a little army of spooks – Sally, Dorothy, Silas P. Warner, and others, each with his own special characteristic.

Then, before I knew where I was, it became impossible to confess without involving others. Another group of spiritualists began to get answers from the Ouija. They didn't know I was fudging. But I knew they were, because they got their answers from the spooks I had invented myself – Silas P. Warner and others. It was a case of,

> "O what a tangled web we weave,
> When first we practice to deceive"

To salve my conscience, I challenged an investigation. Tests, some very difficult, were set. To my own surprise I got through them all undetected.

Half the camp became converted to spiritualism. Seances were held almost nightly. We obtained all sorts of news, including war news. The spook issued a regular war-news bulletin.

Then the Turks came in. First the interpreter. He was an Ottoman Jew called Moise. We called him the "Pimple". He consulted the spook about his love affairs, and he got appropriate answers.

Next came an official order from the Turkish Commandant. It forbade us to mention in our letters home "news obtained in a spiritistic state". I questioned the interpreter and discovered that our Commandant, Kiazim Bey, was a confirmed believer in spiritualism. Indeed he was the patron of a local witch who regularly read the cards for him.

Have you ever fished for trout with a 3x cast and a light rod, and seen a salmon rise to your fly? That is how I felt when I realised what lay behind Kiazim Bey's official order.

Here was my chance at last. I must get Kiazim into my net. How I was to do it I could not see. But from that moment wild horses and the rack and all the tortures of the Spanish Inquisition would not have dragged from me a confession that I was cheating. If this Turkish major believed in spooks, then somehow and sometime I would get him where I wanted him – under my thumb. Once I got him there, I would have a chance of getting away without involving the camp in a "strafe". My plan was to make him an unconscious accomplice in my escape. I would implicate him. I would obtain clear proof of that implication. I would place that proof in the hands of the camp before I left. He would not then dare to "strafe" the camp, for the camp could threaten to retaliate by reporting his complicity to the first superior Turkish officer who came round inspecting.

Such was my plan. But I had only risen him. I still had to get him on the hook. How?

The answer is obvious to every fisherman. Get the right lure. But what was the lure? I could only watch and wait. We had begun spooking in February. I did not find the lure until September, and it was Moise the interpreter, our Pimple, who unconsciously showed it to me.

The Pimple asked me one day if the spook could find buried treasure. My answer was extremely encouraging. Moise asked for a seance. I promised him one. From his talk I learned that the Turks had already been digging for the treasure, but had found nothing. The money they were searching for was the fortune of a rich Armenian in Yozgad – one of the thousands of Armenians in this town who had been massacred by the Turks just before we came. Here was the lure.

Two of the prisoners, Lloyd and Cochrane, had found a useless rusty old revolver buried in our garden. I begged for it. I got it. I buried it again. Then we had the seance. The spook told the interpreter that the treasure was guarded by arms, which must be discovered first. Two Turks were ordered by the spook to be present at the search. I hoped Kiazim, the Commandant, would rise to this fly. He didn't. His bat-man – the lousy villain we knew as "the Cook" – came instead. I guessed that he had been sent by the Commandant, but I did not know.

This was disappointing. I wanted the big fish, not the small fry, but I carried on. I fell into a trance. The spook then guided us to the spot where the revolver was hidden.

When you are spooking for treasure it does not do to dig it up at once. Ceremony is essential. Ceremony counts. So over the spot we built up a fire of shavings. And over the fire of shavings we poured water. And in the mingled steam and smoke, standing with outstretched arms, I recited a mystic incantation, necessary for the discovery of all treasures, which I said I had learned from the Head Hunting Waas of Burma.

The incantation was not Waa at all. It was not even Burmese. It was not even an incantation. It was a Welsh love lyric. But it is surprising how effective Welsh can be as an incantation in a leg pull. For example – "Gwyn fyd na chai Cymru ei diwifr eihun". Yards of this sort of talk make an excellent incantation.

When we dug up the rusty revolver, the Turks were overjoyed. I felt sure that the discovery would bring out the Commandant. But I waited in vain. Kiazim kept hidden, sheltered behind his subordinates, and for months only the "Pimple" came to question the spook about the treasure. This was no good at all to me. If I was to implicate him, I must have the Commandant himself. So the spook refused to say a word about the treasure and would only curse and threaten the "Pimple".

At last the "Pimple" lost his temper with the spook, and challenged the unseen to *do* something, instead of merely cursing and threatening. The spook at once promised to kill him that night. The "Pimple" begged pardon, frantically, and said, "I only wanted you to take off my hat or my move something." "Very good," said the spook, "I shall move something." That night I put six grains of calomel into the "Pimple's" cocoa. He never challenged the spook again. The manifestation of the spook's powers of moving things, next day, did him all the good in the world. Henceforth he was a complete and very obedient convert.

I went on, week after week, trying to build up the prestige of the spook by every trick I could invent. The spook's prestige certainly grew, but it was all no use. The weary days passed on. The Commandant was as far away as ever. I felt pretty certain, but I could not be sure that he was behind the "Pimple" in this treasure hunt. He had never showed himself.

I made one last effort. Without telling the "Pimple" of my suspicion that the Commandant was interested, I managed to convince him that unless everybody concerned with the treasure came forward the medium could never succeed.

A couple of days later a sentry came for me and took me into the Commandant's office. Kiazim and the "Pimple" were there. It was an amazing interview between a junior officer prisoner and the Turkish major in charge. I came away pledged to place my skill as a medium at the service of the Commandant to try to find the treasure.

The fish was hooked at last! What did it matter that I was threatened with death if I sought to betray Kiazim's interest in the treasure to Constantinople? What did it matter that the "Pimple" told me how such things are done – how a prisoner's body is produced with a hole through the back – "shot while attempting to escape". Nothing mattered. The fish was hooked at last.

Hitherto I had kept my own counsel. It had been solitary work, this fishing for the Commandant. Now that he was on the hook, I needed a confederate. In my own mind I had chosen him long ago. I went straight to him now. He was Hill, the Australian flying man. I chose well. He was a companion in a million.

He required no persuasion. When I asked him how far he would go to get away, his answer was, "I'll go the pool – all out. I won't be re-taken alive."

We started at once. Hill made two small tins shaped like shaving soap tins, each with a false bottom. In the false bottom of each we placed a Turkish gold lira, wrapped up in a paper containing directions written by us in Armenian characters.

The top part of the tin was filled with ashes. Hill took the tins outside the camp when he went for exercise, and buried them three miles apart. These were clues to the treasure. The spook was going to find these clues later on.

The spook then set about convincing the Commandant that no good results could be obtained so long as the mediums were in camp. They must be confined somewhere by themselves. We convinced him of this easily enough. But to get him to move us was a much more difficult business.

The spook told him how to do it. The Commandant was to accuse Hill and myself of reading the thoughts of the towns-people and obtaining war news in that way. By a conjuring trick of Hill's the spook provided Kiazim with written evidence to support this absurd charge. He was to convict us for it and to sentence us to solitary confinement apart from the camp, whence, of course, we hoped to escape. Kiazim refused to come up to scratch. Fortunately, just then he got a bad attack of colic. Colic is a painful thing. The spook immediately claimed to be the author of this visitation and threatened Kiazim with a worse attack if he did not comply with orders. Remembering the calomel incident, Kiazim gave in at once. The incredible trial was held, in the presence of four British officers, chosen by myself as witnesses because of their honest belief in telepathy. In complete innocence of our scheme these officers testified that thought-reading was possible. Then, to their horror, they found that Hill and I were being charged with thought-reading, and they saw us convicted and sentenced to solitary confinement on this charge of telepathy.

We were confined in a house by ourselves. At last we were alone. Within twenty-four hours a letter of mine was on its way to England. The letter seemed quite an innocent affair and spoke of the pleasant time we were having as prisoners, but it was really a cryptogram, and that cryptogram told how we had been imprisoned on an absurd charge of telepathy and asked for an inquiry. We had heard of one case where an officer, unjustly condemned, had been granted a compassionate release from Turkey to make up for it. There was a distant chance the same might happen to us. The letter got home all right, the cryptogram was deciphered; it was placed in the hands of Whitehall. Whitehall did nothing. They said it was dangerous to interfere – for our sakes.

We never placed much reliance on this plan, it was merely an alternative sideline. Hill and I set to work on our main line. The first step in our scheme was to obtain proof that the Commandant was implicated. Our idea was to photograph him digging for the treasure in our company, but without his knowledge. We would give this photograph to our friends in the camp. It would be their safeguard. We had a camera and three films hidden away, ready. The camera had been made by Hill out of a chocolate box.

But before we could get going we had to calm the fears of the Commandant. He wanted to know what he was to report about our trial to Constantinople. The spook board was brought out and the spook dictated the letter he was to send to the War Office. He wrote it, and sent it; and if they keep files in the Turkish War Office, it is there to-day.

From that time on the spook ran the camp. Every question that arose was submitted by the Commandant to the spook for advice. Thus there was in Yozgad a ski club, originated by Lieut. Spink. At the end of the ski-ing season the club gave a dinner to which Kiazim was invited as a guest. The spook wrote Kiazim's speech for him, in which he made promises of new privileges to the prisoners. And Kiazim delivered it. There was a hunt club in the summer months, originated by Holyoake. The Turkish War Office sent a letter to Kiazim telling him such clubs were prohibited. The spook told Kiazim to pay no attention to the letter, and the hunt club continued. Again, the senior British officer had put Hill and myself on parole not to escape from Yozgad. The senior British officer was a member of the hunt club. So the spook told Kiazim to put him on parole when hunting. Kiazim got the parole. It is not often a subaltern gets square with his colonel. I do not think the colonel bears us any grudge.

When these minor problems were out of the way we consulted the spook about the treasure.

The story I invented about the treasure was this:

The rich Armenian whose wealth we were seeking had guessed that a massacre was coming. He buried his wealth. At different spots he then buried three clues to where the treasure was. One clue showed the spot from where to measure. The second showed the direction in which to measure and the third showed the distance to be measured. To discover the treasure all the three clues would have to be found.

He did not tell his family where the treasure was because he was afraid they might reveal it to the Turks under torture. But if they happened to escape the coming massacre he wanted them to be provided for. He therefore selected three friends living in different parts of the country. He gave A, B, and C, the three friends, directions for finding one clue each. He also gave them tokens by which to identify one another, and he left instructions that when he died or was killed, friend A was to send for friend B. Friend B, in his turn, knew that he was to send for friend C. The three of them could then go and with their combined knowledge find the clues and dig up the treasure.

Friend A and friend B unfortunately had been massacred about the same time as the owner. Friend C was still alive and lived on the sea coast. But the other two being dead he had never been summoned, so the treasure was still intact as he only knew the position of the one clue.

This was the story the spook told to the Turks. Hill and I did not know a single Armenian name. We got over the difficulty of giving the names and addresses of the Armenians concerned in a manner too intricate to describe here. But the blame for the spook's failure to give the names was fixed on the "Pimple". When the "Pimple" made his report on this seance to the Commandant, the Commandant smacked his face for him. We avenged the "Pimple" later on, when the spook ordered Kiazim not to kiss his wife for a fortnight.

Our programme was to get the Turks to become really hot on the scent of the treasure, in order that they might be willing to take the risks which would lead to our freedom.

At the very first séance the spirit of the dead Armenian owner took charge of the board and announced that he was willing to tell us where the treasure was buried on one condition. The condition was that we were friends of the Armenians. He said he was going to test us, and the "Ouija" spelled out a question in the Armenian tongue. The "Pimple" said he did not know Armenian, so our Armenian spook would have nothing more to do with us. He refused to tell where the treasure was and he went further – he organised an opposition party in the spook world to prevent our finding it. It was the "Pimple's" fault again. Because he did not know Armenian we had lost a great chance.

We therefore decided to find the clues. We soon got into touch with the spirits of friend A and friend B. They were most obliging spooks. They were quite willing to lead us to the clues.

On 31 March we unearthed the first clue. Hill succeeded in taking three photographs of the proceedings without the knowledge of the Turks. That night he developed them while I kept guard. They were not perfect, but the Commandant and the rest of us were clearly recognisable in all of them, and considering cameras are forbidden in prison camps, it was not a bad effort.

We had got our proof.

Next day we unearthed the second clue. That filthy old rascal, the cook, showed his gratitude by kissing Hill and myself before we could get out of his way. The excitement was prodigious. The Turks had the Armenian messages in the tins translated and now knew the direction in which to measure and the distance to measure. All they needed in order to find the treasure was to know the point from which these valuable measurements were to be taken.

When we came back from the treasure hunt we found that a wire had come from the War Office at Constantinople ordering the Commandant to release us from our imprisonment for telepathy and to send us back to camp. Kiazim consulted the spook. The spook told him not to bother about War Office orders, but to carry on with the treasure hunt. He obeyed the spook. There was only one more clue to find. One tiny clue, and the treasure was ours. Enver Pasha and the whole of the War Office could go hang.

Hill and I now got into touch with fellow prisoners whom we could trust. To these we handed the photographs and other proofs of the Commandant's complicity. And in case of documentary evidence was insufficient, we trapped the Commandant irretrievably in a very simple way.

I have mentioned that each of the two clues which we buried contained a gold coin. By the spook's orders each of these coins was cut into three equal parts. I took the third of one coin, Hill took a third of the other. The remaining four portions were given to the "Cook", the "Pimple", the Commandant and the Commandant's wife. The spook ordered us to wear these little bits of gold, night and day and always until the treasure was found, round our necks and next to our skin. We all did so and I knew I could rely upon the Turks continually doing so. If later on the Turks denied that they were implicated in our scheme the Commandant would find it very difficult to explain how we all came to be wearing pieces of the same coin if there was no understanding between us.

Hill and I considered we had now made the game quite safe, so we went bald-headed for the completion of the scheme. The Turks joined in whole-heartedly. For them, completion of the scheme meant finding the third clue and the treasure. For Hill and me it meant getting to the coast.

It was easy enough to combine the two objectives. You remember that the holder of the third clue (Mr. C) lived on the sea-coast. He was still alive so we could not talk to his spook. But being thought-readers we could read his thoughts if we could get near enough. Now you can't read thoughts if you are in mountainous country, because thought waves are like wireless waves – mountains stop them. But if you are at sea level you can pick them up from almost any distance.

Naturally the Turks wanted us to read C's thoughts. They were quite willing to come to the coast to do it. The Commandant at the spook's request agreed to grant leave to the "Cook" and the "Pimple". He himself at the spook's instruction went to the Turkish doctors. The spook told him what to say to get a diagnosis of stone in the hepatic duct. He swung the lead successfully and got a powerful medical certificate. Armed with this certificate, he said, he could get leave by telegram from the War Office at any moment, for he had influential friends there. The Commandant then informed the British senior officer in the camp that he was going to send Hill and myself away from Yozgad. Everything was ready. All we had to do now was to await the arrival of another Commandant to take over charge of the camp from Kiazim. A suitable Turkish officer was actually on his way to Yozgad, in charge of a fresh batch of prisoners. He was due to arrive in a few days and would be available to take Kiazim's place.

Hill and I were also ready. In the handle of my shaving brush I carried enough morphia to put a Turkish battalion to sleep. We had our plans for getting the Turks to supply a boat, for getting them into it, for drugging them with morphia. We had ropes and straps ready to bind them. We had sand-bags ready sewn to fill with sand in case the morphia did not work very well. We hoped that when the Turks woke up, we would be half-way to Cyprus, for we intended to kidnap them. We thought that if we succeeded Mr. Lloyd George might give us an O.B.E. each. But even that did not deter us.

Then the crash came. One of our fellow prisoners warned the Commandant that if he sent us away, as he said he was going to do, Hill and I would escape. This prisoner was a friend of mine. He thought perhaps that we were being sent away in order to be put away. At any rate, the Commandant got alarmed. He drew back. He wouldn't come with us. He wouldn't send us to the coast, but he would send us to Constantinople if the spook would show him how. At Constantinople, being on sea level, we could read the thoughts of friend C and send back word where to find the third clue.

It was a pathetic ending to a jolly little scheme. l could have wept. Hill came nearer to losing his temper than I have ever seen him. But there was nothing for it. We gave up the plan. The spook proceeded to tell Kiazim how to get us to Constantinople. Kiazim only had to say that Hill and I were mad.

Kiazim said so. Tutored by the spook, he went to the Turkish doctors at Yozgad and pitched a pretty tale about our mad behaviour. He brought the two Turkish doctors to see us. We played our part as lunatics in their presence. They certified us. They called me "a furious, who was suffering from a derangement in his brains". Of Hill they wrote that he was "in a very calm condition. His face is long, not very fat. He is suffering from melancholia."

The spook dictated a wire to the Turkish War Office asking permission to send to Constantinople two British officers who had been certified insane by the local Turkish doctors. It also dictated a lengthy report detailing our insane doings and enclosing our medical certificates. A wire came in reply to send us along at once. The Commandant on the spook's instructions ordered the "Pimple" to accompany us.

We had to wait some days for transport. While we waited our own Doctor O'Farrell tutored us. He taught us how to sham mad. We practised on the sentries, whose lives we made a burden, and on our own fellow-prisoners. We were now all out for repatriation as lunatics.

In a few days we started, under close guard, on our specially conducted tour to Constantinople. On the way, at a town called Mardeen, we pretended to hang ourselves. This part of the scheme was too well acted. Owing to a mistake of the "Pimple's" we were both just about unconscious when we were cut down. Next morning we denied that we had hanged ourselves at all. So the Mayor of Mardeen held an inquiry, and his official (the town clerk we supposed) wrote a report to the Turkish War Office to say that Hill and myself were a pair of liars, and that we had hanged ourselves all right. All the way to Constantinople, a ten days' journey, we behaved like lunatics, to the annoyance of our guards, and tutored the "Pimple" as to what he was to say to the mental specialists.

In this way it came about that an immense volume of evidence proving our insanity was produced by the Turkish officials themselves. There were the certificates of insanity from the Yozgad doctors, the report from Kiazim, the officer in charge of the Yozgad camp, the letter from the mayor and corporation of Mardeen, the evidence of our behaviour en route by the "Pimple" and the sentries, and the marks round our throat of where the rope had cut into our necks. We ourselves denied steadily that we were insane or that we had done the insane acts with which we were charged. We also got O'Farrell, our British camp doctor, to write a letter to say that we were not insane – only a bit eccentric. We thought that the Turkish doctors would naturally delight in a chance to disagree with an English doctor.

With all this official evidence of our insanity at our backs the Turkish mental specialists never had a real chance. As doctors, and they were good doctors, they could not get away from our medical history. All we had to do was to act carefully. In less than a month we were certified for exchange. We now only had to keep it up until the arrangements for exchanging sick prisoners were completed. We did not know that we would have to wait for six months for the exchange ship to arrive, and carry on our acting all that time among crazy men in the mad wards of a Turkish hospital. It nearly killed us. But we did it. Hill left the country with the first boat-load of exchange prisoners. I followed in the second boat a few days later. After all our hard work we had gained only a short fortnight over the prisoners who had sat still and done nothing. For the Armistice arrived within a few days of Hill's leaving Turkey. But we had the satisfaction of having done our best.

CHAPTER ELEVEN

AN UNCONDUCTED TOUR
OF ENGLAND

By Heinz H. E. Justus

The first English camp I was taken to as a German prisoner of war in July 1917 was Colsterdale, near Masham, up north in Yorkshire, and I hope it will be taken in good part when I say that I didn't want to stay there. I tried several times to get through the barbed wire and I also took part in one of the tunneling schemes which was, however, discovered by the British just before the tunnel was completed. Then one fine day I hit upon the idea of just walking out through the gate disguised as our English canteen manager, who was about my size and figure – his name was Mr. Budd – I wonder if, by chance, he may read these words and if he still remembers it all. So evening after evening I started observing closely his every movement on leaving the camp, and noticed to my satisfaction that the sentries never asked him for the password. Everybody knew Mr. Budd too well for that. This was also, of course, rather a drawback; but my idea was to do the thing in the evening after dark.

I'd been informed – I think quite wrongly – that every male passenger in those war days was supposed to produce a pass or other document when booking a railway ticket, particularly when travelling to London, and as I didn't feel like walking the whole way there I decided to travel as a woman.

We had private codes between the camps and our people at home so I sent a message to my mother asking her to send me every conceivable thing which I should need for this disguise. After some time I received news that a wig was arriving camouflaged as tobacco; that all sorts of fake jewellery, a compass and similar handy things had been sent off in marmalade jars, or baked in a cake – and, last but not least, that I would soon receive a large quilt with a skirt, petticoat, veil, some sort of a hat, silk stockings and a nice silk coat all sewn up in it. I had asked for everything in black, even the necklace and brooches, as I wanted to look like a poor widow so that people on the trains wouldn't speak to me as freely as if I were dressed as a giddy young girl.

Then I heard rumours of Mr. Budd being transferred to some other camp, so I couldn't afford to wait for the arrival of these mysterious packages and began collecting an outfit in the camp. My skirt was made out of an old blanket and the hat and muff were mostly composed of parts of fur waistcoats. We had plenty of fancy costumes in the camp, beautiful wigs, hats, and so on, but they were all under "word of honour" not to be used except for theatrical purposes, and so of course I couldn't use them.

Then the great day arrived and I put on all the clothes, man and woman's mixed together, so that I was able to change from one to the other with a few slight manipulations.

I approached the gate disguised as Mr. Budd with a false moustache and a pair of spectacles, worn exactly the way Mr. Budd wore them. My cap, mackintosh and bag were also exact replicas of the ones with which Mr. Budd used to leave the camp every evening. Even the most pessimistic of my friends thought I really was Mr. Budd when they saw me.

Mr Budd was in the habit of leaving the camp about 8 p.m. and I had timed my attempt for about ten minutes to eight. Meanwhile a few friends of mine would keep the real Mr. Budd busy in the canteen until shortly *after* eight, and as the sentries were usually changed at 8 o'clock sharp I was sure that the new sentry would not be surprised to see the second and real Mr. Budd leaving camp. So off I went straight to the gate gaily smoking my pipe as if after a good day's work at the canteen. A few yards from it I shouted "Guard," as this was the way Mr. Budd used to announce himself day by day. The sentry called out, "Who's there?" "Budd," I answered. "Right," and opened the big door.

I walked slowly down the street from the camp towards Masham station. I had about a two-hours' walk before me; I hadn't gone more than fifty yards when I espied our Commandant coming towards me. Within a fraction of a second I had torn off the moustache and spectacles as, of course, I didn't want the Colonel to address the false Mr. Budd. As I passed him I just said "Good evening," and so did he.

A little further on I decided to change into a woman. This was only a matter of a few seconds. I exchanged Mr. Budd's cap with the woman's hat and veil which I carried in my bag, and took off my mackintosh, which covered a navy-blue civilian jacket trimmed with all sorts of lace and bows. My skirt was hitched up with a leather belt round my hips so I had only to undo the belt to release the skirt. Luckily for me skirts in those days reached down to the ground, so my leggings were completely covered by the skirt and couldn't be seen in the dark.

I met some Tommies on the road, and they all behaved very decently; they all bade me "good evening," and none of them insisted on starting a conversation with the very reserved woman who did not even reply to their "good evening".

Only once I was a bit troubled, by a shepherd's dog, but he soon withdrew when the strange woman took something out of her muff and sprinkled it on the road. It is very important for an escaper always to carry a box of pepper to defend himself against dogs.

I'd been walking now for quite some time, making good progress towards the station of Masham, when I noticed three soldiers following me and overtaking me. One of them was equipped with a rifle with fixed bayonet and I knew that this must surely be a sentry from the camp as there were no other military in the neighbourhood. I at once thought of throwing away my bag which might so easily give me away, but anything of that sort would immediately have aroused suspicion. The soldiers came steadily closer and closer until finally they overtook me. They then stopped and said "Good evening, miss. Have you by any chance seen a man with a bag like yours? A prisoner of war has escaped and we are out looking for him." Well, I tried for a time, really only for a very short time, to speak in a high voice, telling them please not to bother a decent young girl by starting a conversation with her, but all they said was might they have a look at the bag I carried. I refused, of course, but it was only a matter of another few seconds before I realised that it was all over with me. I was found out. I then learned that my escape had been discovered owing to the sentry not being released as usual at 8 o'clock. So you can easily understand that a mysterious situation occurred when shortly after 8 o'clock a second Mr. Budd appeared and asked the same sentry to be let through the gate. The ensuing confusion was quite amusing, of course, and the bell was immediately rung, but unfortunately I hadn't heard it.

Well, there was nothing for it but to be escorted back to the camp. One Tommy carried my bag, which was not, however, due to gallantry on his part towards a lady, but mainly because he feared I might throw it into the small river we had to cross. I would, however, not have thrown it away as a good deal of my money was in it, which later in the same evening was returned to me by the British, as they never suspected that the small package of Gillette blades did not contain razor blades but six English pound notes folded to exactly the size of a safety razor blade wrapped up in the original Gillette paper and envelope.

There was, of course, great excitement amongst the British officers. The Commandant, the Assistant Commandant, the Adjutant and several other officers had all assembled in the guardroom anxiously awaiting news of the escaped officer, and you cannot possibly imagine the funny faces they made when the door was opened by my escort and in walked a woman wearing a white fur hat. I think the first thing that happened was that everybody burst out laughing. Then the Commandant said that it was not at all customary for a young lady to undress in the presence of so many gentlemen, but that in this particular case an exception to the rule must be made. I could not, however, undo the knot of my petticoat tape, which my friends had tied too tight. I therefore asked if perhaps one of the gentlemen would be kind enough to help undo the thing, and the Adjutant very kindly drew forth his pocket knife, which finally settled the question.

After a few weeks' confinement before trial a court martial was held. I got thirty-five days and was sent down to Chelmsford prison. From Chelmsford I was taken to Holyport, a camp near Maidenhead. This was the best camp I'd been in as regards personal comfort, but it was a very depressing place for an escaper. I took part in several schemes of digging tunnels there, and twice I tried to crawl through the barbed wire entanglement. The second time I was caught right in the middle of it – it had taken me more than four hours to get there, and again I had the thrilling experience of a court martial.

So I was quite relieved when one fine day I was told that, together with forty-nine fellow officers, I would be taken to another camp, which was near Wakefield. You can imagine that when the Holyport officials were asked to send fifty officers to some other place, they didn't miss the opportunity to get rid of their "bad boys".

Well, when we left Holyport, everybody, of course, was very carefully searched, but we had quite some experience already in smuggling – and so when we boarded the train in Maidenhead I had in my pocket a civilian cap, a compass, several maps of England and English money, any single thing of which would have sufficed to bring about another court martial. I was wearing an ordinary English mackintosh which was supposed to resemble a German army coat as there were shoulder-straps sewn on to it. I removed these, however, as soon as we were in the train, and when I turned up the collar of the rain–coat and put on my civilian cap my disguise was perfect. On my legs I was wearing ordinary brown leggings which, especially in those days, were worn alike by civilians and people in any army of the world.

My idea was to get away from the transport in the general rush and turmoil either at Paddington Station, where we would arrive, or at King's Cross, from where our train for the north would leave. But it didn't prove to be easy at all, and I was greatly disappointed when our train left King's Cross for the north.

The only chance now was, of course, just to jump out of the train, and I studied the situation rather carefully, and without saying a word about it to my comrades. We were travelling on a corridor train, with always about six officers in one compartment and one sentry in the corridor to watch two compartments. So it would be necessary to cover the sentry's field of observation for the moment of the jump. But it would be impossible to do the thing in broad daylight and the one great fear I had was that we would reach our destination before sunset. It would be necessary too to find the right place for the jump. The train, of course, would not have to be going too fast and there would have to be no houses or people by the side of the track. So I passed the next few hours in a rather nervous and excited state. It was about a quarter to six when, after a short stop, we left the station of South Elmshall. The train moved very slowly but was speeding up every second – there were fields on both sides of the track, and as it was sufficiently dark already it was quite clear to me that the time had come to do the trick. My fellow officers were, of course, very much surprised when I asked them all of a sudden to stand upright and place themselves before the door and the windows of the corridor so that the sentry would not be able to see me out of the window. They were sporting enough to do what I asked of them, and a few seconds later I found myself on a meadow by the side of the track. The tail lights of the train disappeared into the dark and I was free, absolutely free – nobody who hasn't been a prisoner can possibly imagine what this really means.

The first thing to do now was to put on my civilian cap and I then turned down the collar of my tunic. The German officers' uniforms are so made that the collar fits high round the neck, so in order to hide the German tunic collar I had to roll it down – and as I wasn't in possession of a white collar and a tie I just wound a handkerchief round the neck. This didn't look so very smart but it served the purpose.

I now walked the short distance back to South Elmshall and proceeded to Doncaster, whence I wanted to take a train down to London. My general scheme was eventually to go to some seaport on the west coast, and to smuggle on board some neutral ship, preferably a Spanish one, as I had learnt that language in the camps. I had decided on Cardiff but I thought I would go to London first because it would certainly be easier for the first few days to hide in a big city than in a small place. I arrived in Doncaster at about a quarter past seven in the evening, and found out that there was no train to London before 4.50 or so, I think it was, in the morning. Well, this was really a nuisance, but all I could do was to just make the best of a bad business, and I started out from the station to have a look round the town. There were big signposts advertising a show with the name of "You Are Spotted", which was indeed a rather apposite title for a play from the point of view of an escaped prisoner. I decided to have a look at it. At about half-past eight I made for the theatre, which I deliberately entered a little late because I preferred to take my seat only after the lights in the auditorium had been turned out, as I couldn't even take off my rain-coat, and I had no collar. So when I came in, the show was already in full swing and I was greeted from the stage by a chorus of about twenty or thirty girls waving Allied flags and singing the most exciting rag-times. I can hardly describe my sensations at all this. About three hours ago I was still a prisoner of war, and I couldn't help smiling when I noticed that my neighbour to the right was an English Staff Officer. When the lights went on after the first act he looked at me a little longer than I liked at the moment, and then I heard him say to his companion that I was rather a strange-looking fellow. But that was all, and nobody kept me from enjoying the rest of the show more than anybody else in the house. When the thing was over the band of course played "God Save the King," and I wondered what my neighbours would have said if I had joined in and sung the German words to it, as we have the same tune for a German patriotic song.

Finally the time arrived for me to go to the station. They didn't ask for passes or anything, and I soon had my ticket, and at about 9 o'clock in the morning I arrived at King's Cross, the station which I had left the day before under rather different circumstances. The first thing to do was to buy a good collar and tie, and also a waistcoat to put over my tunic. I then started out for a nice walk through London. Trafalgar Square was one of the few places I remembered from a short visit I paid to this country as a boy in pre-war days, but I was very much surprised indeed to find that it all looked different now. Trafalgar Square in those days was turned into a devastated French village, probably for some Red Cross collection or a similar purpose; there were trenches, shattered houses, barbed wire, shell holes, guns and all that, all of which I inspected with the eye of an expert. I then strolled down the Strand, and after a while I went to the matinee of a show called "Going Up," at the Gaiety Theatre. I have seen a good many shows since 1918 but I do not think I saw a better one than this "Going Up".

After this experience I again wandered around the streets of London, had supper at some small restaurant and then began to think about where to go for the night. I passed a man in the street who looked rather a rough and the right sort of fellow probably to ask for some information of this kind, so I offered him a cigarette and started a conversation. I told him that I was in London for the first time and could he suggest any convenient lodgings for the night where they would not ask for passes, as sometimes you didn't exactly want to give your real name.

He gave me the tip to go to some small hotel near one of the stations where they probably wouldn't be so very strict, but still he wasn't quite sure if I wouldn't be asked to show papers too. I told him that I had been to the Gaiety in the afternoon, and speaking of theatres he said that I should by all means go and see the extraordinarily fine play, "The Hidden Hand" at the Middlesex Theatre. It was awfully good, about War and the Germans and spying and all that. I said I would certainly go, and I did. It was the third time that I had been in a theatre within twenty-four hours, and I very soon realised that this was a very, very thrilling play indeed. But after a while I came to think that it was a little *too* thrilling for a man in German uniform, even if his military attire was covered by a rain-coat. It was the most anti-German performance in the world, and the whole atmosphere around me didn't seem to be very pro-German. I really wondered what would happen if by some chance or other somebody would find out that there was a German officer right in their midst – they would probably have torn me to pieces, and when the lights were switched on after the first act everybody seemed to look at me in a very suspicious way. All of them, just a few seconds ago, had been told from the stage all about German spies and all sorts of nice things about the nice Germans. I fancied I could hear them whisper to one another, "Do you see that funny chap in a mackintosh? Everybody has taken off his coat, why hasn't he?" Well, as a matter of fact, nobody of course said such things, but after all I thought it might be just as safe to leave the house after the first act, which had given me already a complete run for my money. When I went down the stairs I tried to look just as "Allied" as possible and I remember quite distinctly that I whistled the Marseillaise in order to be taken for a Frenchman, or at least for a man with strongly anti-German feelings.

It was about time now to think of going to a hotel. If after all they asked for a passport or something I would just say I'd lost mine and the only consequence would probably be that they wouldn't give me a room. But at all events they would be desirous to know my name, and so I decided to adopt for the night the name of Albert Georges, which could be either French or English, and I thought it might be a good idea to perhaps say that I was a Frenchman if they asked too many uncomfortable questions.

The first two or three hotels were full up, but in the next one they said, "Yes, there was a small room, and would I please fill in this form here." Very well, then, my name was Albert Georges, last address: Southampton. Street? Well, I hadn't thought of that, but I think I wrote Queen Street, hoping that this would be the name of a street in Southampton. Nationality: French. "Oh, you are a Frenchman," the young lady at the hotel said. "There are special forms for foreigners," and so she handed me a great big piece of paper with innumerable questions to be answered. Not only did they want to know absolutely everything about myself, but they wanted to know also all about my parents, and where my grandfather had been born and a thousand questions of that sort. I became quite dizzy and all the time, in order to think of some new name or date, I pretended I couldn't very well write with those extraordinary nibs; in France, of course, we had quite different nibs and all that. Finally I got through with it. I was never asked for a passport, and I smiled when I was shown into my room. But when I was in bed I became uneasy; had I said King Street or was it Queen Street, and what was the number of the house I had given, and what did was my great-grandfather's uncle's first name, and what age had I given? Imagine the consequences if for some unforeseen reason or other they asked me again for one of the many dates and names I had given, and if I didn't remember then the date of my own birthday or something. Well, I switched on the lights again and wrote down on a piece of paper whatever I remembered of all the many dates and names I had given, but I was glad that nobody came to compare my present notes with the ones I had given downstairs.

I had a *very* good night's rest, and felt fine and cheerful when I left the hotel next morning. There was a Red Cross Day on or something, and soon I was stopped in the street by a kind elderly lady who insisted on selling me a little Union Jack which she tried to pin on to my mackintosh. However, the pin wouldn't go through and the trouble was that she always stabbed against the Iron Cross which I was wearing on my tunic. I thought of telling her I was sorry to say that at the moment the Union Jack didn't go so very well with the Iron Cross, but I didn't. I just took the flag out of her hand and fastened it myself on a spot just above my decoration.

I now wanted to get rid of my tunic at the earliest possible moment. I had already thought of throwing the thing into the Thames, but it was a brand new one and it was quite probable after all that one of these days I would find myself back again in a prison camp, where I would miss the nice uniform very much. So I decided just to send the tunic by parcel post to the Commandant of my old camp, Holyport, as I wasn't sure about the exact address of the new camp near Wakefield. I suppose that the Holyport Commandant was much surprised to receive that parcel. I read a few days later in all the papers that he had got it all right.

I now proceeded to buy a pair of trousers and a jacket, and at last I looked like a real civilian and I was now able to take off my mackintosh.

The following night I again tried to register as a Frenchman. I went of course to another hotel, but the young lady there said that no foreigners could be admitted before they had registered at the police station. She told me where the police station was, and I promised to be back in a few minutes – but of course I never returned. I just became an Englishman and spent the night at one of those small hotels near Waterloo Station.

There was much influenza in England in those days, and when I woke up next morning I didn't feel very well, but still I didn't pay any attention to that, and I decided to go to Cardiff in the evening. I was still in possession of a nice sum of money to carry on for quite some time, including a bribe or two to help me to get on a Spanish ship in Cardiff, but I thought it might be good to get some more funds before leaving London, so I decided to sell a valuable platinum and diamond ring I was wearing. My mother had given it to me as a talisman for the trenches, and as I didn't much care for such a showy thing I had accepted it on the clear understanding that I could sell it again once it had done its good work at the front. So I went to offer it at a jeweller's shop, in Fleet Street I think it was, and said I wanted fifty guineas for it. The man said that it was really a very fine ring, but would I produce some proof or something in order to show where it came from. I said my father had given it to me the last time we were in Paris. "Oh, yes," of course he didn't doubt a bit that everything was perfectly in order, and quite all right, but you see these days now you had to be very careful buying things like that – and finally he asked if he might have a look at my registration card or something of that sort which I had never heard of before in my life. I said yes, certainly, but after going through all my pockets I said that I must have left the thing at my hotel and I would go and get it. Everything seemed to be quite all right except that the man didn't seem to care about returning the ring to me. He *knew* that there was something wrong, and he disappeared more to talk the matter over with another man in the back of the shop. For a second or so I thought of just dashing out of the place, but then the man came out again and said, "I'll you seventeen guineas." I protested, of course, but both of us very quickly realised that it must be either yes or no, and so I accepted, and then beat it just as fast as possible. The only thing I failed to understand was why on earth he had offered me seventeen *guineas*; I would just as soon have accepted seventeen shillings.

I now went to Cardiff by train, arrived about 9 p.m., and went to the Royal Hotel. I gave my name as Allan Hinckley, who was an American opera singer in pre-war days in Hamburg. I told the porter right away that I had my luggage at the station, and if anybody had asked me for a passport or something I would just have said that I had that in my suit case. After having written my name in the hotel book I asked if they could send somebody to the station to get my luggage, but I said this, of course, only for show, as I really didn't have any luggage all, and when the porter said of course he could send for it, "Well, I think after all I'll leave it just where it is; I've got to go back to London anyhow early in the morning, and I'd like to turn in right away."

I felt very miserable when I awoke next morning, and I was quite sure now that I had the real 'flu, but I set out in order to see if I could spot a Spanish ship somewhere. I had no idea where the port was and somebody told me that there was a place of the name of Penarth, which was right on the open sea. I went there in a taxi, but was awfully disappointed to find a deserted pleasure resort with no ships whatsoever leaving them for Spain. I went to a small hotel and had a whisky and soda in the deserted lounge. I sat quite by myself by the fireside, and read various articles which had been published in the Press about my escape. One paper had a big headline: "Masquerading Hun Officer in Woman's Dress." Apparently Scotland

Yard thought I was doing the same thing again. While I was reading this a British officer came in, accompanied by two ladies. They all sat down quite close to me in order to get warm at the same fire, and immediately started talking about the war.

The officer had just come from France on short leave, and one of the girls said rather embarrassing things about the Germans – I mean embarrassing for a German officer who sat impersonating a harmless civilian in the same room. She said these Germans must be really frightful people and she was sure that they all were the greatest cowards in the world, and many other delightful things. The British officer, however, had a rather different opinion. He said that he hadn't noticed that the Germans were cowards; he had just come from the Western Front, where he had been stationed opposite a Prussian Guards division, and he had a great respect for them. Well, I tell you, when this officer spoke I very nearly butted in. I felt like saying to him, "Now, look here, I'm a German officer myself, let's talk things over for an hour or so, and we can toss for drinks anyhow. Later on, of course, you must hand me over to the police, but that cannot be helped and I don't want to miss this opportunity of comparing notes with a decent fellow from the other side of No Man's Land."

But I did nothing of the kind as it would have been the immediate and abrupt end of my escapade and I still had faint hopes of getting away to Spain some time and somehow.

My Penarth excursion had not improved my health at all, and I felt very, very miserable indeed when I was back once more in Cardiff. I went to another hotel that night, the Queen's, where under the name of Henry Hughes, I told the people there exactly the same story about my luggage. Everything went quite all right except my health, as I was very sick the next morning. My temperature had gone up in an alarming way and I felt absolutely run down. But I carried on for another day. I went back that night again to the hotel, and the porter was much surprised to see me again, but I had given very liberal tips in the morning and everybody was very kind to me; the whole staff knew already that the so-called Henry Hughes was very much under the weather.

The following day was one of the darkest in my prisoner-of-war history. I felt so ill that I was at last obliged to go to the police station and give myself up; I was too sick a man to carry on with my plans, which after all required perfect health and perfect nerves.

I was sent back next day to the new camp, Lofthouse Park, near Wakefield, where I got the right medical treatment, and when I had recovered there was the usual court martial and the subsequent "vacation" at good old Chelmsford prison. I got fifty-six days this time; and my tunic, which I had sent to the Commandant at Holyport, was returned to me here, in perfect condition.

CHAPTER TWELVE

OUTWITTING THE TURK

By E. H. Keeling

When the garrison of Kut surrendered to the Turks in April, 1916, half the officers were taken to a town called Kastamuni, in the heart of Asia Minor, about 250 miles east of Constantinople. We were interned in private houses cleared for us. During the spring of 1917, Captain Tipton, Captain Sweet, Lieut. Bishop and I made up our minds to escape.

The most vital question was, what point to make for? The only land frontier was the Russian front line, 400 miles away to the east, across extremely wild and mountainous country, and it seemed impossible to escape that way. Our only chance was to get down to the Black Sea, steal a boat and make for a Russian port. If, however, we aimed at the nearest part of the coast we should almost certainly be caught, so we determined to strike for a point much further away, near the mouth of the Kizil River (far off the map to the right), where there was less probability of the beach being watched.

As we should have to walk at least 200 miles across rugged country, to say nothing of a sea voyage afterwards, the problem of food was serious. It was decided that each of us should carry about twenty pounds of food on his back, consisting of biscuits, cheese, chocolate, malted milk and dried goat. We also took a sail in sections, an axe-head for cutting a mast, knives, rope, fishing tackle, two small canteens for cooking, nails, needles and thread, bootlaces, string, spare socks, tin cups, matches, some quinine, Dover's powders and vaseline, various other odds and ends, and of course water-bottles, filled at the start with strong tea. The sail was a patchwork affair made of a sheet, a towel and the lining of two Wolseley valises, roped all round. It was intended for use with a mast to be made with our axe, if we should find a boat from which the gear had been removed, and it would also be valuable as a covering when we slept at night. Each man's load came to about thirty-five pounds, and in order to prepare ourselves for carrying such a weight across rough country we went into strict training. This was fairly easy, as we were allowed to go for long walks under guard, and when whole-day picnics were permitted we made the practical experiment of filling our luncheon knapsacks with sand.

We had a tiny map of the country on a very small scale. It was not accurate, but it told us that we must go almost due east, and it gave the position of the chief rivers and towns. We were able to buy some cheap compasses, and in case they turned out untrustworthy Bishop made a rough compass by suspending a dial with string from magnetized needles.

The question of dress caused much discussion. We decided to wear fezes at night, when they would give us the outline of natives. But we had so little knowledge of Turkish that it was useless to attempt to pass as Turks in daylight. We therefore resolved to wear our uniforms, substituting leather buttons for the brass ones, and to represent ourselves when necessary as Germans. We forged a passport in Turkish, which read as follows: –

To ALL TURKISH CIVIL AND MILITARY OFFICERS:
Give every assistance to the bearer, Captain Hermann von
Bellow, and three soldiers, who are surveying.
(*Signed*) OSMAN,
Commanding Angora Army Corps.

We could not speak German, but we did not anticipate that any Turk we met would do so either.

Sweet was quartered in a house some distance away from ours. To put the Turks off the scent of the direction we had taken he wrote Bishop a letter in which he spoke of making for a town in the south-east. This was crumpled up and left in the room that I shared with Bishop. To get out of the house was the easiest part of the whole business. Kastamuni was so remote and inaccessible that the Turks never dreamed any of us would try to get away. The guard over

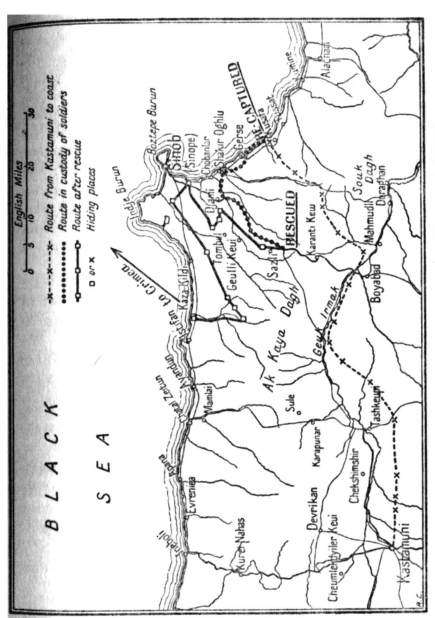

SKETCH-MAP ILLUSTRATING E. H. KEELING'S ESCAPE FROM TURKEY.

the houses was therefore very loose and casual. We had little difficulty in slipping out, at half-past ten one night in August, 1917.

We were guided to the outskirts of the town by one of our orderlies, Bombardier Prosser, who had been in the habit of prowling about after dark in a fez and a false beard. We heard afterwards that the alarm was raised within a few minutes of our departure, and that Prosser had to get back through a cordon of sentries. He knocked over one of them and reached his quarters in safety, and when the Captain of the Guard came round to feel the hearts of all the orderlies, to find out which of them had been running, Prosser could hardly be roused from an innocent sleep. We also heard afterwards that mounted gendarmes were sent in pursuit along the roads, but fortunately we gave a wide berth to all roads.

Our escape had a lamentable effect on the treatment of the officers left behind. Various punishments and restrictions were inflicted upon them for our crime. That they, for the most part, considered that escaping came first, and excused all the discomfort and suffering we brought upon their heads, was only what, knowing them, we would have expected; but it was generous of them, none the less.

Most of the stories in this book are the stories of escapes across the plains of Germany; but the problem that faced us in Asia Minor was very different. Our way lay across mountains covered with forests and intercepted by deep ravines. We were going eternally up and down, over a surface covered with loose stones. One of our greatest difficulties was to find tracks in the right direction.

We marched always eastwards as far as possible, travelling at night and lying up in a forest or gully by day. For guide we relied chiefly on Bishop, who had the best sense of direction of any of us. When we halted in the daytime the forests were a priceless asset, for in them we could light fires with impunity. So far as we could we lived on the country, keeping our knapsacks for emergencies. We picked pumpkins, beans and maize, often in the same field, but it was difficult to find them in the dark. Wheat was plentiful, but the husking of it tedious, and the result not easily digestible. It made Tipton quite ill, and he had severe pain which developed into an abscess, but he gamely carried on. Water was fairly abundant, but not always easy to locate, and this was a constant source of anxiety. One night when we had empty bottles we spent many hours looking for a path down to a stream which we could hear beneath us. After a most difficult descent by the light of two candles, during which Sweet cut his leg rather badly, we were finally brought up by a precipice dropping at least a hundred feet sheer to the stream. We got no water that night.

During our night marches we seemed to rouse all the dogs for miles round, but they never attacked us. On one occasion a man came out and obligingly called the dogs away: it was a good thing we were wearing our fezes. The rifle shots which often followed the outbreaks of barking were trying to our nerves, but the bullets seemed to be unaimed; they probably came from shepherds guarding their flocks and were intended to warn robbers of what they might expect.

So we went on for about a week, but progress was terribly slow. It was essential to get along faster, and we decided to travel by road, in the hope that the search for us there had by now been abandoned. This proved correct, and for three nights we made better progress. But we got little rest by day because of the mosquitoes, and we began to find the night marches very exhausting. Moreover, our boots were giving trouble, and would hardly last for another hundred miles of night work, even on main roads, which in Turkey are no better than English bridle-paths. So we decided to change our tactics again.

Our map showed us that the sea was only thirty miles away across a mountain range to the north-east, and we resolved to leave the road and strike for the nearest point on the coast. We could not hope to find our way in the dark, and we determined to travel openly in the daylight, asking the way and buying food whenever we could. This change of policy was successful. We were able to buy as much food as we wanted, and our appearance seemed to arouse no suspicion. On the second afternoon we reached the top of the watershed, about 4,000 feet above sea level, and the cold was so great that we sought shelter for the night. In a village near the top we were accepted as Germans, given a room in the rest house, and entertained most hospitably. On the following afternoon, thirteen days after leaving Kastamuni, we sighted the Black Sea, just east of Sinope. And next morning we were thrilled to see several boats sailing close in shore. That night we made our way down to the beach, and before dawn broke we started to look for a boat. Our hopes rose high when daylight revealed a small one, complete with mast and sail, moored a little way from the shore, on our right. We hurried towards her.

Bluff had served us so well up to this point that we were over-confident, and disaster followed. We knew it was too early for any inhabitants to be about, but we had only gone a few yards when to our horror we stumbled on a sentry. We passed him with a greeting in Turkish, but he followed and said his sergeant wished to speak to us. We turned back, only to be confronted by an armed guard of ten men.

We told the sergeant the usual story, and showed him our passport. We added that we wished to hire a boat to take us to another Turkish port, and we asked him to negotiate a passage in the boat we had seen. The sergeant suggested that we should go with him by water to a town a few miles westward, to see his officer. We said we couldn't spare the time, but he would take no refusal and compelled us to embark with part of the guard. During the passage we saw several boats that seemed to be unwatched, and we cursed the fate that had made us turn to the right instead of the left when we reached the beach that morning. We had little doubt that we could have secured a boat and got away in it at night, if we had not run into the guard.

On arrival at our destination we stayed in the boat while Sweet, who acted the part of the German officer named in the passport, went to interview the gendarme officer. He actually convinced him that we were Germans, and the officer was conducting him back to the boat when, as luck would have it, they met a naval officer, who probably knew a German when he saw one and insisted that Sweet should visit the Governor of the town. The Governor sent for the rest of us, and said that as we were Germans we would probably like to speak to an officer on the telephone. He gave the receiver to Tipton, who, poor man, knew no German but *Sprechen sie deutsch?* This he gallantly shouted half-a-dozen times into the mouthpiece. Then he put the receiver back in disgust, saying the line was out of order. But the Governor was only amusing himself; he had a description of us, and the game was up. He was politeness itself, and there was nothing for us to do but to try and look pleasant too.

Orders came from Kastamuni to send us back to that town, and we started with heavy hearts next morning, escorted by a guard of nine soldiers in charge of a sergeant. During a halt at a coastguard barrack we found a cobbler who mended our sorely-tired boots. In the light of subsequent events he was godsend.

On the third day's march, we were crossing a pass, about 4,000 feet above sea level, when the incredible thing happened. The road was built into the side of a cliff, with a steep bank, thickly wooded, sloping down on our left. Suddenly we were fired upon. Bullets came in quick succession from the wood, accompanied by shouts of *Askar, askar, teslim ol*! (Soldiers, surrender!) The sergeant of our guard at once ordered his men to lie down and open fire, while Sweet, Bishop and I, feeling the road was no place for us, dived left into the wood; escape was barred on the other side by the cliff. Tipton was riding the sergeant's pony and could not get away at all. After about a minute the firing stopped, and Bishop and myself crept gingerly back on to the road, to find that one of our guard had been shot dead and three wounded, while the others had surrendered to four men who had emerged from the wood. These were alert, weather-beaten men, each wearing a couple of bandoliers stuffed full of cartridges and a long knife in his belt. Two of them turned out to be Circassians, one a Georgian, and the fourth an Armenian.

The change in our fortunes was staggering; but at first we had not the slightest idea what to make of it. Were the attackers brigands, and if so what fate was in store for ourselves? Had we fallen from the frying pan into the fire? But another and more pleasant surprise was to come.

The leader, one of the Circassians, embraced us warmly and cried, *Allons, enfants de la patrie!* To this cordial but somewhat inappropriate greeting we replied in French, but we soon found that this was the only French he knew. So we continued the conversation in halting Turkish. He explained that he and his comrades were not brigands, as we supposed, but political rebels who were "wanted" by the Government and had fled to the mountains. They called themselves *Arkadash* (Comrades). The leader, whose name was Ragib, had been in jail for his share in the murder of the Grand Vizier in 1913.

He heard of our recapture and had arranged the ambush for the sole purpose of rescuing us. Like us, he and his comrades wished to get to Russia, and he undertook to find a boat within a few days.

The offer was much too good to refuse, but before accepting it we had to look for Sweet. He had not reappeared from the wood and we had no idea which way he had gone. All of us, including the soldiers, searched and shouted for him, but without result. After waiting an hour we were obliged to leave without him. What happened to him will be told later.

After releasing the disarmed soldiers, who went away along the road to fetch a cart for their wounded, the outlaws and ourselves set off in the other direction, and lay in a wood till evening. When darkness fell Ragib and the other Mohammadans went off for some purpose which we did not discover, while the Armenian took us back towards the coast. Each of us now carried a rifle taken from the soldiers – no light addition to our load. It was pitch dark, and as our route lay along rough tracks and streams strewn with boulders we all took some pretty bad tosses. We were dead beat when at last, after nine hours, we reached a hiding-place in a wood said to be one hour from the coast. We three fell asleep at once, but the indefatigable Armenian went off immediately to a friendly farmhouse close by and re-appeared with a splendid breakfast of fried eggs, yoghourt, milk, cheese and bread.

During the next four days we changed our hiding-place each night. We were joined by several other men who wished to accompany us to Russia. Not only food but bedding was brought to us; the outlaws could never do enough to make us comfortable and would accept no payment. But we were not the only living things in that bedding.

On the fifth day after our rescue Ragib rejoined us and said that his plans for a boat were going well but the date of embarkation could not yet be fixed. He had heard that 2,000 soldiers and gendarmes were searching for us, and we again changed our bivouac, first to a maize field and then to a wood. To relieve the monotony of the long days a man was sent to the nearest town to get playing cards and tobacco, and we played piquet with the outlaw chief. On the eighth day news arrived that a boat had been chartered, but we continued in hiding while our friends collected food for the voyage. Four days later we left the wood and found a party of ten outlaws assembled, with a pony carrying bread, flour, and honey. They told us that while collecting this food in a village they had been surrounded by gendarmes and had been obliged to cut their way out. One of the band and one gendarme had been killed in the fighting.

Next day we marched five miles to yet another hiding-place, close to the point at which we were to embark, and a messenger was despatched to find out whether arrangements had been made for the boat to pick us up that night. When he returned shortly before dark he made the bitter announcement that the whole scheme had to be abandoned. The Government had ordered that all boats should be hauled up on shore and the sails and oars deposited with the police. They were much incensed by an alliance of rebels with prisoners of war, and were leaving no stone unturned to catch us.

There was nothing for it but to move to an entirely different part of the coast, where the precautions might perhaps be less strict. We marched west throughout that night and the next, and then Ragib and four of the others went off to negotiate for another boat, while the rest of us sought a fresh hiding-place in a thick forest. Here we spent a further week awaiting news. Heavy rain fell, and the nights were very cold, but our friends were past masters of woodcraft and kept a fire twenty feet long burning night and day. Local farmers who knew them brought us food. Coarse unleavened bread was our usual meal, but twice a sheep was roasted whole, tied to a pole which revolved on two Y-shaped posts driven into the ground before the fire. Having gorged themselves with mutton, the outlaws seemed to require no further food for fully forty-eight hours.

At last Ragib returned with splendid news. He had bought a boat from a Turk for £400 in gold, of which our friends seemed to have plenty, including many English sovereigns. The crew had not been told of the sale; they merely received orders from the owner to put in at a certain point on the coast to ship brushwood. The pony was now loaded up with bread, and after marching for eight hours we bivouacked at 3.30 a.m. in a clump of bushes about five minutes from the beach, at a point about thirty miles west of Sinope. We had covered nearly 150 miles since we were recaptured, and 350 since we left Kastamuni.

The next day was the most eventful of all. The boat had arrived during the night, and when dawn broke we hurried down to the shore, seized the crew, and tied them up to trees, according to plan. We then proceeded to ballast the boat with stones from the beach. It was a fishing boat, twenty-five feet long and of about two and a half tons, with dipping lug-sail and four oars. A stream ran into the sea a few yards away, and we filled our water-bottles and a tin and a cask we found in the boat. We had about ten gallons of water altogether.

As we worked a soldier appeared with a rifle, but we wasted no time in arguing with him; we just tied him also to a tree. (We heard afterwards that he was the advance man of a patrol, and that when he reported what had happened motorboats with machine-guns were sent out to look for us.) By sunrise everything was ready and we pushed off. There were fourteen of us on board – eleven outlaws and our three selves.

While we had been embarking, another boat, somewhat bigger than ours, had been creeping along the coast, and we decided to anticipate any attempt she might make to stop us. Accordingly all the rifles were hidden and we quietly pulled alongside. Then we suddenly jumped up and in true pirate fashion levelled our rifles at the crew. There were five of them, but they were unarmed and surrendered at once. We decided to take both them and their boat along with us, and two of the outlaws were placed on board as a sort of prize crew. Being escaping prisoners ourselves we enjoyed having prisoners of our own, but I doubt whether the captured crew saw the humorous side of their position.

Both vessels now hoisted sail, and as a five-knot breeze was blowing from the east we decided to make for the Crimea, straight across the Black Sea, instead of going east along the coast. The Black Sea can be very rough, as its name implies, and to attempt to cross it in a small boat was risky, but we hoped that our luck would hold. Within two hours we must have been out of sight from the land, and there was no sign of any pursuit, nor did the chance of meeting a German submarine seem worth worrying about. Our chief anxiety was for our own boat. She had to be baled out frequently, the boom was badly sprung, and repairs to the sail and rigging were much overdue. In the afternoon the wind dropped and we made the captured crew row. Soon after mid-day we saw the last of the mountains of Turkey that we had known so well.

Our direction was north-east, but our compasses had been taken from us when we were recaptured and we had only the sun and stars to steer by. We were astonished to find that although some of the captured crew had been at sea all their lives none of them had the slightest idea which was the north or any other star. The three of us therefore took watches at the helmsman's side, to make sure that he kept the right course. It is hardly necessary to add that we put everybody on a strict ration of water.

Next morning we were making good progress under a north-east breeze when the other boat lowered her sail and signalled for help. She had broken her rudder, and we decided to take her crew on board and abandon her. Before doing so we changed her boom for ours, and we also took over several bags of grain and flour, a keg containing about two gallons of water, and a pump, which saved us the labour of baling. Our own small boat now carried nineteen persons, and most of the ballast was thrown overboard. The wind again dropped, and for most of the second and third days rowing was necessary. The bread we had brought on board had become mouldy, and after making a fire with floor boards from our boat we concocted a sort of porridge by boiling some of the flour in sea water. You cannot drink salt water, but you can use it for cooking.

Just as it was getting dark on the third day, we sighted to the north-west what looked like a range of mountains, but we could not be absolutely sure they were not clouds, and darkness fell before we could get near enough to decide.

With a strong breeze we made good progress that night, and at dawn next morning we definitely sighted land. Once more the wind dropped, but the captured crew, who cherished the mistaken idea that they would be sent back to Turkey, redoubled their energies at the oars, while we finished off what was left of the bread and water. It took us seven hours to reach the shore, but at noon, after a voyage of two hundred and fifty miles, lasting three and a quarter days, we pulled in to the fashionable watering place of Alupka, on the east coast of the Crimea. It was seven weeks since we had left Kastamuni. Alupka was virtually the nearest point in Russia to the place at which we had embarked, so our rough reckoning had not been far out.

We had learned the Russian words for "English prisoners", and on approaching the shore we shouted out *Angliski plenny* to a man bathing in the sea. But, as so often happens to an Englishman who tries to speak the language of the country he is visiting, he replied "I speak English very well."

Opposite the point at which we landed were the municipal baths. Ever since leaving Kastamuni what we had been looking forward to most eagerly was not good food or drink, linen sheets, or European society, but *hot baths*, and within half-an-hour of landing we were lying in the first we had known for nearly two months.

The rest was easy. Kerensky was still in power in Russia, and Tipton and Bishop got home without difficulty. Not long afterwards, to the sorrow of all who knew him, Tipton was killed while flying in France. Poor Sweet had none of our luck. We learned after the Armistice that when the outlaws opened fire on our guard he decided that the best thing to do was to get clear away, and made no attempt to return to the road on which we waited for him. He pluckily made his way alone to the coast, but was there again recaptured. He was taken back to Kastamuni with a guard of seventy soldiers, led in procession through the town, and kept in the civil jail for six weeks. He was then interned in another prisoners' camp at Yozgad, where I grieve to say he died of influenza just before the War ended.

I stayed on for three months in the Black Sea in an attempt to get some of our comrades away from Turkey, with the help of the Russian Navy and our outlaw friends. One dark night we crossed to the Turkish coast in a Russian destroyer, and the Armenian and two of the Circassians were landed to take a letter to Kastamuni. This letter arranged a rendezvous on the coast, to which these three would guide any prisoners who cared to make the venture, and to which I should return in a fortnight's time. The scheme failed because the Circassians quarrelled with the Armenian and murdered him soon after they landed. When I got back to Russia I found the Bolshevists in power, and I had some difficulty in making my way to England, via Finland, Lapland, Sweden, Norway, the Shetland Islands and Aberdeen.

Most of our outlaw friends settled down in the Caucasus, but Ragib, a prince of adventurers, found employment in the British Secret Service.

CHAPTER THIRTEEN

HIDE-AND-SEEK IN EASTERN SEAS

By Hellmut von Mücke

On Sunday, 9 November, 1914, the 3,000 tons cruiser *Emden* stood in the southern part of the Indian Ocean.

Her raiding activities had caused suspension of trade around the coast of India, and her Commander, Captain von Miller, decided to make use of this pause to destroy the cables and the wireless station on the Cocos or Keeling Islands. I was second-in-command of the *Emden*, and so it was my duty to take charge of the landing party. We went ashore fifty strong and began our work at sunrise, and our relations with the British telegraphists on the islands were quite peaceable. They were civilians, and therefore did not interest us. We learnt from them, to our surprise, that one of the last Reuter telegrams had reported that the Iron Cross had been conferred on our ship for her work. They then invited us to play a tennis match with them, but I am sorry to say that we couldn't accept this invitation. While we were working away on shore under the palms which screened the view on all sides, the *Emden* sighted what appeared at first to be an old coal ship. When it got closer, however, it was recognised as the 6,000 tons Australian cruiser *Sidney*, and before we could get back to the *Emden* she weighed anchor and both ships disappeared fighting over the horizon. The fight ended with the sinking of our ship, but we could not see this and did not hear of it till three weeks later.

I was now left with forty-nine men marooned on British islands in the middle of the Indian Ocean, completely cut off. It was obvious that if we didn't get away at once we would soon be made prisoners of war, and the only thing chance offered as far as we could see was an old sailing schooner of ninety-seven tons named *Ayesha*, which had been lying there at Port Refuge, out of commission and crewless, for many years. Helter-skelter and with all speed we made her ready for sea, and managed to take her through the reefs that very evening. We heard later on that in the darkness we passed quite close to the *Sidney*, which had returned to the islands in pursuit of us after sinking the *Emden*. She was waiting outside the entrance for enough light to enable her to sail in and capture us.

The *Ayesha* leaked badly and her sails kept tearing, which made it very doubtful whether we should get far. Furthermore the monsoon was blowing and caused heavy storms in which we had a number of narrow escapes. In every way it was an uncomfortable voyage. The schooner had been fitted up to accommodate a crew of only five, whereas we were fifty. We had no funds except a single shilling piece which we had happened to find on board, and the absence of razors everywhere produced fine full beards. We had no tobacco either, and tried to make up for this by smoking tea leaves, and we gave up wearing our uniforms so as not to wear them out. Moreover, our navigation equipment was very defective – in fact it consisted entirely of a single chart which covered half the world. We were three weeks at sea in this old hulk, and then we found ourselves in the neighbourhood of the Dutch island of Sumatra, to the north-east.

I expected to find British and Japanese naval forces around Padang, but decided to risk it and enter the harbour there. And the good luck that seemed to be with us did not fail us now. For, when we arrived at Padang, we learned from the Dutch that a Japanese ship, which had been cruising up and down outside the harbour for nearly a fortnight on the look-out for us, had left to coal just three hours before our mast-tops came into sight. Several German merchant ships, which had retreated into neutral waters, were lying at anchor in the roads, and I decided to induce one of them to put to sea and meet me outside. But the Dutch Government made a lot of difficulties. In fact they tried to intern us and the *Ayesha* under some of the so-called Law of Nations. But I appealed to another paragraph of the same Law and declared that violence would be answered with violence. In this way I succeeded in getting our schooner recognised as a man-of-war. Good old *Ayesha*! What would you have thought of that a few days before when you were dreaming among the corals and palms of Port Refuge?

We were twenty-four hours ashore at Padang and when we had completed our secret arrangements with the German merchant steamer, we put to sea again. Our rendezvous was a long way from the coast, and while we were waiting about we twice met hostile steamers and tried to capture them, but without success. In this way we whiled away the time, and a fortnight later the steamer from Padang reached us. We immediately transferred ourselves aboard her and sank the *Ayesha*.

Here, too, fortune favoured us, for at this very time the British auxiliary cruiser *Himalaya*, which was also in pursuit of us, captured a former tender of the *Emden*, not six hours from where we were.

I had learnt at Padang of the alliance between the Central Powers and Turkey, so I decided now to make for the Red Sea and to land in Arabia on Turkish soil. But unfortunately, our new steamer, which had been a coaster in China, had no charts of the Indian Ocean or the Red Sea, so we had to do the best we could without.

However, we got along all right, crossed the ocean and passed the British fortress, Perim, at the narrow entrance of the Red Sea, without being challenged. I now set our course for the Arabian town Hodeida, but since we knew nothing about the situation there we were very anxious about our reception. However we took every precaution and approached the harbour in the darkness, and when we were close in we were delighted to see a row of electric lights. Years previously I had met a French engineer who had told me that he was employed by the Turkish Government in railroad construction from Hodeida to Damascus; so we concluded that this row of lights was a modern harbour, and that the railway was finished. To make sure of this, I embarked my crew in the boats and sent the steamer off with instructions for another rendezvous at sea later on; and this too was a lucky move. For when we had rowed close up to the breakwater with its electric lights, the sun suddenly came out, which happens very rapidly in the tropics and without the warning of dawn, and we saw to our dismay that the breakwater was furnished with two masts, four funnels and armoured turrets. It was the big French cruiser *Desaix*. We had no desire to board her, so we dropped away as quickly as possible. It was three months since we had had any definite news of the war situation, but it looked very much as though Hodeida was now occupied by French troops. However, in spite of that, there was nothing for us to do now but to disembark secretly outside the town, and we planned to hide in the desert during the day and send a disguised officer into Hodeida to reconnoitre at night.

Our boats were overloaded, but we passed through the heavy surf safely and landed. Then we collected our kit and were just about to push off inland, when we suddenly noticed that our landing had not been unobserved and we were by no means alone. Not far away, scattered behind the cover of the sand dunes, was a whole company of men, far outnumbering my own, watching us. They were dressed in red and blue uniforms and I supposed them to be French auxiliary troops. We at once took cover too, and waited for them to open fire. But nothing happened. No doubt they were just as mystified about us as we were about them. Then about a dozen of them stood up without arms and flourished a rag which they evidently hoped would be recognised as a white one. I immediately went forward to meet them and an exciting palaver took place. They were Bedouins, and the whole dozen talked at once, gesticulating violently and shouting themselves hoarse; but it was all in Arabian, which I did not understand a bit. However, it was fairly obvious that what *they* wanted to know was exactly what I wanted to know – whether we were friends or foes. At last I thought of showing them a German coin which we had got at Padang, which had the Kaiser's head on it. They recognised this, and we then learned that they were friends and that the country was still in the hands of the Turks. So we set off to Hodeida, and met on the way the whole Turkish garrison armed with guns and cavalry. Our disembarkation had been reported in the town as an enemy invasion, and they were coming to give battle. However we explained our situation and received information and advice. Alas, the railway I was hoping to find did not exist, and the Turks told us that since there were British and French naval forces in the Red Sea we shouldn't be able to get any further that way.

The best thing we could do, they said, was to march to Sana, up in the mountains, the capital of Yemen, and take the caravan road from there right across Arabia to the Mediterranean. This journey, on camel back, would take seven or eight weeks, but it was better than being captured on the sea in seven or eight hours, and I decided to take their advice. So we set off, and climbed out of the burning desert until we were 12,000 feet up in the Yemen mountains and frequently above the clouds. The days were fresh and the nights bitterly cold, and sometimes there was frost and even snow.

When we arrived in Sana we were not really surprised to find that we could not get any further. The country to the north was in revolt and strong Bedouin tribes were interfering with all communication. The Turks in Hodeida had been perfectly well aware of this, but they had induced us to go to Sana because that town was expecting Arabian attacks at any moment and was so short of arms that it would no doubt find the four Maxim guns which we had with us very useful.

I told the authorities at Sana that I was not at all interested in the Arabians; I only wanted to make my way back to the coast and get on by sea. But they would not hear of this. Such a journey, they said, would mean certain death and they could not undertake the responsibility. I replied that the responsibility for my men was my own affair and they then handed me a paper which they said was a telegram from Mecca which had just been brought in by camel-rider. This telegram purported to be an order from my superiors in Germany that I was not to undertake the hazardous march home, but was to place myself and my men at the disposal of the Turks. I read this and told the Turks that I refused to recognise orders that were not sent in code – although as a matter of fact I had no cipher at hand for decoding messages. I then hurried off to collect a caravan, but I was told that none of the camels in Sana were available.

The Turks were clearly doing all they could to keep me with them. However, I was expecting this difficulty, and I had already got into touch through spies with the tribes outside. If I could not get camels from the Turks, I would get them from the rebels. But unfortunately they wanted a great deal of cash, and my funds did not exceed three shillings. Now there was an old but very rich ex-General named Ibrahim Pasha living in Sana, and I paid a friendly visit to him and scared him out of his wits. I told him that the rebel tribes were advancing and that it was only a matter of days before the town surrendered and was sacked. The rebels, of course, would rob him of every penny he possessed; so I suggested that he should place his cash in my care, and that I would guard it for him and give him also a guarantee in the form of a cheque on the German National Bank, which he could discharge in Berlin after the war. The good old Ibrahim agreed to this, and in a very short time I had bought all the camels I needed from the rebels.

I realised that I must now proceed with great secrecy and cunning, and decided to lay a false trail, for there were a great many spies about, and I did not want the French cruiser, which was still at anchor in Hodeida harbour, to get wind of our real intentions. So I made an arrangement with the Turks that they should get some sailing boats ready for us at certain places on the coast, and as I particularly wanted this plot to be given away I emphasized the necessity for keeping it strictly secret. My real plans were, of course, quite different. I had met by chance a French speaking Turkish soldier, an engineer, who had been called up for military service. He told me that a steam launch, belonging to the government, was lying in a bay north of Hodeida. It was his job to keep this launch in order, and he showed me his last report about its excellent condition and the coal and water supplies. I meant to have that boat, but neither he nor anyone else must know of my intention, and my first step was to get the engineer attached to me as my interpreter. We then collected our caravan of camels and rode off as if to keep our appointment with the sailing ships which the Turks had arranged for us. When we had put a sufficient distance between ourselves and Sana, I took the engineer into my confidence, and told him that if he liked I would take him with me aboard the launch. He was most enthusiastic and expressed the greatest delight at the thought of getting out of this God forsaken country and joining the fighting lines at the Suez Canal. That was his heart's desire, he said. The launch, however, had been put out of commission, and we should need several days to clear her up, so I separated from my caravan and hurried on ahead with a few selected men, including the engineer.

It was a most exhausting journey. Not only had we to move quickly and save as much time as possible in order to have the launch ready for the rest of the caravan when it arrived, but we also had to avoid the usual caravan routes so as not to be seen. So we rushed along for three days and two nights without a wink of sleep and only stopping in order to change our animals. By the time we reached the coast we were practically dead. Then we looked about for the launch. It was there all right, but only the upper part of its funnel was above the surface of the water. I thought that my short stay in Arabia had prepared me for anything; I thought that after living with the Turks nothing would ever astonish me again, but I was certainly unprepared to hear this engineer, who had accompanied me on such an exhausting journey without saying a word, now calmly confessing that the launch had been lying there like this, submerged and in a rotten condition, for years.

I delivered a speech to him of considerable frankness, but he merely interrupted it to ask with a shrug of the shoulders whether I really believed he could report anything so unfavourable to Constantinople. So I gave it up.

But what were we to do now? There remained, of course, the chance of the sailing ships which the Turks had undertaken to prepare for me, but no doubt the enemy already knew about these and I refused to consider them. I ordered the caravan to return one day's journey inland and to wait there until further notice, and I myself rode to Hodeida. Then the expected happened. That morning, at the time fixed for our departure, a gunboat suddenly appeared in the bay and came to anchor near the boats which were awaiting us. So that was that. Both sea passage and land passage were now blockaded; we seemed to be stopped on all sides. But every mouse finds a hole. I was told at Hodeida that they wished to give a banquet in my honour, and I was asked what day would suit me best. I was getting used now to turning life to my own advantage at a moment's notice. No doubt all the nobilities around would be invited to this banquet and there would be much talk about it, and the French cruiser and all the gunboats further out would get to hear of it. All these ships were watching and waiting for the moment when we should attempt to leave by sea. But if there was to be a banquet given for me, on that day they would relax their vigilance. That would be a nice day for us to start. What then would be the best day to suit everyone? Saturday, I said.

Preparations were at once made for a tremendous banquet and it became one of the chief topics of conversation.

Meanwhile, in secret and by bribery, I procured two sailing boats in a bay north of Hodeida, and when I left the town on horseback on the Saturday morning no one smelt a rat, since it was my daily habit. But it was also my daily habit to return, and this time I didn't. My waiting caravan had already received their orders, and in the afternoon everyone and everything was ready at the appointed place. We set sail shortly before sunset at the very moment that I was expected to dinner in Hodeida. In spite of the great heat, I fear that that dinner grew cold. We had no charts at all, so we sailed at a venture, and at sunrise on Sunday morning found ourselves lying becalmed in a position which we did not like at all, that is to say just in front of Kamaran, the harbour of which was used as an advanced base for British gunboats. The calm kept us there until sunset, and at any moment we expected to see the mast-tops of gunboats which relieved each other regularly at that place. But nothing happened. Had I calculated aright? I had chosen Saturday purposely as the day of our departure – for week-ends are sacred.

In our two boats we sailed north through extensive coral-reefs, where larger ships could hardly sail or anchor by day and certainly not by night. I led the way with the smaller boat and a crew of fifteen men; the second boat, which was much larger, carried the rest, and our many sick. Dysentery, malaria and typhoid were rife among us owing to the badness of the climate, the lack of medical supplies and proper clothes, bad nourishment and extreme bodily hardships. Sometimes we had as many as 80 per cent sick.

Even *our* boats could not sail in the reef area at night, and so just before sunset we decided to anchor. But the Arab we had taken along with us, who called himself a pilot, misguided us. My boat struck on a reef, but luckily crossed it without much damage in spite of the now heavy seas. But the second boat, through trying to avoid our reef, struck on a neighbouring one and foundered. In a few moments the heavy waves hammered her against the pointed corals and she broke up. The forecastle remained hanging on the reef, and the rest sank. Then the sun set and total darkness covered everything. The reef between us prevented me from going to the rescue and I was obliged to anchor. Two-thirds of my men were now drifting around in the gloom, most of them seriously ill and unable to swim. Moreover there were sharks about. We tried in vain to direct the swimmers towards us by whistling and calling. We heard their voices drifting past us with the current. We tried to show light, but every lantern was blown out by the stormy wind, and the torches we had brought from the *Emden* missed fire. Nothing remained but our carefully preserved signal cartridges, so we fired these and the white sparkling stars streamed up into the sky, brightly illuminating our surroundings, but also betraying our position for a distance of miles.

However these brought the men struggling towards us, but when scarcely half of them had been hauled aboard it was clear that our load was too heavy for the small boat. So everything unimportant, followed later by nearly all the fresh water and food, went overboard to lighten her. Practically nothing remained but our arms and ammunition, which are the last a soldier parts with. At length, after two hours, we got the last of the wrecked crew aboard, but the gunwale of our own boat was now not more than one and a half feet above the water-line. We were now in a dilemma. We could not continue our general northerly course against the north wind. A southerly course before the wind would have taken us into the open sea. We had only enough fresh water and provisions left to last us for two days, and it would take us about six days to reach the coast against the north wind. But in the middle of the night our luck turned, the wind changed to south and we steered for the Arabian coast, which we reached safely.

We now made a second attempt to get on by land. We had disembarked at a place whose name I have forgotten, and there we managed to procure some camels from an Arab sheik. His son was sick, and from the description given of the illness it sounded like malaria. The sheik asked me if I could do anything for him, and though we had no medical supplies whatever, I wanted his friendship and protection, so I said I could. We then concocted a mixture of water, lime juice and vinegar and added a charge of purgatives and presented it, in a bottle, to the sheik with very careful instructions. It was to be taken three times a day for five days. Any departure from these rules would endanger the patient's life and the father himself must keep the bottle in his control.

We then set off on our camels for the north. A little later, when we were within a day's journey of the small Turkish fortress Djidda, shadows suddenly sprang up all round us in the moonlight among the sand drifts, and a sharp rifle fire broke out in front. We took cover at once and brought our Maxims into action, which succeeded in arresting this surprise attack just in time; but it was not long before the blowing sand got into the mechanism of our guns and jammed them. At day-break we found that we were surrounded by a company of Bedouins, about five hundred strong it seemed, whereas only about twenty-five of my own men were fit for fighting. For three days and three nights they kept us busy with rifle fire, dodging about in front of us and on our flanks among the sand dunes; three days and nights at a temperature of 135 degrees, practically without food and water, since most of the camels which carried our supplies were killed. I lost a number of men too, killed and wounded, but eventually we managed to break through the ambush and got into Djidda. Here we learnt certain things from which we concluded that the recent ambush had been arranged by the Emir of Mecca, who as a Turkish subject was really our ally, but had already made a secret pact with the British Government, which became public three months later.

Several of my men had been killed and many wounded; our ammunition was about exhausted; the mast-tops of enemy gunboats could be seen standing out beyond Djidda harbour, and our allies on land were not to be trusted. It was not a hopeful outlook.

It was not long before the Emir sent a friendly message to us offering his protection. He regretted very much that he could not guarantee the obedience of the wild tribes on the coast, and, so that we should be spared further attacks, he invited us to proceed into the mountains to his sacred city of Mecca. He would send forces to protect us on our way thither and beyond. I accepted this generous offer with the deepest gratitude, and while he was assembling his troops in the narrow defiles round Mecca in order to slaughter us as we passed through, we shipped aboard a sailing boat once more and returned to sea. It was early morning and a stiff southerly breeze carried us along. We had got out of the clutches of the Emir, but there were still the gunboats to be reckoned with. At present there were none to be seen; no doubt they believed that we were already on our way like lambs to the slaughter; but soon they would learn the truth and easily catch up with us at daybreak before we could reach the protecting coral reefs once more. So I anchored in a small concealed bay just out of sight of Djidda, in spite of the protest of my officers who urged me to sail on and take advantage of the favourable wind.

Next day, in full daylight, we sailed on unmolested and anchored safely among the coral reefs. After we had lain there for two hours we saw a bright light about half a mile off steering past us from south to north along the edge of the reefs. It was a gunboat which had clearly been waiting for us at the entrance to the reefs at sunrise and was now going north in search of us, supposing that we must have passed already. So my precautions the previous night had been well taken. When darkness came again the gunboat was obliged to make for the open sea, and with her disappearance our last enemy had gone.

We sailed quietly onwards. In Northern Arabia we had to take to the land once more and so without further incident we reached the southern end of the Syrian railway, where we exchanged our camel saddles for railway carriage cushions. A few weeks later we delivered the flag of the *Emden* to our German Naval Authorities in Constantinople.

So in June 1915, among the roses of Constantinople, ended our journey which had begun in November 1914 under the palms of the Cocos Islands in the Far East.

CHAPTER FOURTEEN

THROUGH THE CAMP SEWER

By Ernest Pearce

The morning of 21 March, 1918, was an eventful one. Eight hours shell-fire had blown to pieces everything required to equip a battlefield, and the few dazed and bewildered soldiers – self included – that remained upright were herded together by the Germans and escorted to their camp at Bullecourt.

We were guests of Mother Nature now, and I didn't blame the dear old lady for her empty larder. There were too many calls made on it by hungry German soldiery and French civilians. When we arrived at Brussels we were given a long black loaf to share among many. It was impossible to collect the crumbs, as they were the same colour as the ground. Cattle trucks to hold fifty were placed at our disposal and we were conveyed to Dulmen in Westphalia, where a basin of barley soup and a staff of German officers were waiting for us. The officers barked orders just the same as our own used to do, and the sentries tried to march us. But we'd done soldiering, so we just ambled along. We were taken to Dulmen Camp, where we were given an emergency parcel and inoculated several times. The parcels were consumed at one meal. The inoculations lingered longer.

I was a boy of eighteen years at this time and filled with the spirit of adventure, and the prospect of being caged behind barbed wire didn't appeal to me. I began thinking of escape at once. But I gathered from inquiries that the camp was almost surrounded by bogs and that several chaps who had tried to get away had all been caught. However, we hadn't been there very long before we were sent to a place named Limburg on the River Lahn, about a hundred miles further south. This was a beautiful town, built on the slope of a great hill on top of which was our camp. The houses were red-topped among trees that looked ever so green and fresh. It would have been a delightful place if we'd had enough to eat. I used to go round the huts of the French and Belgians who had been invalided back from various working-camps. They were receiving parcels from home, and I used to look longingly at them whilst they ate. Some were good natured and gave me a biscuit. Others gave a growl. However, we were soon sent out in sections to various works, and I was sent back north to work in a brown coal mine at Fortuna Griiba, Bergheim, near Cologne, and about ninety kilometres from Holland, where I soon learnt to speak a bit of German, and it wasn't long before I was promoted to interpreter. Up to then the Germans and we had had great difficulties in understanding each other, but now life became a little smoother for some. Not for me. It wasn't an easy job. The Germans thought I was thoroughly efficient and my pals knew I wasn't, and caused misunderstandings more than once to get a rise out of me; so I was harassed all round. However, I mustn't grumble for the job did me one bit of good – it brought me in touch with a Frenchman named Georges Duprez, who also wanted to escape. I soon made a great pal of him, and a better man I have no wish to meet. He had been a prisoner for about three years and had already tried to escape fourteen times. He also possessed a map of the district; so all we wanted now was a compass, and Georges knew of a Russian who had one. So we acquired it by trading him biscuits and tins of conserve for it, and promising him we would let him come with us. I felt sorry for these poor Russian prisoners. They were like men without a country. They received no parcels from home, and had nothing to eat but the German rations of cabbage soup and black bread.

We now looked round for ways and means of escape, and Georges decided that our best way was through the camp sewer. This sewer was a tunnel about three feet in diameter and two hundred yards long, and it drained the various camps into the waste workings of the mine. There were a number of camps, all separate, and the mouth of the sewer came out between the Italian and French quarters and was covered by a sort of gate grid which was only guarded by day. The waste workings were ninety yards below ground, so the gradient of the tunnel from the mine to the surface was about one inch in three. At first I didn't fancy the idea of crawling up this sewer, but I finally fell in with the scheme. We worked in the mine from 4.30 a.m. to 6 p.m. and our plan was to slip away from our gangs one night at knocking-off time, get into the waste workings and crawl up to the surface. The sentry over the grid would have gone off duty by this time. The gangs, however, were closely guarded, and we were counted at the top of the mine by the under-officer every night except one – our weekly bath-night. On this night there was always a lot of disorganisation and we decided to take advantage of it. At about this time a batch of Scots prisoners joined our camp, and one young Scot among them, Alex Miller, a real Highlander, begged of us to let him go with us So that made three of us, and we were now ready.

Next bath-night the list was headed by 500 Russians to be bathed in batches of ten, so taking advantage of the confusion we slipped our gangs and crept up the sewer to the surface. It was an unpleasant journey. The sentry at the top had knocked off, so we opened the grid and were just walking out into the open when a party of French prisoners came by under guard. We dropped down, but the Frenchmen had seen us and whispered "Bon Voyage". Luckily the guard was on the other side of them, so didn't notice us. I should have hated being caught again after that sewer. Georges was so impatient to get going that he was up again and off before the gang was properly out of the way.

We weren't slow in following, and so commenced our international cross-country run. We ran and ran, clear of the works and into the open country, until we were exhausted. It was early morning now, and as we trotted along we came to a stream. Georges said he was thirsty, so grasping a sapling that was growing out of the bank with one hand and his coffee can in the other he lay downsides the bank to catch a canful of water. But the sapling came out, and Georges went in – head first. Alex and I fished him out with a stick that we broke from a small tree. We didn't half laugh; but Georges didn't see the fun of it like we did. In fact he was very cross and let us know it in a few well-chosen remarks. He stripped naked, there and then – everything came off, even his boots and socks – and with his wet garments slung over his shoulder we set off across country once more. Grotesque was nothing to how Georges looked as he hopped, skipped and hobbled stark naked through the fields. He'd been a powerful chap once, but years of captivity and food shortage had made him very thin.

We found a haystack a bit further on and decided to lie up in it till Georges and his things were properly dry. Alex and I hoisted him up pyramid style while he pulled a hole in the top of the stack big enough to hold the three of us. First of all we arranged Georges' clothes at the bottom of the hole and covered them with hay. Then we crept in ourselves and laid on them to dry and press them. Alex was last in, and plugged up the entrance of the hole from the inside with more hay so as to conceal it. Then we slept; but not for long.

We were woken up by voices at the foot of the stack. Then the stack began to shake. So did I. Someone was climbing to the top of it, and in a moment or two we heard voices immediately above us. Blind they must have been, or Alex was an expert at camouflage. They were talking about taking half the stack away; but after a bit they decided that as it was close to dinner-time they'd wait till after they'd had dinner.

They then climbed down the stack again and left the field. So did we. We got out of that hole and made off across the field like hares – Georges still carrying his clothes – and hid in a ditch at the other end of it. While we lay here we discovered that Georges had lost the map and compass. They must have fallen out of his pocket, he said, when he fell in the stream. Luckily, however, I'd taken a compass bearing at the start and checked it up with the stars, so I knew our direction lay between the Great Bear and the North Star. When dark came we set off again and lay up in a wood at dawn.

Georges wanted to light a fire; but Alex and I pointed out that it might draw attention to us. Georges pointed out that his clothes weren't dry yet. So we lighted the fire and it drew the attention of some school-children who were passing. As soon as they saw us they ran away screaming "Gefangene!" – which is German for "Prisoners!" So we had to change our hiding place, and all that day we moved from one part of the wood to another. And all day long we could hear people shouting in different parts of the wood as they searched for us. When night fell I took our bearings by the stars, and we started off again. I got a rick in the neck which didn't wear off for weeks from looking up at the sky so much.

But we hadn't gone fifty yards out of the wood when a man sprang up from behind a manure heap in a cabbage field and shouted "Halten!" Georges whispered to me "Parlez veet!" so I answered the German's question "Wer ist's?" (Who are you?") by replying "Drei Arbeiter nach hause gehend" ("Three workers going home").

He then ordered us to "Come here": we did, and left him knocked out, Georges doing the rough stuff. Another wood befriended us at dawn, and we found a hut in it in which we spent the day. Georges would have his fire again, and since the hut had no vent except the door he nearly choked us. He wasn't even content with a small fire; he made a large one and eventually set fire to the roof. Personally, I wasn't sorry to go, for my eyes were raw with smoke. On and on we went, and a few days later we came to another haystack. This stack stood near two cottages in a field. It was already broad daylight when we saw it, and there were people working the other side of the field. But we were desperate that morning, so we worked our way along until we got the stack between us and the cottages, and then we crept up to it on all fours and burrowed into it as before. But we couldn't sleep, for the voices of the people in the field drew closer and closer to us all day as they worked. We found we'd been hiding on the outskirts of a village – a one-street affair – and, since the street was in line with our route – the Bee Line – we decided to risk it. So we lined up and marched noisily down the street like the German policemen do, myself timing the step by calling out, "Links! Recht! Links! Recht!" ("Left! Right!"). We'd almost got to the other end when suddenly an estaminet door opened and some "Jerrys" came out. As soon as they saw us they shouted, "Gefangene!" and we made off as though a pistol had cracked. They gave chase, but we had a fair start. At the end of the village the road turned to the right, and an old cart track led off in our direction, the direction of the North Star. We dived down this track and I dived into some prickles – nettles, I think – and remembered them for days after. The track ended in a gate which led to what looked like an orchard. We climbed the gate and dropped over – and found ourselves up to our knees in water. The "orchard" was a green-covered pond with trees growing out of it. But we had got used to shocks by this time, so we paddled on, hoping it wouldn't get deeper. It did. When it reached our necks we held a short conference then advanced and got safely across.

We had been living on cabbage leaves, raw potatoes and grass for over a week, and our boots and socks were worn away so that we were walking almost on the dubbing; but we made progress considering. We crossed a canal that was in the way, and reached a railway which we followed for some days. At day-break on our eleventh day out we came face to face with a party of girl plate-layers in blue dungarees, and there was the usual chorus of "Halten, Gefangene!" We didn't obey, but ran down the embankment and into a wood, and the girls didn't follow us very far. We were two days and nights travelling through this wood – the thickest I've ever seen. Georges said it was the Black Forest, and black it certainly was. The trees were so close they formed a sort of roof, so we couldn't tell day from night, let alone see the stars, so we had to chance keeping a straight course. We struggled on through the undergrowth and at last struck a road, and sat down for a rest. Hot sunshine poured on us and speaking for myself I was about famished and all in. But we didn't sit there long. Alex looked up the road and saw something glittering, and Georges said one word "Bayonets!" Sure enough a company of soldiers were marching down the road towards us with steel helmets, rifles and fixed bayonets. We hastily retreated into the wood and waited there till they passed. George said they were the frontier guard and we must go carefully. We didn't get clear of the forest for another three hours, and then at about four o'clock in the afternoon we came out of it and found ourselves facing a hill smothered with heather. Up to then I'd thought it only grew in Scotland. We climbed the hill, up to our waists in heather, and paused on top to look round. The other side of the hill was as free from vegetation as a frog is from feathers, and down below we saw the frontier line – black and white sentry boxes and posts about two hundred metres apart. And the sentries saw us. I thought they were women as they were wearing long black cloaks. They shouted and fired at us, and we flew back down bonny Scotland like the wind. When we were safe in the forest we put our heads together. Our backs were already up. It was Deutschland or the Entente now!

We waited for night, and then crawled back up the Highlands again in extended order, and paused on top to spy out the land. Everything seemed quiet on the north-western front, so we crawled down the barren side on our stomachs. Napoleon was right. The sentries beats were about two hundred metres long, and our idea was to make for the end where the sentry wasn't. When he got to one end we could cross on the other. We got fairly close – about three yards away – and watched the sentry on the right – an industrious chap who never stopped his steady tramp. He turned at our end and started back again, and the other sentry on our right began to approach. This was our moment. Georges gave the signal and we jumped up and dashed forward, and were immediately entangled in trip wire with cans on it and pot-holes dug underneath. The cans made as much noise as Westminster Chimes; both the sentries loosed off into the air, and dogs woke up and barked. But we had new life in us now, and we got through and completed our international cross country race that night. In the early morning we came to some beautiful gardens, with sentry boxes posted here and there. It looked quite nice. The sentries let us pass unchallenged – perhaps the hedge-stake Georges was carrying influenced them – and further on we came to some arc-lights which turned out to be Roermund railhead, in Holland.

Here we met a Dutch policeman. I approached and saluted him and said "Drie gefangeners louven var Deutschland." He said "Gome mit, Camerad," and took us into Roermund Barracks just as reveillé was sounding.

Soldiers rushed out to see us, and an officer who spoke English said, "Your breakfast is ready."

CHAPTER FIFTEEN

ESCAPING FROM ENGLAND

By Gunther Plüschow

After many thrilling adventures during the first year of the War in China and America, which I have described at the beginning of my book, "My Escape from Donington Hall," I attempted to get back to Germany from New York disguised as a Swiss on an Italian steamer in February 1915. But I was discovered and arrested at Gibraltar by the British and eventually found myself in the German officers' camp at Donington Hall, near Derby.

Day and night I planned, brooded, deliberated how I could escape from this miserable imprisonment. I had to act with the greatest calm and caution if I hoped to succeed.

For hours I walked up and down in front of different parts of the entanglements, whilst I unostentatiously examined every wire and every stake. For hours together I lay in the grass in the vicinity of some of those spots that seemed favourable, feigning sleep. But all the time I was closely watching every object and noting the ways and habits of the different sentries. I had already fixed upon the spot where I had decided to climb the barbed wire. Now the question remained how to make headway after this obstacle had been overcome. We possessed neither a map of England nor a compass, no time-table, no means of assistance of any kind. We were even ignorant of the exact location of Donington Hall. I knew the road to Donington Castle, for I had fixed it in my memory on the day of our arrival. I had also heard through an officer, who had been taken by car to Donington Hall from Derby, that the latter lay about twenty-five to thirty miles away to the north, and that he had passed a long bridge before the car turned into the village.

I resolved to make common cause with a Naval officer, Oberleutnant Treffetz, who knew England and spoke English remarkably well.

On 4 July, 1915, in the morning, we reported ourselves sick.

At the morning roll-call, at ten o'clock, our names were entered on the sick-list, and on its completion the orderly sergeant came to our room and found us ill in bed.

Everything was working well.

With the afternoon came the decision.

About 4 p.m. I dressed, collected all that I considered necessary for my flight, ate several substantial buttered rolls, and bade farewell to my comrades, especially to my faithful friend Siebel, whom, unfortunately, I could not take with me as he was no sailor and did not speak English.

A heavy storm was in progress, and rain poured in torrents from grey skies. The sentries stood wet and shivering in their sentry-boxes, and therefore nobody paid any attention when two officers decided to walk about in the park, in spite of the rain. The park contained a grotto, surrounded by shrubs, from which one could overlook its whole expanse and the barbed wire, without oneself being seen.

This is where Trefftz and I crept in. We took a hurried leave of Siebel, who covered us with garden chairs, and we were alone. From now onwards we were in the hands of Providence, and it was to be hoped that Fortune would not forsake us.

We waited in breathless suspense. Minutes seemed like centuries, but slowly and surely one hour passed after another, until the turret-clock struck six in loud, clear chimes. Our hearts thumped in unison. We heard the bell ring for roll-call, the command "Attention", and then the noisy closing of the day-boundary. We hardly dared to breathe, expecting at any moment to hear our names called out. It was 6.30 and nothing had happened. A weight slipped from our shoulders.

Thank God, the first act was a success. For during roll-call our names had again been reported on the sick-list and, as soon as the officers were allowed to fall out, two of our comrades raced back as swiftly as they could through the back entrance and occupied Trefftz's bed and mine. Therefore, when the sergeant arrived he was able to account satisfactorily for the two invalids. As everything was now in order, the night-boundary was closed, as every night, and even the sentries were withdrawn from day-boundary. Thus we were left to our own devices. The exceptionally heavy rain proved a boon to us, for the English soldiers generally indulged in all kinds of frolic in the evenings, and we might have easily been discovered.

At 10.30 p.m. our excitement came to a head. We had to pass our second test. We clearly heard the signal "Stand to", and from the open window of my former room "The Watch on the Rhine" rang out sonorously. It was the concerted signal that all were on the alert.

The orderly officer, accompanied by a sergeant, walked through all the rooms and satisfied himself that no one was missing. By observations carried on for weeks I had made sure that the orderly officers always chose the same route in order to return to their quarters, after their rounds, by the shortest way. So it was to-night. The round began with the room from which Trefftz was missing. Of course his bed was already occupied by someone.

"All present?"

"Yes, sir!"

"All right! Good-night, gentlemen."

And so forth. As soon as the orderly officer had turned the corner, two other comrades ran in the opposite direction and into my room, so that here also all could be reported "present".

It is difficult to conceive our excitement and nervous tension whilst this was in progress. We followed all the proceedings in our minds, and when suddenly silence supervened for an unconscionably lengthy period we feared the worst. With ice-cold hands, ears on the alert for the slightest sound, we lay, hardly daring to breathe.

At last, at 11 p.m., a lusty cheer broke the stillness. It was our concerted signal that all was clear!

All was silent around us. The rain had ceased. The park lay wrapped in darkness, and only the light of the huge arc-lamps, which lit up the night-boundary, streamed faintly towards us. The moment for action had arrived. I crept softly as a cat from my hiding-place, through the park up to the barbed-wire fence, to convince myself that no sentries were about. When I saw that everything was in order and had found the exact spot where we wanted to climb over, I crawled back again to fetch Trefftz. Thereupon we returned by the same way.

When we reached the fence, I gave Trefftz my final instructions and handed him my small bundle.

I was the first to climb over the fence, which was about nine feet high, and every eight inches the wire was covered with long spikes.

Wires charged with electricity were placed two and a half feet from the ground. A mere touch would have sufficed to set in motion a system of bells that would, of course, have given the alarm to the whole camp. We wore leather leggings as protection against the spikes; round our knees we had wound puttees, and we wore leather gloves.

But all these precautions were of no avail, and we got badly scratched by the spikes. However, they prevented us from slipping and coming in contact with the electric wires. I easily swung myself over the first fence. Trefftz handed over our two bundles and followed me with equal ease.

Next we were confronted by a wire obstacle, three feet high by thirty feet wide, contrived according to the latest and most cunning devices. We ran over it like cats. After this we again came to a high barbed-wire hedge, built on exactly the same lines as the first, and also electrically charged. We managed this too, except that I tore a piece out of the seat of my trousers, which I had to retrieve, in order to put it in again later.

But, thank God, we were over the boundary!

Trefftz and I clasped hands and looked at each other in silence.

But now the chief difficulty began.

We opened our bundles, took out civilian grey mackintoshes, and walked down the road in high spirits as if we were coming from a late entertainment. When Donington Castle came in sight, we had to be particularly careful. We had agreed upon all we would do in case we met anyone.

Suddenly, just as we were turning into the village, an English soldier came walking towards us. Trefftz embraced me, drew me towards him, and we behaved like a rollicking pair of love-birds. The Englishman surveyed us enviously, and went on his way, clicking his tongue. Only then, something in the stocky, undersized figure made me realize that it was the sergeant-major of our camp! We stepped out briskly, and after passing the village we were favoured by chance, and came upon the bridge about which we had been told. But we were at once confronted with a critical proposition. The highway branched off here in three directions, and it was impossible to get any farther without knowledge of the road. At last, in spite of the darkness, we discovered a sign-post – an extreme rarity in England. Luckily it was made of iron, and, when Trefftz had climbed it, he was able to feel with his fingers the word "Derby" traced on it in raised letters.

We now fell into a quick step and, taking our bearings by the Polar star, swung along vigorously. Gradually dawn came. About four in the morning, when we arrived within sight of the first houses of Derby's suburbs, the sun rose in majestic splendour, like a crimson ball on the horizon.

We now crept into a small garden and made an elaborate toilet. A clothes brush performed miracles, and a needle repaired the damage done to my trousers. The lack of shaving soap was remedied by spittle, after which our poor faces were subjected to the ministrations of a Gillette razor. We each sported our solitary collar and tie, leaving the brush as well as other unnecessary impedimenta behind us. We entered Derby, looking veritable "Knuts".

Our luck endured, and not only did we soon find the station, where we separated unobtrusively, but we also learned that the next train for London was leaving in a quarter of an hour. I took a third-class return ticket to Leicester and, armed with a fat newspaper, boarded the train. At Leicester I got out, took a ticket to London and when I entered the compartment I discovered, sitting opposite me, a gentleman clad in a grey overcoat, whom I must have met previously, but of whom I naturally took no notice. I believe his name began with a T.

About noon the train reached London. When I passed the ticket collector I must admit that I did not feel quite comfortable, and that my hand shook a little. But nothing happened, and after a few minutes I was swallowed up in the vortex of the capital.

At seven o'clock in the evening I stood weary and downcast on the steps of St. Paul's Cathedral, waiting for Trefftz. I waited until nine, but no Trefftz appeared.

Convinced that Trefftz had already managed his escape on a friendly steamer, I dragged myself, totally exhausted, to Hyde Park which, to my further discomfiture, I found closed. What should I do now? Where should I sleep?

I turned into an aristocratic lane where beautiful mansions were surrounded by carefully tended gardens. I was hardly able to stand on my feet, and at the first favourable moment I jumped with quick decision over one of the garden fences and hid myself in a thick box hedge, only a foot away from the pavement.

After I had lain for about an hour in my refuge, the French doors of the house, leading to a beautiful veranda, opened, and several ladies and gentlemen in evening dress came out to enjoy the coolness of the night. I could see them and hear every word. Soon the sounds of a piano mingled with those of a splendid soprano voice, and the most wonderful songs of Schubert overwhelmed my soul with longing.

At last total exhaustion prevailed, and I slept heavily, seeing in my mind the most beautiful pictures of the future.

Next morning I was awakened by the regular tread of a policeman who marched up and down the street, quite close to where I lay, with the bright, warm rays of the sun shining down upon me.

So after all I had overslept – it behoved me to be careful. The policeman ambled idiotically up and down without dreaming of departure. At last fortune favoured me. An enchanting little lady's maid opened the door, and hey presto! the policeman was at her side, playfully conversing with the pretty dear.

Without being seen by either, with a quick motion I vaulted over the fence into the street. It was already six o'clock, and Hyde Park was just being opened. As the Underground was not yet running, I went into the Park and dropped full length on a bench, near to other vagabonds who had made themselves comfortable there. I then pulled my hat over my face and slept profoundly until nine o'clock.

With fresh strength and courage I entered the Underground, and was carried to the harbour area. In the Strand huge, yellow posters attracted my attention, and who can describe my astonishment when I read on them, printed in big, fat letters, that:

(1) Mr. Trelftz had been recaptured the evening before;

(2) Mr. Plüschow was still at large; but that

(3) the police were already on his track.

The first and third items were news; but I knew all about the second. I promptly bought a newspaper, went into a teashop, where I read with great interest the following notice;

EXTRA LATE WAR EDITION
HUNT FOR ESCAPED GERMAN
High-pitched Voice as a Clue

Scotland Yard last night issued the following amended description of Gunther Plüschow, one of the German prisoners who escaped from Donington Hall, Leicestershire, on Monday:

Height, 5 feet 5 inches; weight, 135 lb.; complexion, fair; hair, blond; eyes, blue; and tattoo marks: Chinese dragon on left arm.

As already stated in the *Daily Chronicle*, Plüschow's companion, Trefftz, was recaptured on Monday evening at Millwall Docks. Both men are naval officers. An earlier description stated that Plüschow is twenty-nine years old. His voice is high-pitched.

He is particularly smart and dapper in appearance, has very good teeth, which he shows somewhat prominently when talking or smiling, is 'very English in manner,' and knows this country well. He also knows Japan well. He is quick and alert, both mentally and physically, and speaks French and English fluently and accurately. He was dressed in a grey lounge suit or grey-and-yellow mixture suit.

Poor Trefftz! So they had got him! I was clear in my mind as to what I was going to do, and the warning gave me some valuable points. First, I had to get rid of my mackintosh. I therefore went to Blackfriars Station and left my overcoat in the cloakroom. As I handed the garment over, the clerk suddenly asked me: "What is your name, sir?" This question absolutely bowled me over, as I was quite unprepared for it. With shaking knees I asked: "Meinen?" (mine), answering in German as I naturally presumed that the man had guessed my identity.

"Oh, I see, Mr. Mine-M-i-n-e," and he handed me a receipt in the name of Mr. Mine. It was a miracle that this official had not noticed my terror, and I felt particularly uncomfortable when I had to pass the two policemen who stood on guard at the station, and who scrutinized me sharply.

I now sought a quiet, solitary spot. My beautiful soft hat fell accidentally into the river from London Bridge; collar and tie followed suit from another spot; a beautiful gilt stud held my green shirt together. After that a mixture of vaseline, bootblack and coal dust turned my blond hair black and greasy; my hands soon looked as if they had never made acquaintance with water; and at last I wallowed in a coal heap until I had turned into a perfect prototype of the dock labourer on strike – George Mine.

In this guise it was quite impossible to suspect me of being an officer, and "smart and dapper" were the last words anyone could have possibly applied to me. I think that I played my part really well, and, after I had surmounted my inner repulsion against the filth of my surroundings, I felt safe for the first time. I was in a position to represent what I intended to be – a lazy, dirty bargee, or a hand from a sailing ship.

For days I loafed about London, my cap set jauntily at the back of my head, my jacket open, showing my blue sweater and its one ornament, the gilt stud, hands in pocket, whistling and spitting, as is the custom of sailors in ports all the world over.

On the second morning I had colossal luck! I sat on the top of a bus, and behind me two business men were engaged in animated conversation. Suddenly I caught the words, "Dutch steamer – departure – Tilbury," and from that moment I listened intently, trying to quell the joyful throbbings of my heart. For these careless gentlemen were recounting nothing less than the momentous news of the sailing, each morning at seven, of a fast Dutch steamer for Flushing, which cast anchor off Tilbury Docks every afternoon.

In the twinkling of an eye I was off the 'bus. I rushed off to Blackfriars Station, and an hour later was at Tilbury.

I went down to the riverside, threw myself on to the grass, and, feigning sleep, kept a lynx-eyed watch.

Ship after ship went by, and my expectations rose every minute. At last, at 4 p.m., with proud bearing, the fast Dutch steamer dropped anchor and made fast to a buoy just in front of me. My happiness and my joy were indescribable when I read the ship's name in white shining letters on the bow: MECKLENBURG.

There could be no better omen for me, since I am a native of Mecklenburg-Schwerin. I crossed over to Gravesend on a ferry-boat, and from there unobtrusively watched the steamer. I adopted the careless demeanour and rolling gait of the typical Jack Tar, hands in my pockets, whistling a gay tune, but keeping eyes and mind keenly on the alert.

This was my plan: to swim to the buoy during the night, climb the hawser, creep on deck and reach Holland as a stowaway.

I soon found the basis for my operations.

After I had ascertained that nobody was paying attention to me, I climbed over a pile of wood and rubbish, and concealed myself under some planks, where I discovered several bundles of hay. These afforded me a warm resting-place, of which I made use on that and the following nights.

About midnight I left my refuge. Creeping on all fours, listening with straining ears and trying to pierce the surrounding blackness, I came closer to my object.

However, I perceived with dismay that the two barges which, in daytime, had been completely submerged, lay high and dry. Luckily, at the stern, a little dinghy rode on the water.

With prompt resolution I wanted to rush into the boat, but before I knew where I was I felt the ground slipping from under my feet and I sank to the hips into a squashy, slimy, stinking mass. I threw my arms about, and was just able to reach the plank, which ran from the shore to the sailing-boat, with my left hand.

It took all my strength to get free of the slime which had proved my undoing, and I was completely exhausted when I at last dragged myself back to my bed of hay.

When the sun rose on the third morning of my escape, I had already returned to a bench in Gravesend Park, and was watching the *Mecklenburg* as she slipped her moorings at 7 a.m. and made for the open sea.

All that day, as well as later on, I loafed about London. I had by then acquired so much confidence that I walked into the British Museum, visited several picture-galleries and even frequented matinees at music-halls, without being asked questions. The pretty blonde attendants at the music-halls were especially friendly to me, and seemed to pity the poor sailor who had wandered in by chance. What amused me most was to see the glances of disgust and contempt which the ladies and the young girls used to throw at me on the top of the 'buses. If they had known who sat near them! Is it surprising that I should not smell sweetly considering my night's work and the wet and slimy state of my clothes? In the evening I was back at Gravesend. In the little park which overlooked the Thames I listened quietly for hours to the strains of a military band. I decided to commandeer unobtrusively, somehow, a dinghy in which to reach the steamer. Just in front of me I saw one which I deemed suitable for my purpose, but it was moored to a wharf over which a sentry stood guard by day and night. But the risk had to be taken. The night was very dark when, about twelve, I crept through the park and crawled up to the embankment wall, which was about six feet high. I jumped over the hedge and saw the boat rocking gently on the water. I listened breathlessly. The sentry marched up and down. Half asleep, I had taken off my boots, fastening them with the laces round my neck, and holding an open knife between my teeth. With the stealth of an Indian I let myself down over the wall, and was just able to reach the gunwale of the boat with my toes. My hands slipped over the hard granite without a sound, and a second later I dropped into the boat, where I huddled in a corner listening with breathless attention; but my sentry went on striding up and down undisturbed under the bright arc-lamps. My boat, luckily, lay in shadow.

My eyes, trained through T.B.D. practice, saw in spite of the pitch darkness almost as well as by day. Carefully I felt for the oars. Damn! They were padlocked! Luckily the chain lay loose, and silently I first freed the boat-hook, then one oar after the other from the chain. My knife now sawed through the two ropes which held the boat to the wall, and I dipped my oars noiselessly into the water and impelled my little boat forward.

When I had entered the boat, it had already shipped a good deal of water. Now I noticed to my dismay that the water was rapidly rising. It was already lapping the thwart, and the boat became more and more difficult to handle as it grew heavier and heavier. I threw myself despairingly on my oars. Suddenly, with a grinding noise, the keel grounded and the boat lay immovable. Nothing now was of avail, neither pulling nor rowing, nor the use of the boat-hook. The boat simply refused to budge. Very quickly the water sank round it, and after a few minutes I sat dry in the mud, but to make up for this the boat was brimful of water. I had never in my life witnessed such a change in the water-level due to the tide. Although the Thames is well known in this respect, I had never believed that possible.

At this moment I found myself in the most critical position of my escape. I was surrounded on all sides by slushy, stinking slime, whose acquaintance I had made before at the risk of my life. The very thought caused me to shudder. About two hundred yards off the sentry marched up and down, and I found myself with my boat fifteen feet from the six-foot-high granite wall.

I sat reflecting coolly. One thing appeared a sheer necessity – not to be found there by the English, who might have killed me like a mad dog.

But the water was not due to rise before the next afternoon. Therefore it behoved me to muster my energy, clench my teeth and try to get the better of the mud. I slipped off my stockings, turned up my trousers as high as I could, then I placed the thwarts and the oars close to each other on the seething and gurgling ooze, used the boat-hook as a leaping-pole by placing its point on a board, stood on the gunwale, and, gathering all my strength to a mighty effort, vaulting into space – but lay, alas, the next moment three feet short of the wall, and sank deep over knee into the clammy slush, touching hard bottom, however, as I did so. Now I worked myself along the wall, placed my boot-hook as a climbing-pole against it, and found myself in a few seconds on top, after which I slid into the grass of the park, where a few hours previously I had been listening to the music. Unbroken silence reigned around me. Unutterable relief flooded me, for nobody, not even the sentry, had noticed anything.

With acute discomfort I contemplated my legs. They were covered with a thick, grey, malodorous mass, and there was no water in the vicinity to clean them. But it was impossible to put on boots or stockings whilst they were in that condition. With infinite trouble I succeeded in scraping off the dirt as far as possible, and waited for the rest to dry; only then was I able to resume a fairly decent appearance.

Could I be blamed if my spirits fell a little, and if I became quite indifferent to my interests? I confess I was so discouraged that the next morning I did not find sufficient energy to leave my hiding-place in time, and only escaped over my fence after the proprietor of the timber-pile had passed close in front of my retreat several times. That day I walked up to London on foot from Gravesend, and returned by the other side of the Thames to Tilbury. All this, in order to find a boat that I could purloin unnoticed. It was quite incredible that I could not do so; several lay there, as if waiting for me; but they were only too well guarded. I gave it up in despair.

That evening I went to a music-hall, with the firm intention of blowing my last pound, and then caught the last train to Tilbury.

After I had passed the first fishermen's huts of Gravesend, I found a small scull. I took it with me. In mid-stream, just near the landing-place of the fishing-vessels, a little dinghy bobbed on the water. Not more than twenty feet away sat their owners on a bench, so absorbed in tender flirtation with their fair ones that the good sea-folk took no heed of my appearance on the scene.

It was risky, but "Nothing venture, nothing have," I muttered to myself. And, thanks to my acquired proficiency, I crept soundlessly into the boat – one sharp cut, and the tiny nutshell softly glided alongside a fishing-boat, on whose quarter-deck a woman was lulling her baby to sleep.

As there were no rowlocks in the boat, I sat aft, and pushed off with all my strength from the shore. I had, however, hardly covered one-third of the distance, when the ebbtide caught me in its whirl, spun my boat round like a top and paralysed all my efforts at steering. The time had come to show my sailor's efficiency. With an iron grip I recovered control of the boat, and, floating with the tide, I steered a downstream course. A dangerous moment was at hand. An imposing military pontoon-bridge, stretching across the river, and guarded by soldiers, came across my way. Summoning cool resolution and sharp attention to my aid, looking straight ahead and only intent on my scull, I disregarded the sentry's challenge and shot through between the two pontoons. A few seconds after the boat sustained a heavy shock, and I floundered on to the anchor-cable of a mighty coal-tender. With lightning speed I flung my painter round it, and this just in time, for the boat nearly capsized. But I was safe. The water whirled madly past it, as the ebbtide, reinforced by the drop of the river, must have fully set in. I had now only to wait patiently.

My steamer lay to the starboard. I wanted to bide my time until the flow of the tide made it possible for me to get across.

I was already bubbling over with cocksureness when the necessary damper was administered. Dawn was breaking, the outlines of the anchored ships became clearer and clearer. At last the sun rose, and still the water ran out so strongly that it was impossible to carry out my flight just then. But at last, happy in the possession of the long desired boat, I slid downstream and, after an hour, pulled up at a crumbling old bridge on the right bank of the Thames. I pushed my boat under it, took both sculls with me as a precautionary measure, and hid them ln the long grass. Then I lay down close to them, and at 8 o'clock I saw my steamer, the *Mecklenburg*, vanishing proudly before my eyes. My patience had still to undergo a severe test. I remained lying in the grass for sixteen hours, until, at eight o'clock that night, the hour of my deliverance struck.

I again entered my boat. Cautiously I allowed myself to be driven upstream by the incoming tide, and fastened my boat to the same coal tender near which I had been stranded the night before. Athwart to me lay the *Princess Juliana* moored to her buoy.

As I had time to spare, I lay down at the bottom of my boat and tried to take forty winks, but in vain. The tide rose, and I was once more surrounded by the rushing water.

At midnight all was still around me, and when at one o'clock the boat was quietly bobbing on the flow, I cast off, sat up in my boat, and rowed, with as much self-possession as if I had been one of a Sunday party in Kiel Harbour, to the steamer.

Unnoticed, I reached the buoy. The black hull of my steamer towered high above me. A strong pull – and I was atop the buoy. I now bade farewell to my faithful swan with a sound kick, which set it off downstream with the start of the ebb. During the next few minutes I lay as silent as a mouse. Then I climbed with iron composure – and this time like a cat – the mighty steel cable to the hawse. Cautiously I leaned my head over the rail and spied about. The forecastle was empty.

I jerked myself upwards and stood on the deck.

I now crept along the deck to the capstan and hid in the oil save-all beneath the windlass.

As all remained quiet, and not a soul hove in sight, I climbed out of my nook, took off my boots, and stowed them away under a stack of timber in a corner of the fore-deck. I now proceeded to investigate in my stockinged feet. When I looked down from a corner astern the fore-deck to the cargo-deck I staggered back suddenly. Breathlessly, but without turning a hair, I remained leaning against the ventilator. Below, on the cargo-deck, stood two sentries, who were staring fixedly upwards.

After I had remained for over half an hour in this cramped position, and my knees were beginning to knock under, there tripped two stewardesses from the middle-deck. They were apparently coming off night duty. My two sentries immediately seized the golden moment and became so absorbed in their conversation that they no longer paid any attention to what was going on around them.

The dawn was breaking, and I had to act at once if I was not to lose all I had achieved at such a price.

I let myself down along the counter on the side of the fore-deck opposite to the two loving couples, and landed on the cargo-deck. Without pausing for a moment I stepped out gently, glided past the two sentries, reached the promenade-deck safely, and, climbing up a deck-pillar found myself shortly afterwards on the out-board side of a life-boat.

Holding on with one hand with a grip of iron, for the Thames was lapping hungrily not twelve yards away, with my other, aided by my teeth, I tore open a few of the tapes of the boat-cover, and with a last output of strength I crept through this small gap and crouched, well hidden from curious eyes, into the interior of the boat.

And then, naturally, I came to the end of my endurance. The prodigious physical exertions, acute excitement, and last, but not least, my ravenous hunger, stretched me flat on the boards of the boat, and in the same moment I no longer knew what was going on around me.

Shrill blasts from the siren woke me from a sleep which in dreamlessness resembled death.

I prudently loosened the tapes of my boat-cover, and with difficulty suppressed a "Hurrah!" for the steamer was running into the harbour of Flushing.

Nothing mattered any longer. I pulled out my knife, and at one blow ripped open the boat-cover from end to end; but this time on the deck side.

With a deep breath, I stood in the middle of the boat-deck, and expected to be made a prisoner at any moment.

But no one bothered about me. The crew was occupied with landing manoeuvres; the travellers with their luggage.

I now descended to the promenade-deck, where several passengers eyed me with indignation on account of my unkempt appearance and my torn blue stockings, which looked, I must say, anything but dainty.

But my eyes must have been so radiantly happy, and such joy depicted on my dirty, emaciated features that many a woman glanced at me with surprise.

I could no longer go about like this. I therefore repaired to the fore-deck, fetched my boots (my best hockey boots, kindly from the English), and, though a Dutch sailor blew me up gruffly, I calmly put on my beloved boots, and slunk down the gangway.

Nobody paid any attention to me, so I pretended to belong to the ship's crew, and even helped to fasten the hawsers. Then I mixed with the crowd, and whilst the passengers were being subjected to a strict control I looked round, and near the railings discovered a door, on which stood in large letters "Exit Forbidden."

There, surely, lay the way to Freedom! In the twinkling of an eye I negotiated this childishly easy obstacle, and stood without.

I was free!

I had to make the greatest effort of my life to keep myself from jumping about like a madman. Two countrymen of mine gave me a cordial welcome, though they would not believe that I was an officer, and, above all things, that I had achieved my escape from England.

How horrible the water in my bath looked!

I also ate enough for three that night.

After I had bought a few small necessaries on the next day, I boarded a slow train for Germany, wearing workman's clothes. I was quite unable to sit still for long. Alone in my first-class compartment I was overwhelmed by the thoughts and hopes which raced through my brain. I ran about my railway carriage like a wild animal in a cage.

At last! At last! It seemed an eternity; the train passed slowly over the German frontier.

Germany, oh, my beloved country! I had come back to thee!

CHAPTER SIXTEEN

RENDEZVOUS WITH A SUBMARINE

By Herman Tholens

I was taken prisoner in the first days of the War, when the German cruisers *Coeln*, *Mainz* and *Ariande* were sunk during a raid of the English fleet into the bight of Heligoland on 28 August, 1914. I was second in command of the *Mainz*, and I was in the water about an hour after she was sunk. I was then picked up by an English destroyer and taken on board. The first ten days of my captivity I passed in the naval hospital at Chatham, and from there I was taken to Dyffryn Aled Camp, near Denbigh, right in the north of Wales. This camp was, I think, one of the best guarded of all prisoner-of-war camps in the whole of Britain – probably because most of its inmates were submarine officers. My thoughts turned to escape at once, but I am six feet two inches in height, and this, I believed, would make it difficult for me to move about English ports and dockyards undetected. So I decided to try to arrange to leave in much the same way that I had come – that is to say, by means of one of our own ships of war. The coast of Wales was only a few miles north, and it seemed to me that if only I could break camp and get there, I might arrange for a German submarine to meet me there and take me off.

This plan for a rendezvous needed, of course, very careful and accurate arrangement; but I talked it over with a fellow-prisoner, my friend, Lieutenant-Commander von Hennig, who had been captain of our Submarine 18. We made a careful investigation of the camp defences, and decided that if we could get our Admiralty to send a submarine to a certain part of the coast at a certain time, we could keep our side of the bargain and be there to meet it. At Christmas, 1914, some of the prisoners of our camp who had lived in England before the War were exchanged by special arrangement against a like number of English prisoners from Germany. By one of these I sent a secret proposal to the Commander-in-Chief of the German submarine flotillas. My proposal was this. My friend, von Hennig, and I undertook to get out of our camp and reach an agreed point on the Welsh coast at an agreed time. Would it be possible for one of the submarines operating in the Irish Sea to be detailed and sent to meet us there? We proposed the most westerly point of the Great Ormes Head as a rendezvous, and a Saturday and Sunday during a new moon as a time of meeting. Our signal would be an electric pocket lamp waved in a circle. The answer to this proposal was given in several letters, in what I can only call "disguised language". It was really very easy. Our friends thanked us for our letters, and said that the wedding of Mrs. So-and-So would take place on 14 August. We quite understood what that meant, and after a further exchange of letters we knew that a submarine was to await us at the proposed point during the nights of 14 and 15 of August, 1915.

Now for our part of the job – reaching the rendezvous. We *must* reach it – for a second chance was not to be expected. And unfortunately, while our negotiations were being made with Germany, the chances to get out of our camp had diminished considerably. In March two of our fellow-prisoners had made a vain escape, with the result that our camp was now guarded during the nights by six sentries instead of by two. The equipment of the camp had also been augmented by four searchlights, which were posted at the four corners and made the nights all round it as light as the days. At the same time the number of roll-calls had been doubled and extra rolls had been introduced. But where there's a will there's a way. These new orders dated from the middle of June, and according to them the searchlights had to be lighted at 9 p.m., which was also the time for the six night guards to take up their stations. Two of them were stationed in front of the house, one at each side and two again in the back. By the middle of August, the time of our rendezvous, the days, of course, would have become much shorter than they were in June, when the above order had been issued. So we agreed that the best time for our breaking away from the camp would be a little before the searchlights were lighted, and the night guards took up their stations, as it would be already pretty dark then.

Our plan was this. We intended to get through the iron-barred window of the room which was inhabited by my two fellow-escapers – for we had added by now a third to our number. Our next obstacle was the first of the two entrance gates, which led through the barbed wire fence which surrounded our prison. If the gate could not be opened, we would have to cut the barbed wire fence next to the room from which we started, and endeavour to crawl through it. Thus our preparations had to consist in cutting one of the iron window bars and in removing the hanging lock from the aforesaid entrance gate as soon as possible before the time fixed for our escape. Further we had to procure a pair of clippers for cutting wire, a map of the coast, a compass, an electrical pocket lamp. Plain clothes were still in our possession, as we had been allowed to wear them during the first two months. When this had been forbidden, and our plain clothes had to be delivered, of course we kept some of them back and concealed them beneath the floors of our rooms.

But one thing was imperative. All our preparations had to be done in absolute secrecy, as some of our orderlies had passed the greater part of their life in England and so were in very close connection with our warders. Under these circumstances if our fellow-prisoners had learnt of our preparations we would probably had been betrayed.

On the date of our escape, everything was in order, and nobody except us had the least idea about our intention. At 7 o'clock in the evening we were in possession of the hanging lock of the entrance gate and by 8.30 it had not yet been replaced by a new one. Sharply at 8.45 we stole through our window, crawled very very slowly to our gate, only twenty yards from the nearest sentry, and one or two minutes later we were outside the camp. Half an hour before we left we had informed two trusted friends of our intentions, and they promised to help us. One of them was to replace the cut iron bar and the other distracted the attention of the sentry, who was stationed in front of the house, by troubling him with some very important question.

On the top of a little hill about one hundred yards away from our prison we made a first short stop to ascertain if we had aroused suspicion. We gave a last look to the house, which had enclosed us one long year, hoping never to see it again; and then started off on our march. We had to cover about twenty miles to reach our meeting place. And this had to be done within the next twelve hours, as we should certainly be missed at the daily roll-call, which took place at 9 o'clock in the morning, and then, of course, the telephones would work and soon all authorities in the neighbourhood would know that three prisoners of war of Dyffryn Aled were at large. So we marched off at good speed, and by 4 o'clock in the morning according to our map we were not very far from the sea. From four till six we took shelter in a small wood, thinking that it would not be good to be seen about at such an early time. At 6.30 we reached the seaboard. A very supreme moment! A little later we entered the town of Llandudno. It was now 7.30 and our warders would just be enjoying their breakfast as usual without any idea of all the trouble which the day had in store for them, so we felt quite safe. We strolled along the streets, crossed a large training field in the middle of the town and admired at our leisure the exercises and drilling of a whole army of soldiers. Before leaving the town we resolved to have a last good English breakfast. We took this in a nice little restaurant near the sea. Then we set off again, and soon made our way to the lighthouse on Great Ormes Head. When we reached this, we looked for a nice spot, where we could shelter all the day and perhaps the following day too. For we had arranged, you remember, that the submarine should wait for us on two consecutive nights.

On 4 August, Submarine 38 left Wilhelmshaven to meet us, and took her course through the North Sea to the Shetlands, where she arrived two days later. From there she sailed through the Atlantic along the west coast of Scotland and Ireland into the Channel and then into the Irish Sea. South of Ireland she sunk some hostile ships with contraband. But in the Irish Sea she made no further attacks in order not to arouse unnecessary suspicion. At midnight on August 13th, she had reached a point fifty miles north-west of Great Ormes Head, where she was to await Submarine 27, which had been sent for the same purpose and to make it as sure as possible that one boat would be ready for us at the fixed time. Here the captain of Submarine 38, who was a special friend of ours, proposed that the other boat should return to her business in the mouth of the Channel, as from now on one boat would be sufficient.

Submarine 27, therefore, went off to the south, while next evening, 14 August, Submarine 38 slowly approached the Hook of Great Ormes Head.

When she sounded about thirty yards, she put off her diesel motors and put in the electrical engines. At the same time the boat was flooded – that is to say, some of her tanks were filled with water, so that if she grounded she could get up again by blowing out the water. The weather and the sea were quiet. There was no traffic and no patrol boat. At one o'clock in the morning she sounded ten yards and stopped her engines. The lamp of the lighthouse on Great Ormes Head showed very high up. The distance from the shore could not be more than a hundred yards. But the rocks of the coast could not be made out, for it was absolutely dark. All the crew was intently on the look out, but no sign of life could be perceived. The small collapsible boat of the submarine was all the while kept ready to row ashore. Hour by hour passed, but nothing happened.

Now to return to us. At 10 o'clock on the night of the 14th, when it was absolutely dark, we left our shelter beneath a couple of brambles, and carefully made our way to a point which we had marked in the morning where it would be possible to climb down the high rocky cliff of the coast. But in the dark we missed the place and could not find our way down. If any of you know the Great Ormes Head you will remember that it is a very difficult place to climb down on a dark night. So we resolved to give our signals from above on this night, rather than to risk some broken arms or legs and so perhaps spoil our chances of being taken on board by our friends on the following night. As we signalled and looked out over the dark sea we thought we saw a periscope, but it was only the mast of a sailing boat, peacefully rowing home after her day's labour. Later on we made out a light, slowly approaching the shore. But this, too, did not belong to our keenly awaited friends, but to some other boat, which soon disappeared round the Hook, probably heading for Llandudno. So the night passed.

It must be understood that as well as the difficulties and dangers of the rocks, we were also in great danger of being detected by the coastguards, who were constantly patrolling the road which led along the cliff and round the lighthouse. At daybreak on the Sunday we carefully revised our position and especially the possibilities of climbing down to the shore. We found that our position was right. We were on the most westerly point of Great Ormes Head, just halfway between the last houses, which bordered the coast, and the lighthouse. Our distance from the lighthouse, which was on the most northerly point of the coast, was no more than a thousand yards. But the part of the coast between us and the lighthouse was extremely rocky. So we again carefully marked the spot, from which we would be able to clamber down to the shore. This was our last chance, we were not going to miss it a second time.

Then we took up our quarters again in our small nest beneath the brambles and tried to sleep a little. But our excitement was too great, and sleep was impossible. Up to now we had been successful in all respects. We had broken out of our camp. We had safely reached the shore, crossed the town of Llandudno, passed the coastguards and found a good shelter in the immediate neighbourhood of the rendezvous. Somewhere, down below, our friends were waiting for us. We couldn't fail now. We lay awake, waiting for dusk. Our shelter lay within a prohibited area, and was, therefore, safe from surprise. The only creatures about seemed to be some cattle, which were grazing the meadows between the road round the peninsula, and the sea-border. Suddenly we heard the loud barking of a dog in our immediate neighbourhood. Soon after we heard his master's voice calling him, and luckily he was a most obedient dog. But his master had to pass our hiding-place again, and so half an hour later the dog gave tongue a second time. Happily it was just before supper time and the master seemed as obedient to his wife as his dog was to him. Thus he did not bother to look for the reason for his dog's excitement. Of course our own excitement and fright had been tremendous, but it had served to give us new confidence for the night to come, and had made us forget the thirst which we had suffered from all that hot August Sunday.

This time we left our shelter before it was dark and got safely down to the coast. At 10 o'clock we began to give our signals – a circle with our electric lamp. It was a wonderful night I remember – absolutely dark, with no moon. The sea was quiet, and only a light breeze was blowing. If the submarine was there – surely she was there – she would certainly make out our signals at a distance of at least two miles. But we got no answer. We began to think that she must have had some mishap and had not been able to reach the rendezvous in time. If need be we would wait for her a third night in spite of our hunger and thirst – but meanwhile we flashed and flashed our light. There was no reply. In desperation we then risked making a large fire from bits of drift wood from the shore, and every ten minutes during the last hour of darkness we waved a large log of flaming wood in a circle. We made our signals as far north as the rocky coast allowed. But no answer came.

How disappointed we were! I can't put that into words at all. We hid again when day broke, intending rather hopelessly to try again the next night. But we had to give up the plan, for a strong gale from the north sprang up in the afternoon, and soon the sea was too rough to make any such embarkation possible.

What had happened? During the day the submarine had lain grounded some miles away. On that Sunday she had come to the surface again and approached the coast. The captain, our friend Valentiner, knew from the previous night that there was no danger from patrol boats, so he approached the shore this time early enough to get as close to it as possible. That was our bad luck. For there it had been all the time waiting for us; but closer in than we'd expected, and just hidden from us by a projecting ledge of rock. It had been waiting for us there not more than 500 yards away, but had not been able to see our signals.

In the evening, after the gale had made it useless to wait for the submarine a third night, I left my friends, who couldn't speak English. My intentions now were to reach London and smuggle on board some Dutch or Scandinavian vessel. But at Llandudno station a policeman stopped me. He said I looked very like a certain Lieutenant-Commander Tholens, who had escaped from Dyifryn Aled three days before. I could only answer "Right you are."

CHAPTER SEVENTEEN

HAZARDS OF ESCAPE

By Lawrence A. Wingfield

In February 1916, No. 12 Squadron, with whom I was serving, went to Avesnes-le-Comte (west of Arras), where we were engaged on every branch of aircraft work. We were equipped with BE2cs. On 1 July, 1916, a special job fell to my lot. I had to go to St. Quentin, a large town then about thirty-five miles on the German side of the lines, there to "lay" a couple of "eggs" on the railway station. I started off at the appointed time, and arrived at St. Quentin and dropped my bombs at the railway station. I observed a column of smoke rise to a great height. On the way home, I met a Fokker monoplane and that was the end of the story.

It took the Fokker about fifteen minutes to shoot me down. On my arrival on *terra ferma*, which I achieved without personal injury, I found myself on a parade ground. My machine and I were immediately surrounded by German infantry, and I found myself amongst men who knew Brighton and London well, and who were all questioning me as to the condition of these places. Did I know them? Had they suffered very much through the War? And so on. I was able to reassure them on these points.

At this juncture there arrived upon the scene a small car containing three German officers, one of them in mufti, the other two in uniform. The car and the contents belonged to the German Air Force, and the gentleman in mufti turned out to be the Commandant of a squadron stationed hard by. This officer apologised to me most profusely for being in mufti, but remarked with mild sarcasm that I had not sent notice of my intention to call. He went on to say, "We've been running along the road firing at you like anything." I then noticed that the car had a machine gun mounted in the centre. Now I expect you know that a machine gun fired from the ground is quite ineffective against aircraft flying at any height over 2,000 feet. I had been flying at about 5,000 feet, so with due courtesy I expressed my regret that my attention had been so centred on the Fokker, who shot me down, that I hadn't noticed him. He looked his disappointment, and I think the score was mine that time.

A guard was placed in charge of my aeroplane and I was invited to get into the car and was then driven by them to their Squadron Headquarters, which were some eight miles north west of St. Quentin. The officers were housed in an old French chateau, and I was very impressed by its condition. The gardens were beautiful, all the flower beds in bloom, the lawn mown and everything tidiness itself. I was ushered into a large dining-room, oak-panelled, where there was a table laid for afternoon tea. I was invited to seat myself next to the Commandant and take afternoon tea. I asked what they proposed to do with my aeroplane and was informed that the "2.C." was considered so ancient and at the same time a survival of such historic interest that it would be handed over to the proper authorities for exhibition in a museum in Berlin.

I was particularly impressed, not to say overwhelmed, by the punctilio with which I was treated by my captors. Each officer as he came in, clicked his heels in the doorway and saluted in the German manner. Possibly this was all intended for the Commandant. With characteristic British conceit, however, I imagined that the salutes were intended for me. I asked the Commandant if a note might be dropped upon the English side of the lines, so that my relatives and my squadron might have news of my whereabouts. I didn't need to tell the Commandant the number of my squadron or its situation. He already knew it, for he said, "I will have a note dropped on to No. 4 Squadron Aerodrome at Albert on our next reconnaissance" – which showed a fairly good knowledge of the position of the squadrons. At a later date a German aeroplane did drop a note, and the note eventually reached my squadron.

When tea was finished the Commandant said, "I am sorry that you must now go. You have to go into St. Quentin and after that into Germany, but you will be well treated there, have no fear." I can't say that the subsequent treatment was always good, and on some occasions it was far from it, but I firmly believe the Commandant was under the impression that it would be. As I left the squadron chateau the car which was to take me to St. Quentin was drawn up to the steps of the chateau. The whole squadron had been paraded on the terrace, and as I got into the car, somebody called them to attention. So they stood, two deep the whole breadth of the chateau. I felt more like a General inspecting his troops than a prisoner of war in the hands of the enemy.

On the way to St. Quentin we passed their aerodrome, and as I had never inspected a Fokker aeroplane close to, I asked if I might be allowed to do so. Immediately they stopped the car, and we strolled across the aerodrome to where a Fokker was standing on trestles in the machine-gun butts. We only restarted when I was quite satisfied. I received the greatest kindness at the hands of that squadron. They were kindness itself.

When we arrived at St. Quentin, I was handed over to one of the Staff Intelligence officers, but he didn't, as I expected, press me for information. He didn't ask me the name of my squadron, who was my squadron commander, or my aerodrome. He told me these things; I felt he would have told me the names and ages of my parents if I but asked. Dazed by his prescience, I was shortly led out and taken to the local gaol. This is the only time I have been in gaol as yet, and while some may be good I don't recommend St. Quentin town goal to anybody. I was only three days there. On the third day myself and about forty other officers and men from the gaol were taken off to St. Quentin Station to go back into Germany.

I told you that my instructions on 1 July were to bomb St. Quentin Station. Apparently I'd been successful in doing so, and the explosion had done the station no good. It was obvious that a considerable expenditure upon glass panes would be required to restore its former beauty. Although three days had elapsed the Railway Transport Officer in Charge, as I suppose he would be called, was still stamping about and displaying every symptom of emotion at the damage done. I was standing in the company of the only other member of the Royal Flying Corps in our party, a man rather older than myself. Evidently the R.T.O. desired vengeance upon the author of the outrage which had been committed on his station, but didn't know which of us was the guilty party. I didn't enlighten him. At any rate, he clearly suspected my companion rather than myself. He was shouting, stamping his feet, and raving at us without being able to make us understand much more than that he loved us dearly. Then he turned and tried to snatch the bayonetted rifle from one of our guards with obvious lethal intent. Happily, the stolid sentry was not used to having his rifle seized in this way by his officers, and, I am pleased to say, he wouldn't let go. The ensuing tug-of-war recalled the R.T.O. to some sense of dignity, and the officer in charge of us managed to pacify him. In the end the R.T.O. contented himself by confiscating all the food we had with us, and entraining us in a fourth-class carriage with Senegalese troops. Late the next day we arrived at Mayence and were conducted to the prisoner-of-war camp, an old fortress on the top of a hill overlooking the town.

I passed from one camp to another as time went on, and about June I went with many others to Strohen. Strohen camp was situated on a sandy moor. The village of Strohen is about ninety miles from the Dutch frontier, and thirty or forty miles from Bremen. We had been housed in a cavalry barracks at my previous camp, but we had only huts at Strohen. The camp was surrounded by steel wire trellis work about nine feet high, topped with barbed wire, and within was a wire fence creating a neutral zone. The whole of the camp was illuminated by incandescent lamps fixed on high poles at intervals of fifty yards or so, and nobody was allowed inside the neutral zone under penalty of being fired on forthwith. Curiosity is so great amongst human beings that if an officer were to be seen lying on his stomach wriggling towards the trellis work, with an eye on the sentries, a pair of wire cutters in his hand, and one or two bundles and haversacks festooned about him, ten or more people would be certain to come and stand and gaze at him as if he were doing it for their amusement. So if you had any idea of attempting to get away from the camp, you had to take great care to keep your idea to yourself.

Many were the ingenious ways of escaping employed. One man concealed himself in a laundry basket and got out of the camp that way; another man made himself a complete German soldier's uniform, even to the belt and bayonet. He gilded the bayonet with the gold foil collected from cigarette butts. Others went out concealed in the camp refuse.

The plan of escape which had been evolved between a brother officer, Lieutenant B. Robinson and myself, was this. There was an old disused gulley running across the camp. Time and rain had shallowed it, but at night it still provided cover to a man lying full length in it, The drain crossed the neutral zone, passed through the wire, and ended in a moat which surrounded the camp. Upon the outer side of the moat was an embankment. The sentries patrolled along the top of this and had a good view down into the camp.

First of all, an escaping kit had to be prepared. I had no civilian clothes, but I took all the stuffing out of my cap, removed my rank badges and blackened my buttons. Then I collected goods of small bulk, such as Oxo cubes, milk tablets, and so on, matches, chocolate, squares of congealed methylated spirit for cooking and spare socks and shoes for the march. I had made large pockets on the inside of my tunic so as not to resemble a Christmas tree when bearing this assortment. I concealed in these pockets everything required for a week's march, plus maps and compass, and found I didn't present an unduly bulky appearance. Such things as maps, of course, were contraband and not easily procured. Malted milk tablets and Oxo cubes were usually obtained from England by parcel post without difficulty. The maps which I had, and which are at present in the Imperial War Museum, were tracings of those belonging to a brother officer in the camp, and how he'd got them I don't know. Many curious articles arrived from England, in spite of the strict censorship of prisoners' parcels, and the constant barrack searches made by our captors never succeeded in unearthing at all the battery of wire cutters, files, compasses and maps which undoubtedly existed in the camp. The wire cutters used by us arrived in a cake, and it may interest you to hear more fully how this smuggling of forbidden things was contrived. The first thing was to make one's needs know to one's friends at home by means of cipher messages in ordinary letters. Numerous methods were used, and they were all difficult to work. One way was to conceal the message in a sentence which wouldn't puzzle the German censor enough to make him suspicious, and yet would puzzle one's friends at home so much that they would scent the trick.

Here's an example from one escaper. He wrote: "I know young Ambrose (which is not his name) better than you do, and if you want to please him send him some of the pictures of the edge of the good old Cheese country." By the next post he was sent motoring maps of the Dutch frontier.

Then there was invisible writing. Several ordinary liquids such as lemon juice, spittle, or on a certain kind of paper, even plain water, make quite good invisible inks which can be developed by heat. You would, of course, have to explain to your friend at home by some means that the letter he had received was to be cooked to make it yield up its true message. Pricked messages were no good. The Germans knew about them.

In this kind of way secret contacts with home were established, and requests for forbidden articles made. The next move lay with one's friends and relatives. They had to procure the required articles, devise ways and means of packing them in food parcels so that the German censors wouldn't find them, and finally return word to the prisoner concerned – also by code – so that he would know in what parcel and article the thing was concealed. Major Evans, who has also contributed to this series, describes in his book, "The Escaping Club," how he decoded a postcard from home and got the message "maps in oswego." But what was "oswego?" He had no idea, and he naturally felt a bit nervous when the Germans opened that particular parcel. One of the first things they picked up was a yellow paper packet. They felt it carefully, but passed it to Evans without opening it, and he saw "Oswego" marked on it. It was a packet of flour and contained a large bundle of maps in the middle of it. He also tells another amusing story – how one prisoner borrowed another prisoner's dried fruit to make a stew for the mess and, when he was cooking it, found messages from home floating about on top. Apparently they'd been substituted for the stones in the dried prunes.

Many and various were the ways and places in which these messages and contraband articles were concealed, and the final move lay with the prisoner again – to get them out of the parcel room undiscovered. Sometimes, of course, the Germans just handed them over as in the case of "oswego" – but it was often advisable to try to prevent the guilty article receiving too close a scrutiny and many devices were successfully tried. One way was to tempt the censor by offering him a tin of food and then, while his attention was thus agreeably distracted, pocket the particular article in the parcel one didn't want examined. At one camp the censor used to cut cakes of soap in half to see if there was anything inside – as there often was. This went on until a prisoner showed him how he could see right through the soap if he held it up to the light. This interesting experiment was carried out with a cake of Pears transparent soap, and thereafter the intelligent censor held up all kinds of soap to the light and never cut another cake. Well, now to get back to my own escape.

The outstanding difficulty of the "getaway" was that it would take us three or four minutes at least to cut through the wire. We had to wait until the two sentries who ordinarily patrolled the embankment were both standing still at the opposite ends of their beats. The attempt was to be made after dark on a wet night. My friend and I waited for a fortnight without obtaining favourable conditions, and during this period we took a third officer into our scheme. We arranged with him that he should be the first to enter the drain and cut the wire, and we would watch how the two sentries were behaving and signal to him by a prearranged series of taps upon a china plate. This method of signalling was adopted because we proposed to use the kitchen window as our vantage point, and because in the general noise of the camp it was less likely to attract attention than whistling or using lights.

At length our patient waiting night after night was rewarded. It was a very dark night, raining hard, and the sentries were still. At about 9 p.m. Somerville, our third confederate, entered the gully and crawled along it to the wire. He cut through the wire and crawled through the hole he had made without making a sound. In some miraculous way he managed to pass, running, through the zone of light into the darkness surrounding the camp, without being seen by either of the sentries.

We gave him four minutes start and then Robinson and I entered the gully at a point about seventy-five yards from the wire. We began to wriggle on our bellies keeping one eye on the sentries. When they moved we waited. Unknown to us we had been observed by brother officers in the camp, and two of them, seeing what was happening, had joined the escape procession and entered the gully behind us. I don't know whether you've ever done it, but it's quite exhausting to wriggle seventy-five yards on your face, in mud and water, clad in a raincoat and encumbered as we were, I was fairly tired when I reached the wire. So when my coat caught in the loose strands of wire, I stuck, but the chap behind me, with herculean strength, seized hold of my legs and shot me through the hole like a cork from a bottle. The noise attracted the attention of the two sentries, who came up at the double. I have an impression of scrambling over the embankment, and of the fleeting figures of my comrades receding into the darkness. There was a lot of noise and shouting as the whole of the camp guard, numbering about twenty, turned out. Luckily there were so many that those who had rifles could hardly fire for fear of hitting the others. My friends' speed was so much greater than mine that I sought safety by cover rather than flight and dived into a ditch nearby. I stayed as nearly as possible below the surface of the water, with only my head out. The guards continued to fire in all directions in the pitch dark, which chiefly endangered themselves. The bugle sounded throughout the camp, and the roll-call was taken, all while I was lying in this ditch close by. My most vivid impression of that time was the wish for some means of taking a photograph of myself, because I am sure that a more unhappy looking object would be impossible to find.

I was about three quarters of an hour under water in the ditch, and when the commotion had died away I got out and made off across the moor. When I had put some distance between myself and the camp, I stopped and took stock of my stores. I had left my light raincoat in the ditch, because it was so wet; I found that my matches and cigarettes were spoilt, also my compass wouldn't work. It was a home-made one, consisting of a card swinging upon a gramophone needle which had been magnetised by rubbing it on a magnetic steel razor. The whole thing was encased in a cardboard pill box, and although it was still intact the bath hadn't improved it. Everything else was soaked.

For the first two days I tried to avoid roads and go across the country. In a dry country this might have been all right, but the country in this neighbourhood was very low-lying with a lot of water about, and when I left the roads I got into trouble. So I wasted a great deal of time stumbling into back gardens and arousing dogs by the hundred or getting soaked by falling into streams. At this rate I didn't make much headway to begin with. I only travelled by night and very soon discovered a good plan for keeping warm during the day. Hay in Germany is invariably kept under cover in open barns, so I would find a good stack and bury myself about four feet down in it. This would keep me very warm, without in any way interfering with breathing. Towards the end of the second night, after I'd been soaked by the rain, I took cover in the straw of one of these barns. I hadn't been there long when I heard voices, and found to my horror that someone was removing the straw. The voices turned out to belong to French soldiers, prisoners of war. I should explain here that non-commissioned prisoners were usually employed on some work not connected with the war, such as farming, and were only under lock and key at night. When I realized who they were, I took them into my confidence and they were most anxious to help me. That night they brought me a black cloak, took me back with them to their quarters, and found me a hiding place up in a loft. So there I was, back again in a prison camp, although not as a prisoner. I stayed with them two nights to recuperate. They were naturally rather anxious to get rid of me, as my presence was a danger to them, and at the end of the two days they gave me a clay pipe, three pounds of the strongest tobacco I have ever come across and quantities of provisions and saw me off down the road. I had only two whiffs of that pipe before I hurled it and the tobacco over the hedge, and as the rain continued I went back to the same place again unknown to them. I thought I might just as well stay in such a good place during the rain and was actually there three days and nights. In this way I got through the Sunday, the day when all Germany takes to the country, which was dangerous for me as it increased the possibility of an encounter with someone.

It took me four days more to get to the Dutch frontier, travelling always at night, in stages of about twenty miles. It rained every single day and the rest of the journey was without serious incident. The French prisoners had given me an old great coat, to replace the raincoat which I had lost. I must have looked like an animated scarecrow. I had long since lost collar and tie but I had five socks in my possession; I wore two on my feet, two on my hands as gloves, and one round my neck, and I used to change them over occasionally to dry them when they got wet. I followed railway tracks, rather than roads, whenever possible, as naturally they were deserted. One had, of course, to avoid being run down by passing trains.

On the eighth day after leaving Strohen I came to the river Ems, near the Dutch frontier. It was about ten o'clock at night, and I went down into the marsh and reeds which fringed the east bank and was looking for a narrow place where I might swim across when a man came up behind me and said something. I don't speak German, so I didn't understand what he said, but as he waved his arms and his revolver, I thought I'd better stop. He was in uniform – a frontier patrol. As I appeared so dense he said: "Do you speak French," and I explained in that language that I was an English officer, a prisoner of war. He said "I can help you, I am an Alsatian, and will show you where to cross." He told me to follow him at about fifty paces and if I saw anybody coming to slip into the wood and hide, until they were gone. In my excitement I didn't ask his name, and unless this book should get into his hands there is no hope of my being able to find him and express my gratitude. He led me about a quarter of a mile, and then said: "There you are." The river at this point was only about one hundred yards wide. I went down to the water's edge, found a plank of wood and tied my clothes on to it with my puttees. Then I asked him if there were any patrols on the opposite bank, and he said "No." It was certainly lucky for me I met him. I swam over pushing the plank in front of me, dressed on the far bank, and started off west again. I got lost once or twice during that night and at about two o'clock I arrived at a new canal in course of construction, and presumed that I had arrived in Holland. I had.